George MacDonald
Literary Heritage and Heirs

essays on the background and legacy of his writing

Roderick McGillis

editor

George MacDonald: Literary Heritage and Heirs
Copyright © 2008 Zossima Press
Wayne, Pennsylvania

All rights reserved. Except in the case of brief quotations embodied in critical articles or reviews, no part of this book may be reproduced or transmitted in any form or by any means, electronic or mechanical, including photocopying, recording, or by any information storage or retrieval system, without written permission of the publisher.
For information, contact Zossima Press www.Zossima.com

Zossima Press titles may be purchased for business or promotional use or special sales.

ISBN 0-972322-132

10 - 9 - 8 - 7 - 6 - 5 - 4 - 3 - 2

For Kate and Kyla again

And in memory of Muriel Hutton and Bill Raeper

TABLE OF CONTENTS

Introduction   1
Roderick McGillis

Part 1   Precursors and Sources

Chapter 1.   "Perhaps He Will Need To Love Scotland Too":   7
David Robb   The Importance of MacDonald's Scottish Sources

Chapter 2.   Poets, Dreamers and Mediators: the Metaphors of   25
Gisela Kreglinger   Dreams, Night and Death in Novalis' *Hymns to the Night* and George MacDonald's *Lilith*

Chapter 3.   Mr. Vane's Pilgrimage into the Land of Promise: 45
Robert Trexler   MacDonald's "Historical Imagination" in *Lilith*

Chapter 4.   Kore Motifs in the Princess Books: 65
Fernando Soto   Mythic Threads Between Irenes and Eirinys

Chapter 5.   George MacDonald and Universalism   83
David L. Neuhouser

Part 2   His Master's Voice

Chapter 6.   "More is Meant Than Meets the Ear":   99
Jan Susina   Narrative Framing in the Three Versions of George MacDonald's *The Light Princess*

Chapter 7.   An Ambivalent Marriage of Heaven and Hell: 113
John Docherty   Some Aspects of Irony in *Lilith*

Chapter 8. Ginger Stelle	Phantastic Parallels in George MacDonald's *Phantastes* and *St. George and St. Michael*	139
Chapter 9. Kirstin Jeffrey Johnson	Curdie's Intertextual Dialogue: Engaging Maurice, Arnold, and Isaiah	153
Chapter 10. Susan Ang	George MacDonald and 'Ethicized' Gothic	183
Chapter 11. Roderick McGillis	Fantasy as Miracle: Tentative Beginning Without Conclusion	201

Part 3 Some Children

| Chapter 12.
Geoffrey Reiter | 'Travelling Beastward':
George MacDonald's Princess Books and Late
Victorian Supernatural Degeneration Fiction | 217 |
| Chapter 13.
Colin Manlove | Parent or Associate?
George MacDonald and the Inklings | 227 |

Part 4 MacDonald's Reputation

| Chapter 14.
John Pennington | A 'Wolff' in Sheep's Clothing:
The George MacDonald Industry and
the Difficult Rehabilitation of a Reputation | 239 |

| **List of Contributors** | 260 |
| **Index** | 263 |

Illustrations

	Page
Sir Henry Vane & Four Authors, Illustrators unknown	44
Frontpiece to *Adela Cathcart*, F. A. Fraser	82
Frontpiece to *The Light Princess*, F.D. Bedford	98
From *St. George & St. Michael*, Sydney P. Hall	138
From *The Princess and Curdie*, Dorothy L. Lathrop	152
From *The Princess and Curdie*, Dorothy L. Lathrop	216

About the cover

Culzean (pronounced "Cullane") Castle is considered the finest example of a Georgian castle in Scotland. Between the years 1777 and 1792, the great architect Robert Adam turned a dowdy fortress into this grand, romantic and fashionable castle.

Introduction

Roderick McGillis

George MacDonald died at Ashstead, Surrey, on September 18, 1905. Between September 16 and 19, 2005, a number of scholars from around the world gathered at the Armstrong Browning Library, Baylor University in Waco, Texas, for a centenary celebration of the great nineteenth-century writer's passing. The conference, organized by the Library's Director Stephen Prickett, had the title: "George MacDonald and His Children: the Development of Fantasy Literature." Perhaps the title captured the spirit of the conference, but not its letter. Over three full days, attendants at the conference heard papers on MacDonald's precursors, on his own work, and on the writers he has influenced. Scholars who presented papers included those familiar with MacDonald studies and those beginning to take MacDonald studies in new directions. This conference was not only excellent in its organization, but it also marked an auspicious development in MacDonald studies. I dare say, this conference will stand as a crucial moment; perhaps for the first time the various voices who speak about and for George MacDonald came together and shared ideas. At the Armstrong Browning Library in 2005, theologians and literary theorists and literary historians, mythographers and biographers, fans and professionals, formalists and moralists came together in a genuinely productive conversation that focused on George MacDonald, the sources of his work and vision, and his legacy. The Baylor conference gives notice that MacDonald studies not only continue as an important but modest academic pursuit, but that these studies are also expanding and expanding provocatively. The MacDonald who emerges from this conference is a writer no longer under the shadow of C. S. Lewis' famous assertion that the "texture of [MacDonald's] writing as a whole is undistinguished, at times fumbling" (14).

The essays collected in this volume derive from the Baylor conference. They deal not only with MacDonald's fantasy and its progeny in the twentieth century, but also with the connections of this fantasy with MacDonald's full vision in realistic novels and in his theological writing. The impact of the essays here is to illustrate the cohesion of MacDonald's work, and its consistency. Like Blake, MacDonald is a writer whose vision may expand as the years pass, but it does not fundamentally alter. MacDonald's deep-rooted Romanticism, his acceptance of Romanticism's challenge to the Enlightenment, is as clear in his last works as it was in his first ones. We might quibble over whether MacDonald begins in youthful optimism and ends in the bitterness and pessimism of old age, as Wolff seems to argue in *The Golden Key* (1961), but we cannot deny the fierce belief that for MacDonald a great good is coming. In 1880, at the age of 56, MacDonald published the following poem in *A Book of Strife in the form of 'The Diary of An Old Soul'*:

> Well may this body poorer, feebler grow!
> It is undressing for its last sweet bed;
> But why should the soul, which death shall never know,
> Authority, and power, and memory shed?
> It is that love with absolute faith would wed:
> God takes the inmost garments off his child,
> To have him in his arms, naked and undefiled.
> (August 11; p. 163)

The vision of a return to the pristine celebrates, as it were, the aging process. MacDonald, rarely considered an accomplished poet, here uses rhyme masterfully. Growing leads to knowing; beds and weddings connect intimately; and the child is, thoroughly, undefiled. The "shedding" here is absent, like death to the soul. The rhymes "bed," "shed," and "wed" fold nouns and verbs, and in the middle is "shed," both a verb and a noun. MacDonald's vision is unifying, blending, and, we might say, loving. This short verse concerns the immaterial (the soul), and yet reminds us just how material the immaterial is. MacDonald's fantasy is a fantasy of desire's fulfillment, a fantasy consistent (even in its clothing metaphor) throughout MacDonald's career. We might even think of Lord and Lady Cokayne in *Lilith*, that grotesque skeletal pair who are completely without clothing (fabric or flesh), naked, and on the path to a condition we can call "undefiled." In a late letter to his old friend J. S. Blackie, in November 1894, MacDonald writes:

> Next month I shall be 70, and I am humbler a good deal than when I was 20. To be rid of self is to have the heart bare to God and so to the neighbour – to *have* all life, own and possess all things. I see, in my mind's eye, the little children clambering up to sit on the throne with Jesus. My God, art thou not as good as we are capable of imagining thee? Shall we dream a better goodness than thou hast ever thought of? Be thyself, and all is well with us. (Sadler 362-363)

For MacDonald, hope is eternal as is the vision of eternal childhood.

MacDonald's Romantic spirit is intricate in both derivation and expression. His work derives, to a great extent, from German and English (including Scottish) literature of the late eighteenth and early nineteenth centuries. This is a literature that hails the oral culture and folds it into the still-emerging literary culture. MacDonald finds such a combination of the literary and the oral stimulating and suggestive. Logos represents such a combination. The Word is both heard and seen, both material and immaterial. Accordingly, MacDonald's writing delights in paradox, oxymoron, synaesthesia, polysemy, metaphor, and allusion. The attention to language apparent in such rhetorical intensity pursues the Romantic desire for a language that is itself "naked and undefiled," an unmediated language that brings subject and object, material and immaterial, word and deed together. The essays in this volume trace MacDonald's sources in Romantic literature. They place him in the context of his precursors and also in the context of his contemporaries. Finally, they consider his continuing reputation and influence.

The first section, Precursors and Sources, includes essays on MacDonald's Scottish sources, on Novalis, on American transcendentalism and its seventeenth-century origins, on MacDonald's refashioning of Greek myth, and on his universalism. David Robb traces connections between MacDonald's writing and such Scottish forbears as Scott and Hogg; he also demonstrates the extent of MacDonald's borrowings from Sir Thomas Dick Lauder's *Account of the Great Floods of August 1829 in the Province of Moray, and Adjoining Districts* (1830). Robb places MacDonald squarely where he belongs – among the major Scottish writers who preceded him. And he shows how a great writer – MacDonald – uses a minor writer and historian such as Lauder. Although the English and German Romantic writers proved hugely influential on MacDonald when he was a university student and continued to inform his work throughout his life, his first exposure to literature was surely to that of his own country. The folktales and literary tradition of Scotland are the ground of MacDonald's literary life.

But from first to last MacDonald openly testified to the importance of the German writer Novalis (Friederich von Hardenburg) to his own writing. Gisela Kreglinger carefully outlines the influence of Novalis's *Hymns to the Night* on MacDonald, especially on MacDonald's last great fantasy, *Lilith*. From here, the essays take a less familiar turn. Robert Trexler painstakingly and convincingly demonstrates a connection between MacDonald's character Mr. Vane, in *Lilith*, and the seventeenth-century divine, Sir Henry Vane. This essay is a model of literary archaeology. Another sort of literary archaeology appears in Fernando Soto's densely focused study of MacDonald's recasting of Greek mythology in his work, especially the two "Princess" books. We see in Soto's reading a MacDonald deeply familiar with myth and deeply understanding of myth's spiritual implications. Finally, this first section offers an explanation and consideration of MacDonald as a "Universalist." David Neuhouser carefully places MacDonald among other universalists in the nineteenth century not to argue for this position, but to explain the context for MacDonald's apparent claim that all will be saved once the final bell has rung. Universalism is a potent idea for MacDonald, and a full understanding of his work requires that we set him in the context of nineteenth-century approaches to it. Neuhouser does this, and he does this with scholarly grace.

In section two, His Master's Voice, we have essays that focus directly on MacDonald and his writing. Jan Susina gives a thorough description of the three versions of "The Light Princess," explaining along the way the thematic implications of the various framing devices. This is a masterful reading of one of MacDonald's most accessible stories, and Susina goes a long way to confront the question of audience. This story appeals to both an adult and a child audience, and MacDonald appears to have intended this embracing of what we now think of as "cross-writing," writing for both adult and child. John Docherty, always a meticulous reader of MacDonald's literary conversations with other writers, analyzes the connections between the work of William Blake and MacDonald's *Lilith*. Ginger Stelle demonstrates, in her study of *Phantastes* and *St. George and St. Michael*, the consistency of MacDonald's ideas and images in his realistic fiction and his fantasy. Kirstin Johnson's focus is the "debate" between MacDonald and Matthew Arnold in regard to the Old Testament *Book of Isaiah*. She concludes that MacDonald's Maurice-influenced fantasy, *The Princess and Curdie*, offers a counter reading of *Isaiah* to Arnold's. Whereas Arnold looks to the strict letter in any interpretation of the biblical text, MacDonald is more willing to allow the language of Isaiah to mean many things. MacDonald's Bible thrives on many readings and re-readings; its great code is interpretively rich. From the Bible to the Gothic, the next essay is Susan Ang's study of MacDonald's use of the Gothic in his short story, "The Cruel Painter." This is the only sustained reading of this story that I know of, and Ang brings a fresh approach that will prove useful to future commentators of this and the rest of MacDonald's work. Clearly, MacDonald has something of a "Gothic" imagination; he delights in mystery, the unknown, and the teasingly transgressive. His fantasies and realistic novels contain much of the *mise en scène* of the Gothic: large and labyrinthine houses, dark and even stormy nights, pale women and demonic men, hints of taboo subjects, the grotesque and the fearsome, and even vampires and werewolves. We might see MacDonald as a writer who sets out to rehabilitate a form – the Gothic – that traditionally plays with blasphemy. All in all, this section presents a MacDonald who is willing to experiment and debate in his public discourse. Finally, this sections contains my own contribution, "Fantasy as Miracle: George MacDonald's *The Miracles of Our Lord*." This essay attempts to show how MacDonald's sermons can inform our reading of his fantasies.

Section three is shorter than the previous sections, containing just two essays. The first is Geoffrey Reiter's, "'Traveling Beastward': George MacDonald's Princess Books and Late Victorian Supernatural Degeneration Fiction," a study of MacDonald in the context of what Max Nordau termed "degeneration." Once again, we have MacDonald placed in the company of Gothic writers such as Bram Stoker and Arthur Machen. Reiter makes a connection between the impact of Darwin on Victorian literature and the late-century slide into the *fin de siècle* darkness. The second essay in this section is Colin Manlove's response to the question of MacDonald's ties to the Inklings. He concludes that MacDonald "differs from Williams, Lewis and Tolkien much more than he is like them," and that the practice of linking him with the other three writers has more to do with arguing for MacDonald's importance than it does with MacDonald's real similarity with them.

Serving as something of a coda to all the essays is the single essay in the final section: John Pennington's "A 'Wolff' in Sheep's Clothing: The George MacDonald Industry and the Difficult Rehabilitation of a Reputation." Pennington reflects on the influence of C. S. Lewis' well-known commentary on MacDonald, and on recent treatment of MacDonald by Evangelical writers such as Kathryn Lindskoog and Michael Phillips. He takes a close look at how such writers appropriate MacDonald for their own purposes, and in the process turn the focus on MacDonald awry. Pennington's essay fittingly closes this volume because it argues for a full, disinterested treatment of MacDonald as a writer. And if the essays in this volume are any indication, then this is precisely what is happening. I know of two other collections of essays on MacDonald in publication as I write this Introduction. Clearly, MacDonald studies are as healthy as they have ever been, and what a reader will be left with from a reading of this volume is a more complete sense of MacDonald than we have yet had, as well as a clear sense of what remains to be done.

Without doubt, the MacDonald who works through these pages is a writer worth caring about and worth serious study not just for the myth that may be inherent in his writing, but for that writing itself. We need close rhetorical analyses of MacDonald's work, and not just the fantasies. We also need a fuller understanding of the various contexts in which MacDonald situated his writing. Many of us tend to fix on Romanticism as the most important context for MacDonald, but a book such as *England's Antiphon* ought to remind us just how expansive MacDonald's knowledge is. Over and above the literary, however, we have the Protestant legacy stemming from at least the seventeenth-century Cambridge Platonists, through William Law to Frederick Denison Maurice. Then we have teasing allusions to the likes of Dante and Origen, and the even more silent echoing of Greek myth that Fernando Soto has begun to locate in MacDonald's work. This volume presents a beginning in these areas. My hope is that it stimulates further research on a great writer whose work continues to inspire both academic interest and personal faith.

Note: contributors to this volume wish to express appreciation to Stephen Prickett, and the Armstrong Browning Library for their generosity in organizing the centenary celebration of George MacDonald's passing. They would also like to record their gratitude to Randall O'Brien, Provost of Baylor University, for his financial support. Without the September 2005 conference at the Armstrong Browning Library, this volume would not exist.

Works Cited

Lewis, C. S. *George MacDonald: An Anthology*. London: Geoffrey Bles, 1946.
MacDonald, George. *A Book of Strife in the form of 'The Diary of An Old Soul'*.
    Printed for the Author, Chelsea, London, 1880.
Sadler, Glenn Edward, ed. *An Expression of Character: The Letters of George MacDonald*. Grand Rapids. MI: William B. Eerdmans, 1994.
Wolff, Robert Lee. *The Golden Key: A Study of the Fiction of George MacDonald*. New Haven: Yale UP, 1961.

Part 1: Precursors and Sources

Chapter 1:

"Perhaps He Will Need To Love Scotland Too" The Importance of MacDonald's Scottish Sources

David Robb

C. S. Lewis' well-known essay on MacDonald, the Introduction to his 1946 collection of quotations, contains the judgment on MacDonald's novels – "none is very good"– which still stands to this day (17). The quotation in my title sets one of Lewis' three preconditions for getting anything out of them at all (the others are a love of holiness and a love of MacDonald), and the conjunction of these conditions would appear to be still sufficiently rare in the world of literary academia (even in Scotland) for the pleasures of the realistic novels continue to be largely ignored. Yet when any substantial discussion of MacDonald includes an element of biography, MacDonald's Scottishness is always made much of, as if his peculiar northern roots and family background help explain the extraordinarily idiosyncratic writer he became. In such discussions, however, more emphasis tends to be given to his family history and to his psychological and religious inheritance than to his Scottish literary background, and when discussion of previous Scottish writers who may have influenced him does take place, it tends to be the obvious ones (Burns and Scott) who are gestured towards. In this chapter, I investigate this aspect of the influences on MacDonald a little more. It seems to me that to best understand MacDonald and what he wrote, we have to acknowledge a Scottish literary background alongside the other major sources of literary influence upon him although when one has contemplated the immense scope and wealth of the writing from German and English directions which filled his awareness, it is easy to feel that one has largely accounted for the nourishment which sanctioned and fed his distinctive creative originality.

I suggest, therefore, that elements of a distinctively Scottish kind helped make him the writer he became. In particular, his sense of fantasy and fairy tale obviously began in Huntly in the 1820s and early 1830s long before he encountered much else in the way of great literature, and the oral folk-material he encountered there and then has to be regarded as his literary starting-point (the Bible apart). The latter part of this chapter, therefore, is a reminder of the influence of such material on his mature writing. Scottish fairy tales were not simply a juvenile starting-point for his literary and creative journey, but a conscious companion throughout its long route. The same can be said, also, for his awareness of Scotland's well-known writers, not merely those of the great generation that preceded him (in particular, Scott and Hogg) but also, in at least one unexpected instance, of Stevenson as well.

I want to begin, however, with a far less widely known and now unread volume, and to use it to consider the balance in MacDonald's adult awareness between the Scotland that he actually lived in during his first twenty years, and the Scotland he encountered in a variety of literary sources. How much did he get from life, and how much did he get from books? In *Sir Gibbie* (232-3), MacDonald (bringing to a close the novel's major episode of the flood) cites as his source *Sir Thomas Dick Lauder's Account of the Great Floods of August 1829 in the Province of Moray, and Adjoining Districts*, which was published in 1830. Indeed, at this point MacDonald has just incorporated several actual lines from Lauder's book, giving them to a farmer's housekeeper as her description in a letter of how she had discovered that the receding waters had deposited a pile of edible game and vegetables at the back of the house – one of the rare instances of the calamity offering sustenance rather than its more usual cataclysmic destruction (see Lauder 181-182).

Lauder's book describes in great and systematic detail the events and devastation visited upon a large part of the north-east of Scotland when terrific storms caused all the leading rivers, in particular the Spey, the Findhorn, the Don and the Dee, with all their subsidiary streams, to suddenly burst their banks and rise to an almost unheard-of extent. This occurred in August 1829, and while there was a comparatively small loss of life there was an immense amount of destruction in a region which had recently been making substantial economic strides thanks to the greatly improved infrastructure post-1745 and also to the developments in agricultural practices in the same period. Lauder (1784-1848) was a local landowner and a minor novelist and man-of-letters. This book on the great flood is his masterpiece, however, thanks to his painstaking research and his identification with the area and with its inhabitants. It might seem a wearisome prospect to read nearly four hundred pages of disaster and destruction. Lauder seems to describe the loss of every bridge, the fall of every cottage and the destruction inflicted upon every mansion house and estate throughout North-East Scotland. He recounts how abnormally high each body of water became on the 3-4 August 1829, and on page after page sketches the terrors experienced by countless families and communities, both in the region's towns and villages, and in innumerable isolated spots. Deeds of heroism, miraculous escapes and the occasional tragedy are sprinkled throughout his account, as well as the various bizarre details which a freak of nature such as this produces. In fact, the book is surprisingly readable, thanks to the author's evident knowledge and love of the region, and to his combination of scientific and what we might call 'romantic' interest in the phenomena and spectacle of the episode.

It seems to have been one of those books that helped consolidate the Highlands of Scotland in the imaginations of people in the Victorian period. In it, the terror implicit in the acknowledged sublimity of these highland and northern districts was made manifest. The 'awfulness' of those high, wild, rocky regions had proved capable of inflicting an awesome degree of destruction, and the image of life-threatening, home-destroying storms and floods became part of what people associated with the Scottish Highlands. In Aberdeen Art Gallery, for example, there is a spectacular large painting by Sir Edwin Landseer (he of 'The Monarch of the Glen') entitled *Flood in the Highlands* and painted between the mid-1840s and 1860. It depicts a three-generation Highland family (and their sheep and goats, and dogs, and cats, and poultry) clinging to the thatched roof of an inn as agonized cattle and an ominously driverless horse and cart are swept past. Lauder's cumulative account, similarly awe-struck and detailed, is imaginatively memorable and transcends its lamentations to become a positive evocation of what was then a still fairly out-of-the-way and very distinctive part of Scotland.

Even so, the warmth and personal involvement of MacDonald's commendation is noticeable. In the *Sir Gibbie* footnote, he describes Lauder's account as,

> an enchanting book, especially to one whose earliest memories are interwoven with water-floods. For details in such kind here given, I am much indebted to it. Again and again, as I have been writing, has it rendered me miserable – my tale showing so flat and poor beside Sir Thomas's narrative. Known to me from childhood, it wakes in me far more wonder and pleasure now, than it did even in the days when the marvel of things came more to the surface. (232-3)

The book clearly intertwined with and helped fix his own dim memories of the event – he would have been just over four and a half years old when the flood struck. MacDonald's description of events in the novel is vivid, but closely follows the spirit, and many of the letters, of Lauder's account. That earlier volume provided him with quite a few idiosyncratic details, including (189-90) the woman who managed to float on the floods on a 'brander' (a word normally reserved for a gridiron but which was also used for a makeshift raft or for any lattice-like wooden structure) – a detail which MacDonald utilized to invest Mistress Croale with something of the aura of a witch. Mistress Croale, however, may also have derived something from Lauder's account elsewhere (151-2) of a "strange witch-looking woman" perilously isolated on a tiny piece of solid ground.

Nor was *Sir Gibbie* the only novel of MacDonald's to make use of Lauder's volume. The other great flood MacDonald unleashed was in *Alec Forbes of Howglen*, where we also find that he is writing his account with Lauder's book at hand, once more drawing from it details along with the general spirit of the event. In particular, the account of Alec's single-handed rescue of Annie Anderson from Tibbie's flooded cottage closely parallels one of Lauder's many heroic tales, as well as the latter's story of Isabella Morrison who, trapped in a cottage with her elderly aunt, failed to keep her alive as the waters rose about them and who deliriously thought that a drowned hen which kept floating into her was a detached head, a detail MacDonald uses to vivify his account of Annie's dire situation. Similarly, the account of the deaths of Malison the schoolmaster and the crippled lad Truffey when the town bridge is swept away can be related to several different incidents recounted by Lauder.

Others before me have noted MacDonald's fondness for fictional floods and the late William Raeper in particular, in his biography of the writer, noted a number of other novels of MacDonald's in which floods feature (394n.). Raeper concluded, surely correctly, that MacDonald was able to remember the 1829 event as seen through his own young eyes – the *Sir Gibbie* footnote suggests as much – and no doubt the memory would have remained with him under any circumstances. But it seems to me that we have enough evidence to suppose that Lauder's account played an immense part in the vividness with which the memory stuck, and in the importance that the image of a great flood retained for him. By MacDonald's own account Lauder's book was an important part of his childhood, and its narrative must have developed into a strong influence, perhaps even a dominating influence, in his memory of the event itself. It is clear that MacDonald, in adult life, leaned heavily on Lauder's work when he came to write his fictions. After all, what is MacDonald likely to have retained from his own unaided childhood observation? Perhaps a single image of vastly flooded fields, and nothing much more. It seems to me highly probable that his sense of the 1829 floods, in all likelihood, derived from literature rather than from his own memories.

Lauder's book seems to me particularly characteristic of its Scottish time and place and one which, moreover, helps underline how MacDonald was also a product of his Scottish time and place. While the driving force of Lauder's account is simple and straightforward (but indefatigable) journalistic reportage, his narrative frequently takes the opportunity to recount many of the striking episodes of history and legend with which, for the native of the place, the landscape was steeped. Just as Tam o' Shanter does not simply ride home across an empty tract of country, but rather traverses a dark region throbbingly alive with the memories of deaths, disasters and murders, so Lauder's North-East is a network of recollected episodes of clan warfare and civil war, and of human interaction with fairies. Equally, however, Lauder's perspective includes the analytical and scientific. His explanations and descriptions of what has happened to the landscape are geologically informed, just as his explanation of the meteorological events which brought about the catastrophe in the first place would not disgrace a television weather presenter. The awareness that he brings to his task covers a spectrum running from the scientific, through a lively immediate response to the world of the senses, and on to a more imaginative and at times near-superstitious openness to legend and folk-lore. I doubt if this combination of characteristics can be claimed as exclusive to nineteenth-century Scots, but I do wonder if that particular spectrum – and its shortness, with the scientific responses to reality living cheek by jowl with the archaic, folkloristic and the imaginative in the mind of a writer like Lauder – was not particularly marked in this small country where a technological and rational future co-existed especially closely with a primitively heroic and legend-filled past for these early-nineteenth-century generations. It is a combination which is perhaps most especially exemplified by a prominent contemporary of both Lauder and MacDonald, namely, Hugh Miller (1802 – 1856), an immensely talented journalist, self-taught geologist and scientific communicator of something approaching genius, loving apologist for the landscape and people of the Highlands, and assiduous collector of legends and fairy-lore – this last encouraged by his own openness to belief in the supernatural. Whether or not the contradictions in Miller's ways of apprehending reality contributed to his eventual suicide is still not clear. MacDonald, fortunately, was a far less fiery and aggressive person than Miller, and in him the spectrum I'm considering here ran far less to extremes – but he retained his undergraduate interest in chemistry in particular, and maintained (equally) a disposition to want to believe in ghosts even though he found that he lacked the Celtic faculty of the Second Sight.

Even with all these considerations, however, one wonders why MacDonald was so fond of this book, and equally why he was so fond of putting floods (and, perhaps, their near relatives, storms and blizzards) into his own works. Why did he relish this tale of disaster so much? He seems to have responded with positive warmth to its tale of woe, as if it were a monument to life-enhancement rather than a mere tale of destruction. The destructiveness of the storm produces sublimity, and makes for exciting Romantic reading, just as canvases by Turner, John Martin and several other Romantic painters of Nature at its most titanic made for attractively awesome and appalling viewing. Furthermore, Lauder's work is a poem about mutability, a vision of the transience of earthly things and of human endeavor. One recalls that another favorite work of MacDonald's, the *Fairie Queene*, ends with a focus on mutability. One recalls, too, how MacDonald was attracted to any vision in which the world leaned towards the transient, the insubstantial and the dreamlike. There is in Lauder's book, also, an awareness of extraordinary forces within the normal benignity of nature, a hidden life which may be terrible but which is also deeply vital and appealing. Is there an echo of MacDonald's response to the drama of natural cataclysm in Greville MacDonald's unexpected image applied to Huntly's hidden depths when he writes on the second page of his account of his father's life, "The ancient River of Romance runs through the town silently for most part, but at times, as if in sympathy with the rebel blood in every true Celt's veins, defies its banks, flooding and even wrecking a homestead here and there" (*George MacDonald and His Wife* 20)? Did MacDonald associate floods with a romantic vision that transforms or disrupts the security of the everyday?

In addition to all this, one realizes that Lauder's book succeeds in being, in spite of itself, a celebration of the Scottish North-East. The one catastrophe striking the region as a whole becomes a prompt for the contemplation of the region as a whole — its people, its way of life, and its economic and geographical variety. And in Lauder's book the North-East becomes a scene of wonder and marvel, a place where the world's grandeur, and some of the fundamentals of human experience, are exhibited. And so the book was MacDonald's confirmation that what he had witnessed with his own eyes was indeed as awe-inspiring as his childhood response to the flood had no doubt suggested. The young MacDonald, reading and re-reading the book, had in his hand a connection between his own experience and his own place in the world, and a world of wonders. The everyday could indeed be transformed into the marvellous; the marvellous was indeed a dimension of the everyday.

The example of Lauder's obscure book, however, suggests to me that the sense of a Scottish reality that MacDonald acquired from literature played a substantial part in enabling him to shape the visions that we find in his works. It seems to me that both his major fairy tale writings and at least his Scottish novels (half-way to fairy tales themselves) were partially moulded by his knowledge of, and exposure to, a variety of Scottish literary sources.

Apart from Lauder, which sources? The first possibility which springs to mind is, for every reader of MacDonald's generation, one of the keystones of their literary awareness: Sir Walter Scott — still, arguably, Scotland's greatest novelist. One would expect that MacDonald would revere him, and so he did, as various asides throughout his works suggest. So, in *David Elginbrod*, "what a character David would have been for Sir Walter" (19) thinks Hugh Sutherland as he reads *The Heart of Midlothian*, and when Hugh begins to bestow a literary education upon David's daughter, "Sir Walter's poems" (30) are lent to her early on. Scott is now primarily appreciated for his intellectually impressive achievement in finding a fictional way of contemplating the rhythms of history, a focus which links him directly to the eighteenth-century Scottish Enlightenment. MacDonald, prescient in literature and thought in so many ways, was not so prescient as to respond to Scott in this twentieth-century way. Rather, he saw him as a creator of memorable characters, and as a poet, and as a teller of Romantic narratives. When Scott's writing approached the Gothic, in particular, MacDonald's enthusiasm quickened, a response glimpsed in *Sir Gibbie* in yet another of MacDonald's many scenes of spiritual growth through literary encounter: Donal Grant the cowherd boy reduces Gibbie the waif, recently escaped from the horrors of Aberdeen, to helpless ecstasy by reading him "the Danish ballad of Chyld Dyring, as translated by Sir Walter Scott" (84). This is a supernatural ballad in which a mother's ghost returns from the grave to frighten her remarried husband and his household into treating her children properly despite the enmity of the wicked stepmother. (Actually, MacDonald is wrong here: the infrequently reprinted translation, part of the notes to the early editions of *The Lady of the Lake*, was by the Rev. John Jamieson, creator of the first substantial modern dictionary of the Scots language.)

Another kind of Scott-derived influence which we might perceive is one in which a story-idea of Scott's is taken up by MacDonald. A few years ago, I suggested that some of MacDonald's novels might reveal a recollection of some of Scott's lying behind them (Robb 174-177). *Malcolm* (1875) resembles in certain respects Scott's early novels of lost heirs and seacoast adventures, *Guy Mannering* (1815) and *The Antiquary* (1816), and it may be, also, that *Sir Gibbie* (1879) draws upon Scott to some extent. Once again, we need not doubt that MacDonald was well acquainted with those novels of Scott's, though one notes that it is *The Antiquary* which Alec and Kate attempt to read at the outset of Kate's holiday at Howglen. Like *Sir Gibbie* and *Malcolm*, Scott's two novels are tales of lost heirs who are eventually found and reinstated. They contain, too, character types also used by MacDonald, such as morally weak fathers and stickit ministers. Like *Malcolm*, *Guy Mannering* makes prominent use of a mysterious seaside cave. Also like *Malcolm*, *The Antiquary* gives a prominent part to a female servant who smuggles the newborn child away and is a repository of the family secret. And if one considers *The Antiquary* further, in the wider context of MacDonald's writing, one notes that the motifs of buried treasure and of the truth-imparting dream are similar to what is found in *Castle Warlock* (1882), while Lovel's dream-experience of the tapestry coming to life (chapter 10 of *The Antiquary*) seems suspiciously similar to the transformation scene in the second chapter of *Phantastes* (1858). Perhaps most intriguingly of all, the antiquary himself is a scholar who has experienced the mockery of the girl he loved and who, like Malcolm's mentor Alexander Graham, had lost her to the hero's aristocratic father. Robert Lee Wolff, for one, thought that MacDonald's repeated use of this motif pointed to a real-life flirt in the library (16-17). Might not the idea's source lie in literature, perhaps in *The Antiquary*, rather than in life?

MacDonald wrote only one full-dress historical novel, however: *St George and St Michael* (1876). Like all other Victorian historical novels, this one owes the deepest debt to Scott by its very existence and there can be little doubt that MacDonald was fully conscious of the earlier writer as he wrote it. It is an impressive and convincing imitation of a Waverley novel. Following Scott's habitual practice, MacDonald sets it at a decisive turning-point in the nation's history, in this case the English Civil War of the 1640s. The personal tale of hero and heroine, following Scott's formula, is enmeshed in a conflict between two opposed historical groupings, Royalists and Roundheads. Serious matter, of battles and of the nation's fate, is counterpointed (both Scott and MacDonald following Shakespeare here) with comedy and personal intrigue. Furthermore, MacDonald strives to emulate Scott in scholarly accuracy and solidity, grounding his tale on historical sources to which he directs the reader, weighting his narrative with period details of dress and domestic appurtenances and making regrettable gestures towards seventeenth-century speech (Stevenson's 'tushery') (Stevenson 116). And perhaps it is possible to go a little further than merely comparing MacDonald's tale to the whole genre which Scott had established. Two specific Waverley novels were surely in his mind as he wrote – *Old Mortality* (1816) (another tale of seventeenth-century Royalists and Whigs, in which a besieged castle figures prominently and which includes a decisive battle on a bridge) and *The Heart of Midlothian* (1818), which shares with *St George and St Michael* a heroine of startling scrupulousness and conscience, to whom lying is anathema.

And yet, the differences are as stark as the similarities. MacDonald is not interested in taking over from Scott his perennial and deeply considered theme of history's progress. Where, in Scott, one finds (in novel after novel) a party of the past and a party of the future – be it Jacobites against Hanoverians, supporters of an independent Scotland against adherents of the 1707 Union, or those of an ancient cast of mind against embodiments of eighteenth-century rationalism, peace and justice – one finds in MacDonald's novel simply a destructive and unnecessary partisanship, neither side the clear standard-bearer of the nation's future. Equally, while Scott's Tillietudlem Castle (in *Old Mortality*) embodies a way of life caught uneasily between the violent propensities of past ages and the peaceful promise of the impending Glorious Revolution, MacDonald's Raglan Castle, elevated (in a way characteristic of MacDonald) almost to the status of a character equal in importance to the humans, becomes a living creature, a vision of the individual human personality striving to preserve its echo of God's completeness. MacDonald may have been quite interested in history's stage-trappings; Scott, however, had been passionately interested in history's meaning. Scott's reading of history tells of the emergence of the modern; MacDonald's reading of history tells of mankind's instinctive and timeless factionalism. Both write historical novels which serve, in part, as comments on their own times but where Scott's perspective makes history itself a central dimension, MacDonald's perspective sees history dwarfed by eternity.

St George and St Michael may seem, at first, an unnecessary excursion by MacDonald into fictional realms better colonized by a great predecessor, yet the historical novel proves surprisingly capable of expressing his unique vision, radically different as it is from Scott's concerns. Where MacDonald's favorite technique for compromising between his transcendental message and the confines of fictional realism was to carry his readers to the unfamiliarity of early nineteenth-century Scotland, here he makes similar use of the unfamiliarity of the English seventeenth century. The result is far from being the least rewarding of his novels.

Scott was not the only major nineteenth century Scottish novelist whose writings perhaps served as a model for the necessarily industrious MacDonald. In the same article I also suggested an alternative model for *Castle Warlock*: its tale of hidden treasure may contain recollections, as I have just mentioned, of Scott, but it seems to me possible that it reflects, even more, that best-known novel of hidden treasure, *Treasure Island*, especially the opening Billy Bones section of Stevenson's famous novel. Briefly, in both works an isolated household of parent and adolescent son find themselves forced to play host to an old man, an interloper quite alien in his personality and behavior, who brings with him the influences of ways of life and experience remote from those of his hosts. Both old men are alcoholics with their health seriously impaired by drink. Their language is bad, their behavior towards their hosts ungracious, rude and domineering. They have outsized, dominating personalities, capable of arousing dislike which those around them must stifle. Each has a background linking him with piracy, and their stays with their reluctant hosts are to a certain extent imposed upon them: they are trapped, by weather in the case of MacDonald's Lord Mergwain, by fear of detection in the case of Billy Bones. Both are threatened by the resurgence of a piratical past and both expire in a moment of supreme conflict with it, succumbing to drink and ill-health. Even the shared wintry weather, differently but powerfully evoked by Stevenson and MacDonald, is prominent. Both novels, too, contain enigmatic quatrains relating to hidden treasure, though Stevenson's 'Fifteen men on the dead man's chest —/ Yo-ho-ho and a bottle of rum!' has caught on better than MacDonald's

> Catch yer naig an' pu' his tail;
> In his hin' heel caw a nail;
> Rug his lugs frae ane anither —
> Stan' up, an' ca' the king yer brither.

Ingenuity can find even more echoes and resemblances, but perhaps the point has been made. If I am correct in this, however, then MacDonald's enthusiasm for Stevenson's story predated the first book-publication of *Treasure Island*, which occurred in 1883. *Castle Warlock* was published in 1882. Stevenson's story first appeared, however, in serial form under the title *The Sea Cook* in the periodical *Young Folks*, beginning in October 1881. My case is perhaps further bolstered, however slightly, by a detail recounted in that little-regarded source of information about MacDonald, Joseph Johnson's biography of 1906, where we are informed how an unnamed friend of MacDonald recalled "how enthusiastically he spoke of men and books; of Stevenson and his stories, in the early days of his writing, before his star was much above the horizon. Once, before leaving for a long train journey, he asked his friend to inquire if the new story by Stevenson was out. On its being brought from the bookstall, he took the volume in his hands with the glee of a schoolboy, saying: 'Now I shall have a pleasant journey'" (62)

The Scottish influences on MacDonald, however, did not consist merely of the impact on him of individual books and writers: the general Scottish literary environment should also be considered. A yet deeper and more pervasive influence on his work is possibly to be found in that tradition of writing about Scottish everyday life which idealizes it, and which eventually gave rise to that late nineteenth-century phenomenon, the Kailyard novel. From this tradition comes MacDonald's vision of the cottage, or of the impoverished household, as the domain of virtue, and the source of the power which rescues endangered or corrupt palaces. It is the source of his insistence on rural piety — and/or of distinctively Scottish piety — as a regenerative force. Indeed, within several of his books (such as *David Elginbrod*, *Robert Falconer* and *The Marquis of Lossie*) instinctive heroic Scottish righteousness is brought into direct confrontation with un-ideal contemporary Englishness (embodied both as an environment, such as the slums in which *Robert Falconer* works and the brittle London society from which Malcolm rescues his sister Florimel and her friend Clementina, and also in characters such as the crudely materialistic English incomer to the Highlands in *What's Mine's Mine*, Peregrine Palmer.) Indeed, the Scottishness of MacDonald's own image, both as a person and as a writer, was surely an expression of his sense that Scotland had something especially spiritual to give, and something notable to say about "the condition of England."

In his invaluable biography of MacDonald, William Raeper touches on this aspect of MacDonald and Scotland when he discusses *David Elginbrod*. Raeper describes the Elginbrod household as "an idealized family possessing all the noble virtues that MacDonald associated with old peasant Scotland, and which are also to be found in Scott's novels" (184-185); once more, we encounter the suggestion that MacDonald's lived experience of Scotland was overlaid by his reading about Scotland. Instances of this vision of Scottish humble life can certainly be found in Scott: most of all in the story of Jeannie Deans in *The Heart of Midlothian*. Yet Scott does not seem to me to be a principal carrier of this tradition, and I would suggest some other names.

Central to the tradition is Burns' controversial poem, 'The Cotter's Saturday Night'. Burns was one of MacDonald's favorite poets and his most popular topic during his lecture tour of America. It is unlikely that MacDonald would have shared the hesitations which twentieth-century readers have had about the poem; rather, its idealized depiction of the simple but powerful piety of the cotter family at their domestic worship must have been to him one of the clearest proofs of Burns' essential spiritual rightness. The poem describes the peasant family gathering together in the parental cottage at the end of the working week, eating their evening meal then turning to an act of family worship led by the father as head of the household. Burns presents their piety as a pervasive characteristic of ordinary Scots, and insists that it is one of the key strengths of the Scottish people. There is an echo here, in fact, of that Reformation-derived claim by the Scots to be a nation specially chosen by God. Burns' poem, however, was one of the principal means by which that old notion was kept alive, to some extent, into the nineteenth century.

Yet it was far from being the only literary expression of that idea to be influential on Victorian readers. Much of the minor, and no-longer-read, Scottish fiction of the early and middle decades of the nineteenth century reflects the notion to a greater or lesser extent, fiction which would have contributed to the literary air MacDonald breathed as he grew to adulthood. One thinks, for example, of the once-popular tales of humble Scottish life gathered together in 1822 under the title *Lights and Shadows of Scottish Life*. These are by the author perhaps still best remembered under his pseudonym "Christopher North," in which guise he wrote the bulk of the ponderous (but still entertaining) satirical series for *Blackwood's Magazine*, "*Noctes Ambrosianae*." Second-hand copies (there is no other kind) of *Lights and Shadows*, however, and of his novels of a similar would-be exalted cast, are likely to give the author on the spine as "Professor Wilson." John Wilson (1785-1854) had obtained the politically selected post of Professor of Moral Philosophy at Edinburgh in 1820, and was a howling success in the position, despite knowing very little about the subject. For years, his crowded lectures were based upon material secretly sent to him on a regular basis by an old undergraduate friend: Wilson supplied the rhetoric, of which he had an inexhaustible supply. And that sense of how to woo his audience is clear in the tales in *Lights and Shadows*, which are sketches of Scottish peasant experience – a peasantry rich in piety, in sound moral judgment, in openness to the influence of high principle and of God, in trust and in acceptance of whatever good or ill the Almighty chooses to bestow upon them. These are tales in which lowly Scots make all the right decisions at life's major turning-points and challenges. It is often said that what particularly marks such writing in nineteenth-century Scotland is its piety, and it is true that Wilson steeps his stories in Christian idealism.

But one can detect much of the same impulse to idealize the Scottish peasantry when religion is thrust down the reader's throat far less vigorously, as in (for example) a famous essay-cum-short story entitled "Rab and his Friends" by Dr John Brown (1810-82). This first appeared in 1858. Rab is a dog, a great mastiff, owned by a humble Edinburgh carrier, but although the story does justice to Rab (in a Landseer-like way), the heart of the essay is the account of the mastectomy undergone (without anesthetic) by the carrier's elderly wife followed by her death a week or so later. Her husband dies soon after and Rab has to be put down. The tale is a celebration not of humble piety, but of humble fortitude, emotional strength and capacity for love and fidelity. Rab the mastiff becomes a symbol of the outstanding sturdiness, combined with vulnerability, of ordinary people. The story contains as much idealizing as Wilson's do, though it draws on much more immediate contact with the realities of humble life. There is the same air of representativeness, too; these characters and their story are indicative of the fineness which can be found (always with a faint hint of surprise on the part of the authors or narrators) in the lowest orders of society. (The influence of Wordsworth, of course, is subtly pervasive through so much Victorian writing of this kind.)

This way of perceiving, and writing about, ordinary Scots and their ways is characterized by several things, therefore: an insistence on their moral strength (whether due to their religiosity or not) and a tendency towards the stereotype, with the simplifying and standardizing of life, relationships and emotions. There is often a concentration upon strong, life-changing situations. Above all, perhaps, there is a consciousness of the characters' otherness, with regard to the author and reader. They are always perceived as special, and consequently surprising: their obscurity is both a cause of, and an unexpected context for, their moral stature. We the readers, and the authors, look in at their world from the outside, amazed and challenged by what we see. And it is upon that discovery of strength, help and moral leadership in the most unexpectedly humble locations that MacDonald builds so much of his writing – an idea which regularly takes crystallized form every time a MacDonald hero (whether it be Gibbie fleeing from man's cruelty, or Anodos exhausted in his physical and moral wanderings) pushes upon a humble cottage door to find within a maternal figure overflowing with strength and compassion. MacDonald is entirely happy to write in this tradition with its strong sense of the iconic, but he attempts to achieve a new degree of strength in his figures of piety, truth and moral significance. Furthermore, it is worth pointing out that this vision of the moral and social strength associated with an older, simpler, more pastoral Scotland was not simply a literary concept but one which people held to in their real lives. Thomas Chalmers (1780-1847), for instance, the great leader of the Scottish Evangelical movement in the 1830s and first Moderator of the Free Church of Scotland after the Disruption of 1843, based his major attempt at social reform and amelioration in one of industrial Glasgow's worst parishes, in the early 1820s, on the idea that what was required was a return to the values and outlook of Scottish rural and small-town life. In Scotland during the period we are concerned with, the ancient pastoral ideal took on a new force and urgency as Scottish society struggled to respond to the challenges of having suddenly become the world's first industrialized economy. MacDonald's version of the pastoral ideal was part and parcel of that feature of his age.

Finally, in addition to all these influences from the writings of MacDonald's contemporaries, we must acknowledge what is, I think, an equally important source that MacDonald surely encountered earlier and even more naturally than he did Burns and Scott. In Chapter 10 of *Ranald Bannerman's Boyhood* (1871), Ranald and his friends cluster round an old woman in the village to hear her recount "an old Highland legend, which she adorned with the flowers of her own Celtic fancy" (73). I have little doubt that in some such way as this MacDonald himself imbibed many a legend and folktale, both Highland and Lowland, during his childhood, and I suspect such scenes of being another major source of the wonder and fairy-matter which so distinguishes his writing. Folktales are, of course, a vast and specialised area of study in their own right, nor is material for study in short supply, as the publishing of collections of folktales in books and journals has been a common practice at least from MacDonald's time to the present day. Even a brief survey of some of this material, however, reveals that not only can various story elements in MacDonald's fantasies and fairy tales be paralleled by original tales, but also that MacDonald must have lived his Huntly childhood in a world in which belief in fairies was not the habit of another, earlier and far more distant age than we perhaps assume, but a more recent element in people's minds which must still have been contributing strands to the fabric of the communal outlook. I have earlier touched upon the capacity of someone as intelligent and well-read as Hugh Miller to believe in a supernatural dimension, but what perhaps needs saying here is that throughout rural Scotland in the early decades of the nineteenth century there was clearly a recollection of a recent time when fairies were believed in as immediate neighbors of humans and when there was, in all probability, strong traces of a continuity in that belief. Fairies were still, however faintly, part of the texture of life in the world in which MacDonald had his childhood. Not that there appear to be many contemporary anecdotes of encounters with fairies. Instead, there are tales of the departure of the fairies, either as individuals or as a race, a departure told about in many parts of Scotland. As Hannah Aitken has written, "whatever took place, or was imagined, round about the year 1790, descriptions of it recorded as far apart as Nithsdale and Caithness are detailed, vivid and surprisingly alike" (121). Miller, for example, in *The Old Red Sandstone* (1841), recounts how, "on a Sabbath morning nearly sixty years ago," a little herd boy and his sister "saw a long cavalcade ascending out of the ravine . . . The horses were shaggy diminutive things, speckled dun and grey; the riders stunted, misgrown, ugly creatures, attired in antique jerkins of plaid, long grey cloaks and little red caps from under which their long uncombed locks shot out over their cheeks and foreheads." On being asked who they were and where they were going, they replied, "Not of the race of Adam. The People of Peace shall never more be seen in Scotland" (qtd in Aitken 122). And this incident was paralleled in many similar folktales current into the nineteenth century. Folklorists agree that it was the Agrarian Revolution which put paid to the Fairies and drove them out, but that revolution was still very much under way around Huntly, and in Aberdeenshire generally, during MacDonald's childhood: The Farm, for example, owned and worked by MacDonald's father and uncles, was still in the course of being reclaimed from bog, and Aberdeenshire as a whole, now one of Scotland's principal farming areas, had to be cleared of boulders and stones in the early nineteenth century before the land could be farmed at all.

Surviving, therefore, only in the tales still being told about them, the fairies in MacDonald's time were understood to have been living surprisingly close at hand, often in underground regions, and capable of interacting on a daily basis with humans. Sometimes they were helpful, but "the race of Adam" did well to be wary of them, as they could be malevolent, especially in their habit of making off with human children – whether or not they substituted one of their own. Often, a district would have a Wise Woman, however, who could give advice on how to deal with the difficulties brought about by the fairies (as well as with all the other difficulties arising in everyday life). Often, too, the fairies and their doings were invisible to ordinary human sight, but the second sight (when someone possessed it either temporarily or as a permanent gift) would enable a mortal to see what was going on. We find tales of fathers with afflicted daughters (as in "The Light Princess") who promise their hands to whoever can relieve the daughter of the affliction. Tales, too, of children, sometimes abandoned and sometimes not, who stumble into the household of a giant and escape only through quick-wittedness. After sunset is the time when one can be caught and captured by malevolent fairies – being kidnapped by fairies seems to have been a constant fear. Brownies are common in these tales, as is the association of witches and cats. Sometimes fairies can be very small (as in the opening of *Phantastes*). In several, heroes or heroines are sent on journeys to successive old men each of whom is hundreds of years older than the last. MacDonald's tales and fantasy novels are compounded from materials like these. We need not be surprised that MacDonald in particular remained alive to these stories throughout his life: as Alan Bruford of Edinburgh University's School of Scottish Studies has written, fairies "represent in anthropomorphic form the mysterious and numinous in wild nature, the part of the world which is beyond mankind's understanding" ("Introduction" ix).

It would take a whole new chapter to illustrate the full range of apparent parallels which anyone familiar with MacDonald's fiction would be able to spot between it and even a moderate selection of Scottish folktales. To the best of my knowledge, it is an area of MacDonald study that has been little explored. (William Raeper in his biography makes a similarly brief gesture towards the still glowing embers of belief in folk superstition which marked MacDonald's boyhood world.)

MacDonald, I have no doubt, drew directly upon his own encounters with the tales of the common people of Scotland, but he was also the beneficiary of the work of at least two crucial predecessors who, a generation earlier, had mediated between the ancient vision of the folk and the taste of an enlightened literary readership. Scott, with his *Minstrelsy of the Scottish Border* (1802-3) had bridged the gap, in Scottish writing, between the world of folk tradition and the literature of the nineteenth century. With the appearance of that collection, the writers of Scotland (to look no further) were given both the material and the encouragement to let the fairies, and the supernatural generally, into their writing. As Scotland moved on from the sharpest contrasts of the previous century, between Enlightenment rationalism and uneducated superstition, to an outlook in which superstitions and folk culture could themselves become a focus of enlightened interest, study and entertainment, so supernatural material became one of the most regularly appearing strands in Scottish writing, finding a more natural place in it, perhaps, than it did in English writing of the same period (despite the great number of set-piece Victorian ghost stories). As such, it survived well into the twentieth century, even in such classic Scottish Renaissance novels as Lewis Grassic Gibbon's *Sunset Song* (1932) and Neil Gunn's *The Silver Darlings* (1941). In novels like these, the supernatural is still being treated as a part of reality, and of human experience, with no attempt to explain it away. It is as if an ancient wisdom, different from the wisdom of eighteenth-century rationalism, could still survive and be acknowledged. It was from this outlook that MacDonald drew much of his vision.

And if Scott was a necessary instigator of this trend, his contemporary James Hogg showed better than anyone else what literary potential there was in the kind of material Scott had made available. Hogg's writings, above all, are steeped in the folklore of his class and culture, and he gloried in being (as he put it himself) "King o' the Mountain and Fairy School" (Hogg 118). His influence on MacDonald, I am sure, was very real. MacDonald's famous reference to Hogg's poem "Kilmeny," in *At the Back of the North Wind*, along with Greville MacDonald's references to his father's reading of Hogg's verse, are probably all the hard proof we need of MacDonald's knowledge of the work of his predecessor, but it is reassuring to find him also writing of the boy Alec Forbes eagerly reading "the *Arabian Nights* and the Ettrick Shepherd's stories" (MacDonald *Alec Forbes* 68). Hogg's fiction was widely available during the Victorian period, although in extremely poor texts. Even so, MacDonald seems to have responded to Hogg's constant juxtaposition of the commonplace world and the realm of the otherworldly, a vision which amounted to seeing the supernatural as a dimension of the real (rather than, as in the standard ghost story, offering an escape from the real into a daydream of the supernatural). MacDonald shared with Hogg, too, a willingness to enliven his renderings of the everyday Scottish world with action which is striking, often suddenly melodramatic, and frequently bordering on the unbelievable. Hogg, too, like MacDonald, was fully aware of how Nature, in Scotland, is capable of sudden awesomeness and destructiveness, and full of deadly traps for the unwary human. Despite his love of writing about the everyday world of humble Scottish country dwellers, Hogg's tales form no part of the comfortable, idealizing tradition of 'The Cotter's Saturday Night' that I discussed earlier. They represent an alternative vision, an insider's vision, the vision of one steeped in the wisdom of rural traditions and beliefs, in opposition to the rationalism of post-Enlightenment Scotland and the materialism of the emerging Victorian age. One can say much the same about MacDonald's writings, as well, though by the time he came to maturity MacDonald was both insider and outsider as regards the world of Victorian Scotland.

Note: Attendance at the conference at which an unrevised version of this paper was delivered was made possible by the generous provision, by the British Academy, of an Overseas Conference Grant.

Works Cited

Aitken, Hannah. *A Forgotten Heritage: Original Folk Tales of Lowland Scotland.* Edinburgh & London: Scottish Academic Press, 1973.
Bruford, Alan. "Introduction." *Highland Fairy Legends: Collected from Oral Tradition* by Rev James MacDougall. 1802-1803. Ipswich & Cambridge: D. S. Brewer; Totowa, NJ: Rowman & Littlefield, 1978. v-xi.
Hogg, James. *Memoirs of the Author's Life and Familiar Anecdotes of Sir Walter Scott.* Ed. Douglas S. Mack. Edinburgh & London: Scottish Academic Press, 1972.
Johnson, Joseph. *George MacDonald: A Biographical and Critical Appreciation.* London: Sir Isaac Pitman & Sons, 1906.
Lauder, Sir Thomas Dick. *An Account of the Great Floods of August 1829 in the Province of Moray, and Adjoining Districts.* Edinburgh: Adam Black; London: Longman, Rees, Orme, Brown & Green; Elgin: Forsyth & Young, 1830.
Lewis, C. S. "Introduction." *George MacDonald: An Anthology.* Ed. C. S. Lewis. London: Geoffrey Bles, 1946. 10-22.
MacDonald, George. *Alec Forbes of Howglen.* 1 vol. London: Hurst & Blackett, n.d.
MacDonald, George. *David Elginbrod.* 1 vol. London: Hurst & Blackett, n.d.

MacDonald, George. *Ranald Bannerman's Boyhood*. London, Glasgow & Bombay: Blackie & Son, 1911.
MacDonald, George. *Sir Gibbie*. 1 vol. London: Hurst & Blackett, n.d.
MacDonald, Greville. *George MacDonald and his Wife*. London: George Allen & Unwin, 1924.
Miller, Hugh. *The Old Red Sandstone; or, New Walks in an Old Field*. Edinburgh: John Johnstone, 1841.
Raeper, William. *George MacDonald*. Tring and Batavia, Illinois: Lion Publishing; Sutherland, Australia: Albatross Books, 1987.
Robb, David S. "George MacDonald's Scottish Novels: Three Notes." Notes & Queries (new series) 33.2 (1986): 174-177.
Stevenson, R. L. *The Letters of Robert Louis Stevenson*. 2nd ed. Ed. Sidney Colvin. 4 vols. London: Methuen, 1911. Vol. 2 (1880-1887).
Wilson, John. *Lights and Shadows of Scottish Life. A Selection from the papers of the Late Arthur Austin*. Edinburgh: William Blackwood, and London: T. Cadell, 1822.
Wolff, Robert Lee. *The Golden Key: A Study of the Fiction of George MacDonald*. New Haven: Yale UP, 1961.

Chapter 2:

Poets, Dreamers and Mediators:
the Metaphors of Dreams, Night and Death in Novalis'
Hymns to the Night and George MacDonald's *Lilith*

Gisela Kreglinger

The influence of Friedrich von Hardenberg, better known as Novalis, is commonly attested in MacDonald scholarship. Wolff (1961)[1], Reis (1972), Raeper (1987), Robb (1987), McGillis (1990), Docherty (1990), Broome (1991), Prickett (1991), Manlove (1991), Kranz (1991), Dearborn (1994), and Hein (1999) all acknowledge the influence. However, most discussions have focused on the relationship among *Phantastes*, *Heinrich von Ofterdingen*, and MacDonald's translation of the *Spiritual Songs* by Novalis, and are always introductory. A more in-depth study of Novalis is necessary if we are to understand Novalis himself and the extent to which he shaped MacDonald's thinking. Commentators more often than not neglect the influence of *Hymns to the Night* upon MacDonald even though MacDonald translated these hymns and included some of them in his poetical works (see *Poetical Works*, Vol. 2: 324). John Docherty and Giorgio Spina mention these hymns, Adelheid Kegler briefly discusses their influence on *Lilith*, but only Deirdre Christine Hayward, in her doctoral thesis, discusses the *Hymns* in any detail.[2] The extent of Novalis' influence on MacDonald, especially in regard to Christian faith, remains undiscussed, but it is clear in MacDonald's appropriation of Novalis' *Hymns to the Night*. In this chapter, I argue that Novalis' *Hymns to the Night* influenced MacDonald's *Lilith*. I focus on a discussion of *Hymns to the Night* in light of Novalis' understanding of dreams and of poetics, and I offer suggestions for how MacDonald appropriated some of the imagery and theology of these hymns for his last visionary fantasy.

Owen Barfield rightly cautions the reader not to read these hymns superficially. They are complex and deserve careful attention. Barfield writes, "In a sense one has the feeling that only dead people ought to be allowed to read this *Hymn*. This is where the consciousness soul, like a spiritual policeman, steps in. It never forgets death. It is not going to allow us to forget that, before there can be a resurrection, there must be a death" (Barfield 139). We need to heed Barfield's warning. Furthermore, we cannot understand *Hymns to the Night* apart from a broader understanding of Novalis' life and other works. Particularly, *Heinrich von Ofterdingen* is important for understanding these hymns as they were written about the same time, right before Novalis' death in 1801. In *Heinrich von Ofterdingen* we will focus our investigation on the discussion of dreams between Heinrich and his father to provide an entry point into Novalis' thinking and context.

Novalis and his context explored through dreams:

It is striking that both *Phantastes* and *Lilith* end with the same quotation from Novalis. MacDonald introduces the last chapter of *Phantastes* with this aphorism and the very last sentence of *Lilith* reiterates it: "Our life is no dream, but it should and will perhaps become one" (*Lilith* 252).[3] It is also worth noting that Novalis is one of only two writers that MacDonald quotes from directly in *Lilith*.[4] While most MacDonald scholars mention the Novalis quotation, no one has yet discussed its importance for understanding *Lilith*, even though the image of dreams is very prominent in *Lilith*.[5] MacDonald's citation of Novalis calls for a closer investigation of Novalis' influence on MacDonald in this regard. It is important therefore to investigate the significance of dreams in Novalis' thinking and how this has shaped MacDonald's understanding of the role of dreams, thereby shedding some light on MacDonald's most difficult novel.

Novalis' understanding of dreams is complex and closely related to his understanding of aesthetics, poetics, fairy stories, the imagination, revelation, and eschatology or, in Novalis' words, his longing for the "Golden Age" (Novalis, *Werk*, vol. I: 198, 271, 323, 396). In the beginning of *Heinrich von Ofterdingen*, Novalis provides one of his most comprehensive discussions of dreams. Heinrich has a dream about a blue flower and he believes that this dream has deeper significance than an ordinary dream (Novalis, vol. I: 243). He shares this dream with his parents, but his father is not keen on Heinrich's new fascination, urging his son to pursue his studies rather than dwelling in the world of dreams. Heinrich's father argues,

> Dreams are *spindrift* [lit. foam], whatever your learned men may think of them; and you will do well to turn your mind away from such useless and harmful reflections. The times are past when ...[the divine face] appeared in dreams, and we cannot and will not fathom the state of mind of those chosen men the Bible speaks of. The nature of dreams as well as of the world of men must have been different in those days. In the age we live in there is no longer any direct intercourse with heaven. The old stories and records form our only source of knowledge, in so far as we need it, of the supernatural world; and in place of those express revelations the Holy Ghost now speaks to us indirectly through the minds of wise and well-disposed

men and through the way of life and the fortunes of the pious.[6]
(*Henry Von Ofterdingen* 18)

Heinrich, on the other hand, has a much more open stance towards dreams:

> But my dear father, what makes you so opposed to dreams? ... Dreams seem to me to be a defence against the regularity and routine of life, a playground where the hobbled imagination is freed and revived. Without dreams we should certainly grow old sooner; and so we can regard dreams, if not as directly sent from heaven above, at least as divine gifts, as friendly companions on our pilgrimage to the holy sepulchre. Certainly the dream I dreamed last night will not have been an ineffectual accident in my life, for I feel that it reaches into my soul ... [like a] giant wheel, impelling it onward with a mighty swing. (*Henry Von Ofterdingen* 19)

The above dialogue shows Novalis' awareness of the contemporary debates concerning dreams, and it also sheds some light on his own understanding of dreams. Heinrich's father is skeptical about the whole idea of dreams and seems to represent an attitude that reinforces Enlightenment skepticism towards the imagination, dreams and supernatural revelation.[7] Reason is now the sole category by which revelation is evaluated and since dreams lack order and cannot be always interpreted rationally, they stand in opposition to the pursuit of truth. The way we can know things, according to Heinrich's father, is through "the minds of wise and well-disposed men," in short, through the intellect.

Manfred Engel, in his careful analysis of dreams in the period between Enlightenment and late Romantic thought, shows that the pre-Enlightenment discourse about dreams focused on fictional and supernatural dreams. Actual dreams, as opposed to literary dreams, were only of marginal interest then, and they were mainly discussed by physicians. With the Enlightenment, however, a significant shift occurred. The emphasis completely changed and supernatural dreams diminished in significance. The idea of a direct revelation from God was challenged and thus dreams had to be interpreted on merely natural grounds. God does not intervene in the natural order of things and therefore he does not send dreams anymore (Engel 145-147).[8]

Christian Wolff (1679-1754), an important German enlightenment thinker, first clearly differentiated between dreaming and waking.[9] Wolff was able to draw attention to the phenomenology of dreams, and he also included a category of untrue dreams. For Wolff, the primary criteria for the evaluation of dreams are the truths and certainties accessible through reason. These truths are marked by a great sense of order and since dreams often lack order and cannot be always interpreted rationally, they stand in opposition to truth. Wolff writes, "In the truth everything builds upon one another sensibly, but not so in dreams" (qtd in Engel 145).[10] Order has now become the sole category by which dreams are evaluated.

The discussion of dreams in enlightenment thought continued in the context of the enlightenment battle against supernatural revelation and superstition. While dreams were still important, it was denied that God would still send dreams, because he does not intervene into the natural order of things anymore. As a consequence of this denial of a supernatural source for dreams, popular enlightenment thought attempted to explain dreams naturally, i.e. either rationally or, at a later stage empirically and psychologically.[11] The German university preacher Richerz writes in 1785, for example, that his nightmare can be explained on the grounds of experiences of the previous day, physical sensations and his personality (qtd in Engel 147).

Novalis, as we have seen in the dialogue above, opposes a mere rational and scientific understanding of the world and he bemoans his own time as a period where "divinely, magically and poetically oriented people cannot develop under such conditions" (Novalis, *Werk*, vol. II: 322). For him, divine interventions cannot be encapsulated sufficiently in a mere rational outlook, which deliberately excludes the possibility of divine intervention. Nor can the possibility of God's speech be constrained to a previous time, but must be contemplated in the present. In *Heinrich von Ofterdingen*, Novalis, as we have seen, has Heinrich regard dreams as "divine gifts," and "friendly companions on our pilgrimage to the holy sepulchre" (*Henry Von Ofterdingen* 19).

The development of later enlightenment thought into German idealism proved fruitful for Novalis. A new interest in the role of the imagination and poetics in relation to metaphysics also brought with it a renewed interest in dreams and their metaphysical significance. Herder and Jean Paul, for example, closely associate dreams and poetics. Jean Paul calls dreams the mother country of the imagination and for Herder dreams are the ideal of the fairy tale genre as well as all novels (Engel 151). Here, at the beginnings of German idealism, one has to locate the early Romantic voice of Novalis. For Novalis, the imagination — or to render the German more literally, the power and ability to imagine (German: *Vorstellungskraft, Einbildungsvermögen*), becomes the foundational force for all knowing and the role of dreams is crucial (Engel 152). In dreams, "the hobbled imagination is freed and revived" (*Henry Von Ofterdingen* 19) as Heinrich says when he argues with his father. Thus, in response to a merely ordered and rational understanding of the world that privileges the use of prose, Novalis puts forth the poet-dreamer as a person who guides his readers to a renewed and more comprehensive vision of the world, especially a renewed vision for the supernatural and divine.[12] The task of the poet, so Novalis argues, is to point to the Golden Age.[13] The poet, according to Novalis, should employ stylistic devices such as an arbitrary use of the world of the senses, non-coherence in the plot and non-closure in the narrative (Kasperowski 176). Hayward calls this technique a "strain[ing] against the barriers of conventional narrative" (209). The subversive use of images and symbols is another important device. In this way the rational world has to submit to and serve a fresh poetic expression.

Symbols are important in Novalis' work. Symbols suggest things, and create associations that are meant to open up one's vision in contrast to a more mechanical prose, which, for Novalis, has a tendency to narrow down meaning. Even though *Heinrich von Ofterdingen* consists of a considerable amount of prose writing, it is saturated with symbols. Novalis continually creates associations through symbols that can express complex realities. Novalis argues: "Our language is either mechanical, atomistic or dynamic. The true poetic language ought to be organic and alive. How often do we feel the poverty of words, which seek to express several ideas with one swoop" (*Werk* vol. II: 255). Of course MacDonald's view of poetics is very similar and it is no surprise then that MacDonald would refer to and lean on Novalis for the creation of his two most "Romantic" fantasy novels, *Phantastes* and *Lilith*.

In this context of Novalis' Romantic view of language as a response to enlightenment thinking and its refusal to believe in supernatural revelation, one has to understand Novalis', and also MacDonald's, use of dreams. Of course, true to the Romantic spirit, dreams in Novalis are complex and fluid rather than systematic. I will focus on just one aspect here, where dreams serve as a poetic device to open one's vision to the divine. Novalis distinguishes between various qualities of dreams. There are of course ordinary dreams with no deep significance. The highest form of dreams happens in a synthesis of dreaming and waking. In this synthesis the experience of the individual is brought into the spiritual world created by the imagination. And for Novalis this synthesis of waking and dreaming is best mediated in poetic dreams of the fairy tale genre (*Werk* vol. II: 448; also Engel 164). Novalis' privileging of the fairy tale as a dream form provides the context for our understanding Mr. Vane's state at the end of *Lilith*, where he is not sure whether he is dreaming or awake. Mr. Vane is awaiting the fulfillment of the "other" world that he has begun to discover in the world of the seven dimensions. "I wait; asleep or awake, I wait" are his last words and the novel closes with Novalis' words: "Our life is no dream, but it should and will perhaps become one" (MacDonald, *Lilith* 252).

Dreams and fairy tales have become poetic strategies for drawing the reader into the world created by the poet. Novalis does not differentiate between dreams and fairy tales anymore. It is in this context that one has to understand the Novalis quotation translated by MacDonald in *Phantastes*:

> One can imagine stories without rational cohesion and yet filled with associations, like dreams; and poems that are merely lovely sounding, full of beautiful words, but also without rational sense and connections-with, at the most, individual verses which are intelligible, like fragments of the most varied things. This true Poesie can at most have a general allegorical meaning and an indirect effect, as music does. (*Phantastes* 3)

Stories without rational cohesion, images that seek to suggest and cause one to make associations are thus literary tools by which Novalis, and MacDonald in his own way, sought to defamiliarize the reader aesthetically. Fairy tales become the place where a certain rationality is destroyed so that the narrative can establish a fresh and more profound vision of the world.[14] Engel writes, "dreams are for Novalis, like other insertions as poems and fairy stories, a model for a specifically romantic, anti-realistic style of writing, in which 'dream-like' streaks break out the enclave of a clearly defined dream sequences and enter into the main body of the narrative"(167). The line between dreaming and waking is purposefully blurred and a literary style is created that seeks to transcend the orderly, rational and systematic world in order to awaken the reader to the supernatural and spiritual world that Novalis (and MacDonald) so strongly believed in. In this way dreams can become for Novalis prophetic.

It is important to emphasize that neither Novalis nor MacDonald understood such literary creation as irrational. Reason was still a crucial dimension of these newly created worlds. They sought to re-establish a "rationality" that views the spiritual not in opposition to the rational and empirical world (Engel 164).[15] It was important for Novalis to seek an integration of the physical with the spiritual rather than a mere transcending from the physical to the spiritual. Novalis' elevation of the state between waking and dreaming as the superior state emphasizes this very important concern of integration.

Dreams to what end? Dreams, revelation and the face of God

As I mentioned above, Novalis sought to recover a more comprehensive view of the world for his own time, especially in regard to the integration of the spiritual world into a time and culture that focused on the physical and rational. However, his poetic expression was not so much for the discovery of something new, but rather for the recovery of something old. Novalis writes: "All truth is ancient. The allure of the new lies in the variety of expression. The greater the contrast in appearance, the greater the joy of recognition" (*Werk*, vol. II: 290). Dreams have a revelatory dimension; they reveal something that exists, but that is not easily grasped. In the conversation between Heinrich and his father in *Heinrich von Ofterdingen*, Novalis offers us important insights into what this revelation might refer to. While Heinrich's father argues that the times are past when "the divine face appears in dreams," Novalis, in the voice of Heinrich, holds to a more medieval understanding of revelation.[16] While he does not equate dreams with a direct revelation from God, he does understand them as "divine gifts, as friendly companions on our pilgrimage to the holy sepulchre" (*Henry Von Ofterdingen* 10). Novalis would certainly not attribute to every dream a deeper meaning. However, he does consider the possibility that God can reveal himself in dreams and that they have therefore revelatory dimension with an eschatological significance. Heinrich, in response to his father's skepticism, says about his dream: "Certainly the dream I dreamed last night will not have been an ineffectual accident in my life, for I feel that it reaches into my soul ...[like] a giant wheel, impelling it onward with a mighty swing" (*Henry Von Ofterdingen* 19). Dreams have thus the potential of revealing truth, but only because they are sent by God as "a divine gift." The source of such revelations is not dreams in themselves, but God who reveals in and through them.[17]

George MacDonald holds to a very similar view of dreams and revelation. In *Lilith*, he firmly situates Mr. Vane's dreams in the reality of God's presence in the world. The source of Mr. Vane's dreams is not his own subconscious, but God who gives dreams. Mr. Vane is unsure whether he is dreaming or awake, and he questions where his dreams have come from. He wonders:

> "Could God Himself create such lovely things as I dreamed?"
> "Whence then came thy dream?" answers Hope.
> "Out of my dark self, into the light of my consciousness."
> "But whence first into thy dark self?" rejoins Hope.
> "My brain was its mother, and the fever in my blood its father."
> "Say rather", suggest Hope, "thy brain was the violin whence it issued,

and the fever in thy blood the bow that drew it forth. — But who made the violin? and who guided the bow across its strings?" [. . .]

Man dreams and desires; God broods and wills and quickens.

When a man dreams his own dreams, he is the sport of his dream; when Another gives it him, that Other is able to fulfil it.[18]

(*Lilith* 251)

It is in the context of this understanding of revelation in dreams that one needs to understand the Novalis quotation that MacDonald was so fond of. "Our life is no dream, but it should and will perhaps become one," becomes now a metaphor for an understanding of life, where the spiritual dimension of reality becomes integral and finds its ultimate fulfillment only in the future. In dreams one can be freed from a fixation on a mere material world and open up one's eyes to the spiritual world. The open-ended nature of this statement has eschatological and, as Engel calls it, prophetic overtones (Engel 163). Dreams have the ability to "impel one onward" towards the ultimate destination of humanity, one's homecoming and this homecoming is for Novalis closely linked with his belief in Christ as both *Hymns to the Night* and his *Spiritual Songs* suggest.[19]

Hymns to the Night

In *Hymns to the Night*, Novalis creates a cycle of hymns that seeks to "reach into one's soul like a giant wheel," impelling the reader onward "with a mighty swing" (*Henry Von Ofterdingen* 19). In what follows, I discuss Novalis' employment of subversive imagery in order to help the reader to rediscover an important aspect of the Christian journey. Novalis' theory of poetics and dreams as well as his belief in God now take on concrete form. These hymns literally function like "a divine gift, a friendly companion on our pilgrimage to the holy sepulchre," and I argue that it is because of their subversive nature as well as their emphasis on Jesus as the fulfillment of Novalis' longing that they had such a strong hold on MacDonald and served as an inspiration for his last fantasy, *Lilith*.

As the title of this cycle of six hymns suggests, the main subject is the night. It is surprising then that these hymns begin with an appraisal of the light. Novalis writes, "Before all the wondrous shows of the widespread space around him, what living, sentient thing loves not the all-joyous light, with its colors, its rays and undulations, its gentle omnipresence in the form of the wakening Day?" (Novalis in George MacDonald *Rampolli* 3).[20] After such an introduction one would expect a continuation of the praise of the day and the light, but already in the second paragraph an important turn occurs, which Novalis continues throughout these hymns. Rather than turning towards the light, Novalis turns downwards to the "holy, mysterious, inexpressible night" (*Werk,* vol. II: 149).[21] Thus, in the very beginning, Novalis sets up a stark contrast between night and light. It is also important to notice that he uses these symbols in a subversive way, as the century of enlightenment associated the light and the day with reason, darkness with sin and guilt and the night stood in contrast to the light of God's revelation. Such subversive imagery seems at first confusing and disturbing.

However, in light of the conversation between Heinrich and his father discussed above, Novalis' intention becomes clearer. In true Romantic spirit he challenges the contemporary over emphasis on reason and a mere rational understanding of reality by subverting the use of light and night and he reconstructs a reality in which the symbol of the night becomes central. In this way he emphasizes both the limitations of enlightenment thinking as well as the fact that some of the most important aspects of the Christian faith cannot be apprehended on a merely rational basis; they have to be experienced by a turn towards the night, an important idea in Christian mysticism.[22] Novalis' final aim, however, is not to set up a false dichotomy between reason and a Romantic mystical outlook. The final goal is their integration, a concern very close to MacDonald's own heart. Thus Novalis reflects in hymn four: "Now I know when will come the last morning: when the light no more scares away the Night and Love, when sleep shall be without waking, and but one continuous dream" (*Rampolli* 6).[23]

Hayward describes Novalis' subversive use of traditional imagery well when she calls it a "re-orientation of classical Christian Doctrine" (206). Novalis describes his own poetics as a way "to defamiliarize in a pleasant way, to make an object strange, and yet familiar and enticing, that is Romantic poetry" (*Werk* 839). But what is this reorientation and what is it exactly that Novalis wants to entice his readers into? Hayward suggests that death and absorption have become the prime impulses of an erotic mystical love affair and she concludes that these hymns "offer anarchic ideas. Love is seen in terms of erotic desire, spiritual union in terms of overt sexual activity; death is seductive and alluring " (206). It is significant that Hayward, in her discussion of these Hymns, leaves out a very important part of *Hymns to the Night*, where Novalis reflects on Christ's death and resurrection. For Novalis, only in Christ's suffering, death and resurrection can we find redemption. Death in itself does not offer life or redemption as Hayward suggests when she writes, "For Novalis, as for MacDonald, death was the great link between the two worlds, the absolute necessary step towards finding the way home" (240).[24] I shall challenge Hayward's view by showing that the erotic and sexual language that Novalis employs in these hymns has to be understood in his return to medieval imagery and mystical ideas in order to express a profound Christian mystery. A couple of examples shall suffice here to support my argument. Novalis, before moving into erotic language, praises the victorious cross of Christ in Hymn four:

> Inconsumable stands the cross,
> Victory-flag of our race.

He then continues in the voice of a passive lover:

> Oh, powerfully suck me, beloved,
> Draw till I'm gone;
> That, fallen asleep, I
> Still may love on! (*Rampolli* 8) [26]

In hymn five, after reflecting on Christ's resurrection, Novalis points to Christ's death that calls the believer to the wedding feast; he notes that to Mary thousands will lift their hearts.[27] Novalis ends this cycle of hymns by calling the reader once more down into the night:

> Blest be the everlasting Night,
> And blest the endless Slumber! ...
> To our home we have to go
> That blessed time again to know. ...
> Down to the sweet bride, and away
> To the beloved Jesus! (*Rampolli* 15, 16)

The bridal imagery used interchangeably for Christ, his beloved Sophie, and Mary was quite common in medieval Germany and some of the erotic language is reminiscent of the *Song of Songs* in the Old Testament. Already in *Heinrich von Ofterdingen* can we see this return to medieval imagery in Novalis. The novel is set in medieval Germany and medieval imagery abounds. Novalis weaves into one of the fairy stories the red carbuncle, a medieval symbol for Christ. At another place, Heinrich compares his beloved Mathilde to a sapphire, a medieval symbol for Mary as well as wisdom.[28] The experience of the death of Mathilde now becomes like a higher revelation of life.[29] Thus the lost Mathilde, like the lost bride in the above hymn, referring to Novalis' real loss of his fiancée' Sophie, has taken on the role of a mediator. Novalis clothes this conviction in yet another medieval image when he has the miner explain to Heinrich at another point in *Heinrich von Ofterdingen* that the gems of life are only found in the depths of the mountain.

But what has this melting of Romantic love with imagery of Mary, the beloved Mathilde/Sophie, and Christ to do with the night? Eugen Biser argues convincingly that the key to understanding *Hymns to the Night* is an experience that Novalis had after the tragic loss of his fiancée, Sophie (12-13).[30] Novalis struggled with depression and suicidal thoughts, wanting to follow his beloved into death. However, one day, at her grave he had a profound spiritual experience through which his grief and depression was transformed into a new hope:

> The hillock became a cloud of dust, and through the cloud I saw the glorified face of my beloved. In her eyes eternity reposed. I laid hold of her hands, and the tears became a sparkling bond that could not be broken. Into the distance swept by, like a tempest, thousands of years. On her neck I welcomed the new life with ecstatic tears. Never was such another dream; then first and ever since I hold fast an eternal, unchangeable faith in the heaven of the Night, and its Light, the Beloved. (*Rampolli* 6)

Novalis' own experience of loss and the subsequent mystical encounter beside Sophie's grave made him understand a central and yet seemingly paradoxical mystery of the Christian faith: the very place one would naturally consider as "dark," one's losses, one's suffering and the harsh reality of death, becomes now the very place where God reveals himself. This is why Novalis can write *Hymns to the Night*, not because he intends to celebrate death, loss and suffering as such but because of what is revealed in the night.

In the first hymn Novalis asks of the night: "What holdest thou under thy mantle, that with hidden power affects my soul?" (*Rampolli* 4). In hymn four and five Novalis answers this rhetorical question: "the Night became the mighty womb of revelation" (*Rampolli* 11, *Hymn* 5). This revelation is centered for Novalis on the birth, life, death and resurrection of Christ, which he reflects upon in the last four hymns. Novalis writes, "Inconsumable stands the cross, victory-flag of our race," and "In death eternal life was made known, you are death and thou first makest us whole" (*Hymn* five, translation mine). Thus, I argue that Novalis' fascination with the night and death is not with death as such, as Wolff and Spina have argued (Wolff 22-23; Spina 30). Rather, it is because of Christ's death and resurrection that one's own experience of suffering and loss can become the very place we encounter God. In Christ, one's own experience of loss and suffering can be redeemed. This is why Novalis urges his reader again and again to go down into the holy and blessed night (*Rampolli* 3, 15), resonating the Latin *exsulet* and its praise of the Easter night: *o vere beata nox*. This journey downward into the night and his longing after death really reflect a longing after home, which is for Novalis closely connected with his faith in the beloved Jesus. Thus he writes at the very end of these *Hymns*, "Down to the sweet bride, and away to the beloved Jesus! Courage! The evening shades grow grey, of all our grief to ease us! A dream will dash our chains apart, and lay us on the Father's heart" (*Rampolli* 16). Death in itself cannot save or redeem or give birth to hope and new life. But the experience of loss and death can become the very place where Christ meets us and where we can come to know Christ and be unified with him in his suffering and somehow, also in his resurrection. And for Novalis this great mystery is best expressed in poetical dreams which in turn help the reader both to imagine and learn to participate in this great mystery and somehow be laid into "the Father's heart" (*Rampolli*, 16).

The uniqueness of *Hymns to the Night* lies in its employment of Romantic poetics as a way to enter into one of the most difficult and profound Christian mysteries.[31] Thus, these hymns do not offer anarchic ideas as Hayward suggests. On the contrary, they seek to provide guidance in the midst of a frantic existence where the experience of loss and suffering does not necessarily have to lead to despair and hopelessness. The movement down into the night becomes a way through the abyss to a solid place, which Novalis calls "the beloved Jesus" (*Rampolli* 16). Poetics, for Novalis, thus serves the greater purpose of expressing the mystery that is revealed to all and yet remains forever "unfathomable" as Novalis puts it in *Heinrich von Ofterdingen* (*Werk* 361).[32] For Novalis the task of the poet and priest is intimately connected and he sees it as the task of his time to recover their unity. He writes:" Poet and priest were one in the beginning and only in later times were they separated. The true poet is always priest, just as the true priest remains always a poet – and should the future not seek to re-establish the old order of things?" (*Werk*, Vol II: 255. My translation). This unified vision of the role of the priest as poet as well as Novalis' profound grasp of the mystery of Christ's death and resurrection in light of his own suffering had a strong appeal to MacDonald as he sought to bring these two callings together in his own life, while facing tremendous suffering and the loss of many of his loved ones.

A few suggestions as to how *Hymns to the Night* helped shape *Lilith* shall suffice here. Mr. Vane, the protagonist, finds himself mysteriously transported into another world and is challenged by a sexton, who is also a raven, to lie down in the chamber of death. Mr. Raven speaks: "Do not be a coward, Mr. Vane. Turn your back on fear, and your face to whatever may come. Give yourself up to the night, and you will rest indeed. Harm will not come to you, but a good you cannot foreknow" (36). However, Mr. Vane is not so easily persuaded to enter into the chamber of death and lie down and sleep. Mr. Vane's story is that of someone who struggles to give himself up to the night. He wants to follow his own ideas.

But why should one think that MacDonald employed these symbols of death and the night like Novalis to express the implications of Christ's death and resurrection for the Christian faith? No direct references to Christ occur in *Lilith*. A careful look at MacDonald's employment of biblical imagery will show, however, how important and central Christ's death is for understanding Mr. Vane's own journey. I focus on one biblical reference in particular, one that recurs in *Lilith* at very important turns in the story. When Mr. Vane first enters the sexton's cottage he asks for food and drink that will quench his thirst and he receives bread and wine. Bread and wine are, of course, the central elements of the Eucharist, the place where Christians enter the mysteries of Christ's death and resurrection. After Mr. Vane eats and drinks, he remarks: "the bread and wine seemed to go deeper than the hunger and thirst" (30-31). Towards the end of the novel Lilith herself is offered bread and wine and Eve tells her: "This food will help thee to die"(214), but Lilith refuses to eat it. At the very end Mr. Vane is finally ready to lie down in the chamber of death, but he must first be forgiven by Adam and Eve (220). After his final test, Mr. Vane is served bread and wine once more and he literally "partakes of it" (229); MacDonald's language here is liturgical and hence indicative of the Lord's Supper. Clearly these references evoke associations of the Eucharist and tie Mr. Vane's journey to the Christian story.

Both the influence of *Hymns to the Night* and the biblical references show the importance of Christ's death and resurrection for understanding Mr. Vane's journey. Just like Novalis, MacDonald grappled with the great Christian mystery that as we partake in Christ's suffering we will also somehow take part in his resurrection. And just like Novalis, so did MacDonald employ subversive imagery to speak to a Christian context that seemed unable or unwilling to enter more deeply into this difficult mystery. Novalis was a great inspiration for MacDonald in this regard and there is no other writer, friend or thinker of whom MacDonald would say, "It is, indeed, well with him who has found a friend whose spirit touches his own and illuminates it. … Shall I not one day, 'somewhere, somehow,' clasp the large hand of Novalis, and gazing on his face, compare his features with those of Saint John?" (*A Dish of Orts* 229-230).

Endnotes

1. Wolff's discussion of the influence of Novalis is an early and comprehensive discussion. However, his evaluation of Novalis is not careful. He argues for example that Novalis desired death and that MacDonald toyed with similar inclinations. Careful studies of Novalis have shown though, that he overcame his suicidal period after his spiritual encounter by Sophie's grave and his writing on death has to be understood symbolically rather than a literal desire for death. See especially Wilhelmine Maria Sepasgosarin, *Der Tod Als Romantisierendes Prinzip Des Lebens* (Frankfurt: Peter Lang, 1991). Sepasgosarin provides a very careful discussion of Novalis' very complex understanding of death in the context of his Moravian tradition and his period of depression and recovery. See esp. pp. 148-162.
2. Deirdre Hayward's treatment of the influence of Novalis upon MacDonald is the most comprehensive and most helpful so far.
3. The citation in *Phantastes* is slightly different: "Our life is no dream; but it ought to become one, and perhaps will."(*Phantastes* 182)
4. The other direct quotation is from Thoreau's essay "Walking". MacDonald also inserts two footnotes in chapters XLV and XLVI citing Dante.
5. Wolff provides a very careful discussion of Novalis' citation in the beginning of *Phantastes* but only mentions the dream citation. Hal Broome discusses dream imagery in MacDonald's works from a scientific angle which is helpful, but he neglects the theological importance of dreams which is so important for MacDonald. Frank P. Riga provides a general discussion of dreams in MacDonald, using *At the Back of the NorthWind* as his prime example, but he fails to recognize the importance of Novalis' influence upon MacDonald. Hayward provides an overview of the dream imagery in Novalis and MacDonald's work and draws out MacDonald's more critical stance towards it (Hayward 229-233).
6. Unfortunately, the English translation available and used here is at times not correct. Thus, I will add my own translation in brackets as needed.
7. For a similar argument see Kristin Pfefferkorn, *Novalis: A Romantic's Theory of Language and Poetry* (New Haven: Yale University Press, 1988), pp. 171-72. Engel shows in more detail how much Novalis was familiar with the dream theories of enlightenment thinkers. See Manfred Engel, "Träumen Und Nichtträumen Zugleich. Novalis' Theorie Und Poetik Des Traumes Zwischen Aufklaerung Und Hochromantik," *Novalis Und Die Wissenschaften*, ed. Herbert Uerlings (Tübingen:

Max Niemeyer Verlag, 1997), p. 160.
8. Engel relies here on an article on dreams published in the Grosses *Vollständiges Universal-Lexikon aller Wissenschaften und Künste*, published in Germany in 1745.
9. This is important to notice, as MacDonald completely blurs the lines between waking and sleeping in the character of Mr. Vane at the end of *Lilith*.
10. Christian Wolff, *Gesammelte Werke*. I. Abt. Bd. 2, p. 76, as quoted in Engel, "Träumen," p. 145. Translation mine.
11. Engel, "Träumen," pp. 147-51. With the rise of empiricism, the study of dreams became a main focus with anthropological studies as it sought to understand the experiences of the soul ("Erfahrungsseelenkunde") on empirical grounds.
12. Novalis' understanding of the role of the poet has at times strong idealist tendencies and thus becomes problematic, especially because he seeks to recover a theological understanding of the poet. At times the poet becomes deified and seems to be the sole mediator between the finite and the eternal. See for example Novalis, *Novalis Das Philosophisch-Theoretische Werk*, ed. Hans-Joachim and Richard Samuel Mähl, vol. II, III vols. (München: Carl Hanser Verlag, 1978), p. 322.
13. The Golden Age is an important idea in Novalis' thinking and closely connected to his eschatological understanding of the world. In *Christenheit oder Europa* Novalis bemoans the loss of faith in the modern world and envisions an undivided Christian Europe. The pre-reformation period is seen as the ideal world where people still had a childlike faith. Through the Reformation and the scientific discoveries the Europeans lost their respect for the earth and their heavenly home. Novalis, *Die Christenheit Oder Europa* (Stuttgart: Philipp Reclam, 1984), p. 69. It is no accident that Novalis places *Heinrich von Ofterdingen* in the medieval period where Heinrich can discover his poetic gifts quite freely. While both of these works seem to idealize the medieval world, in a sense it is clear that this is only a stylistic device. Novalis reflects quite critically on the Crusades in *Heinrich von Ofterdingen* for example.
14. For a similar argument see Deirdre Christine Hayward, "George Macdonald and Three German Thinkers," PhD, University of Dundee, 2000, p. 213. Hayward defends both Novalis and MacDonald against accusations of irrationality and meaninglessness and argues that "the way to new kind of rationality (the project of MacDonald and Novalis) goes via a deconstruction of ordinary logic."
15. MacDonald's novel *At the Back of the North Wind* is a great example of such an integration of dream sequences into the realistic framework of the story.

16. In the medieval period dreams and dream visions were often thought to be divinely inspired. See Steven F. Kruger, *Dreaming in the Middle Ages*, Cambridge Studies in Medieval Literature (Cambridge: Cambridge University Press, 1992). He provides a careful discussion of the role of dreams in the medieval period.

17. Novalis is not always as clear about the source of revelation as he is in this part of *Heinrich von Ofterdingen*. See Hayward, "George Macdonald and Three German Thinkers," p. 219-20. She discusses Novalis' more idealist understanding of poetry.

18. MacDonald makes a similar argument in his first essay on the imagination. See MacDonald, *A Dish of Orts*, p. 25.

19. See also Sepasgosarin, *Der Tod Als Romantisierendes Prinzip Des Lebens*, pp. 220-24, 55.

20. Unless otherwise indicated, the translation of the *Hymns* is taken from George MacDonald in *Rampolli*. There are two different German versions of *Hymns to the Night*. MacDonald's translation relies on the later published version. It is noteworthy that the handwritten version does not have "waking day" but merely "day". Novalis, *Novalis Das Dichterische Werk, Tagebücher Und Briefe, Novalis Werke*, ed. Hans-Joachim and Richard Samuel Mähl, vol. I, III vols. (München: Carl Hanser Verlag, 1978), pp. 148-49.

21. In the last verse, the move downwards is stressed once more (see p. 177).

22. Gerhard Schulz argues along similar lines when he states these hymns seek to explore a dimension of the Christian faith that the enlightenment world with its focus on the day and the light is unable to grasp. Gerhard Schulz, "Novalis (Friedrich Von Hardenberg)," *Deutsche Dichter Romantik, Biedermeier Und Vormärz*, ed. Frank Rainer and Max Gunter Grimm, Deutsche Dichter (Stuttgart: Reclam, 1989), p. 46. See also Eugen Biser, *Abstieg und Auferstehung: Die geistige Welt in Novalis Hymnen an die Nacht* (Heidelberg: Lambert Schneider, 1954), pp. 34-36.

23. As the hymns develop, he works towards an integration of the light and the night. The most perfect state will be when the two are integrated into one another or, to use Novalis' words, when the day does not scare away the night anymore. Literally, Novalis writes: "Now I know when will come the last morning: when the light no more scares away the Night and Love, when sleep shall be without waking, and but one continuous dream." Novalis in George MacDonald, *Rampolli* (Whitethorn: Johannesen, 1995), p. 6.

24. Hayward's discussion of death in Novalis is problematic for various reasons. While she begins her discussion of Novalis with an analysis of *Hymns to the Night*,

she then establishes her understanding of death in Novalis on various quotations taken from Novalis' *Fragments*. Methodologically speaking, this is very difficult to do, as these fragments were written over a long period of time and Novalis' understanding of death was rather complex. For a more careful discussion of Novalis' understanding of death see *Sepasgosarin, Der Tod Als Romantisierendes Prinzip Des Lebens*.

25. Roder provides a careful analysis of a variety of medieval symbols that Novalis employs. He also discusses Novalis' use of mystical ideas. Florian Roder, *Novalis Die Verwandlung Des Menschen* (Stuttgart: Urachhaus, 1992), pp. 427, 636ff.

26. The line, "Oh, powerfully suck me, beloved," is my own translation as MacDonald's translation does not capture the force of the German "*O! sauge, Geliebter*". The word "*sauge*" expresses a very strong degree of drawing or pulling someone near. The English word "sucking" seems to capture this German word best.

27. It is noteworthy that MacDonald does not directly name Mary, as Novalis does, but refers to her as "mother maiden" which might indicate that MacDonald was quite uncomfortable with Novalis' adoration of Mary and the prime place that she had in his theology.

28. "There is engraved an enigmatic token, full deep into the jewels' glowing blood. The stone is comparable to a heart, in which the image of the unknown woman rests." Novalis, *Henry Von Ofterdingen*, trans. Palmer Hilty (New York: Frederick Ungar Publishing Co., 1964), p. 41. The last two lines are my own translation. Roder, in his careful biography of Novalis, provides a collection of medieval images that depict the relationship between Christ, Mary/Sophia in mystical fashion. See especially the German medieval depiction of the Trinity with Sophia/Mary in the middle as well as the image of Mary and Jesus with the blue flower linking the two. Roder also provides a discussion of the meaning of these symbols, both lining out their historical significance and how Novalis appropriates these symbols for his own purpose. His emphasis lies with their aesthetic and metaphysical significance. Unfortunately, he does not stress their theological import enough. Roder, *Novalis Die Verwandlung Des Menschen*, pp. 261, 433, 689-92, 733.

29. Novalis, *Vol. I*. P. 370-371. The idea that the loss of a beloved, in this case Mathilde and Sophie, becomes a revelatory experience is also based on a medieval image, where a young man has to break a sapphire in order to get to the carbuncle which is enclosed in the sapphire. See the image in Roder, p. 733.

30. Roder, p. 639, argues along similar lines. Hymn three bears such striking similarities to an entry into Novalis' diary for May 13. 1797 regarding a profound spiritual experience by Sophie's grave that the connection between the two is commonly acknowledged.

31. Christianity is for Novalis superior to Ancient Greek mythology, for example, precisely because it is able to make sense of death in light of Christ's death and resurrection. In hymn five Novalis incorporates the Ancient Greek myths and gods into his hymn, a popular undertaking in the Romantic period, and he laments the inability of the Greek gods to make sense of death.

32. The relationship of poetics and religion in Novalis' works is complex and the question of whether art is subservient to religion or the other way around is difficult to answer and beyond the scope of this chapter. In *Hymns to the Night* one can clearly argue for poetics as a handmaiden to religion but at other places in Novalis' works it might seem the other way around. See Pfefferkorn, pp. 187-190. She discusses this issue and concludes that "his stronger inclination is toward the service of art to the truth, to the divine, and that for this reason his truly religious poems, the *Geistliche Lieder*, are his most successful poetic work" (189). And the same can be said for *Hymns to the Night*.

Works Cited

Barfield, Owen. *Romanticism comes of Age.* London: Rudolf Steiner Press, 1966.
Biser, Eugen. *Abstieg und Auferstehung: Die geistige Welt in Novalis Hymnen an die Nacht.* Heidelberg: Lambert Schneider, 1954.
Engel, Manfred. "Träumen Und Nichtträumen Zugleich. Novalis' Theorie Und Poetik Des Traumes Zwischen Aufklaerung Und Hochromantik." *Novalis Und Die Wissenschaften*. Ed. Herbert Uerlings. Tübingen: Max Niemeyer Verlag, 1997. 143-68.
Hayward, Deirdre Christine. "George Macdonald and Three German Thinkers." PhD. University of Dundee, 2000.
Kasperowski, Ira. *Mittelalterrezeption im Werk des Novalis.* Tübingen: Max Niemeyer Verlag, 1994.
MacDonald, George. *A Dish of Orts.* 1996 ed. Whitethorn: Johannesen, 1893.
---. *Lilith. A Romance.* Grand Rapids: Eerdmans, 1895, 2000.
---. *Phantastes.* Grand Rapids: Eerdmans, 1858, 2000.

---. *Rampolli*. Whitethorn: Johannesen, 1897, 1995.
---. *The Poetical Works of George MacDonald Vol. 2*. London: Chatto & Windus, 1911.
Novalis. *Henry Von Ofterdingen*. Trans. Palmer Hilty. New York: Frederick Ungar Publishing Co., 1964.
---. *Novalis: Das Dichterische Werk, Tagebücher Und Briefe. Novalis Werke*. Ed. Hans-Joachim and Richard Samuel Mähl. Vol. I. III vols. München: Carl Hanser Verlag, 1978.
---. *Novalis: Das Philosophisch-Theoretische Werk*. Ed. Hans-Joachim and Richard Samuel Mähl. Vol. II. III vols. München: Carl Hanser Verlag, 1978.
Spina, Giorgio. "Contrapositions, Correspondences and Symmetries in George MacDonald's fiction." *Inklings: Jahrbuch fuer Literatur und Aesthetik* 13 (1995): 27-45.
Wolff, Robert Lee. *The Golden Key: A Study of the Fiction of George MacDonald*. New Haven: Yale University Press, 1961.

Sir Henry Vane

Thoreau

Emerson

Maurice

Hawthorne

Chapter 3

Mr. Vane's Pilgrimage into the Land of Promise: MacDonald's "Historical Imagination" in *Lilith*

Robert Trexler

> *I learnt from [Coleridge], by practical illustrations, how one may enter into the spirit of a living or a departed author, without assuming to be his judge; how one may come to know what he means without imputing to him our meanings. I learnt that beauty is neither an accidental nor an artificial thing, that it is to be sought out as something which is both in nature and in the mind of man, and which, by God's law binds us to nature.*
> F. D. Maurice – From the 1842 dedication of *The Kingdom of Christ*

George MacDonald's artistic debt to German and Scottish writers is an established fact. However, it will be a surprise for many to learn that American writers also influenced MacDonald. The general purpose of this essay is to link MacDonald's book *Lilith* and its protagonist, Mr. Vane, with Puritan history and American literature – in particular, to what Thoreau calls "American mythology" ("Walking" 620).

My American theories about *Lilith* began, as theories generally do, with some accidental discoveries. While reading the collected poems of John Milton I found a memorial sonnet he wrote entitled "To Sir Henry Vane, The Younger." I had never heard of Sir Henry Vane. I had never heard of anyone with the name Vane except Mr. Vane, the protagonist of *Lilith*. I learned that Sir Henry Vane was a pivotal figure in both English and American history – a Puritan statesman, theologian, mystic and martyr – who lived from 1613 until he was beheaded in 1662. Knowing MacDonald's love of Milton and his interest in Puritan history, I filed that away as an odd coincidence. When I read F. D. Maurice's book *The Kingdom of Christ*, published in 1838, I was surprised to find a very favorable mention of Sir Henry Vane. Another coincidence, I thought.

Then, while reading a biography of Robert Browning, a favorite poet of MacDonald's, I was intrigued by a comment Browning recorded in one of Nathaniel Hawthorne's notebooks. During a visit by the Hawthorne family to the Brownings in Italy, Browning commented that his favorite Hawthorne book was *The Blithedale Romance*, the least critically acclaimed of all Hawthorne's romances (Ward 272). I was curious about Browning's opinion and wondered whether MacDonald would have had a similar opinion. I was impressed, in reading Hawthorne's Preface to

The Blithdale Romance, by his description of artistic imagination; the book itself contains significant parallels in plot and characters with *Lilith*. I began to wonder if Hawthorne's and MacDonald's interest in Puritan history had a common source.

Another inspiration took me to Thoreau's essay "Walking." MacDonald chose a paragraph from that essay as an epigraph for *Lilith*. The essay's central motif is of a pilgrimage to the Promised Land and what Thoreau calls "American Mythology" ("Walking" 620). One of Thoreau's early essays was on Sir Henry Vane. Other New England Transcendentalist writers, Emerson and Hawthorne, also mention Sir Henry Vane in their writings, Emerson in *Nature* and Hawthorne in *Legends of the Province House*. I came to the conclusion that there was more to this than coincidence. There was something about the historical imagination of these Victorian writers that gravitated toward Puritan history.

As unlikely as it seemed to me at first, it now seems very likely that Sir Henry Vane, the Younger, is the prototype for MacDonald's character Mr. Vane. Evaluating the historical and fictional Vanes produces at least three benefits: 1) it deepens our understanding of MacDonald's theological foundations, 2) it uncovers common interests with some of his contemporary writers – especially F. D. Maurice and the New England Transcendentalists, and 3) it offers evidence that Puritan history and American myth stimulated MacDonald's historical imagination and provided a context for him to write an ironic, apocalyptic, anti-utopian romance.

Sauntering to Eden

A good place to begin is with Thoreau's essay "Walking." Thoreau first delivered this essay as a Lyceum lecture in Concord, Massachusetts in 1851. He refined and presented the essay frequently in the following years. But it was not published until after his death in 1862. The epigraph chosen by MacDonald describes Thoreau as being in a "stately pine wood" where he has the impression of walking into the hall of some "ancient and altogether admirable and shining family" living in Concord, Massachusetts ("Walking" 628). The description compares with Mr. Vane's impression of what he calls a "moving panorama" as he imagines people who looked upon his own estate years ago (*Lilith* 8). Mr. Vane, who has just taken possession of his estate, does not realize he is about to embark on a fantastic journey through space and time. The form of that journey is a spiritual pilgrimage.

Thoreau's essay begins with these words: "I want to speak a word for Nature, for absolute Freedom and Wildness, as contrasted with a Freedom and Culture merely civil" (597). When Thoreau speaks of Freedom contrasted with Culture he is not merely being poetic; he is also writing serious philosophical and political commentary. Thoreau writes, "I walk out into a nature such as the old prophets and poets Menu, Moses, Homer, Chaucer, walked in. You may call it America, but it is not America. Neither Americus Vespucius, nor Columbus, nor the rest were discoverers of it. There is a truer account of it in Mythology than in any history of America" (604).

One indication that MacDonald, while writing *Lilith*, considered themes of the American and English myth of hope and freedom is Thoreau's theme about a pilgrimage to the land of promise, where the city of Concord, Massachusetts represents the New Jerusalem. Thoreau uses the image of the sun, traveling daily westward, as a symbol of man's desire reflected in literary Utopian destinations. He writes: "The island of Atlantis, and the islands and gardens of Hesperides . . . appear to have been the Great West of the ancients, enveloped in mystery and poetry" (609). He mentions the voyage of Columbus, praises the beauty of wild nature, and extols the virtue of freedom. Thoreau writes with a note of sarcasm: "Perchance, when, in the course of ages, American liberty has become a fiction of the past, – as it is to some extent, a fiction of the present, – the poets of the world will be inspired by American mythology" (620). If MacDonald has used Sir Henry Vane as a symbol of American mythology – as an example of the fiction of American liberty – then he could have chosen no better essay than Thoreau's with which to give a clue to the careful reader.

Thoreau says that only one or two people he has met "understood the art of walking" and he uses the word "sauntering" which he says can be interpreted two ways. The first interpretation is:

> from idle people who roved about the country, in the middle ages, and asked for charity, under the pretense of going *a la sainte terre* – to the holy land, till the children exclaimed, "There goes a *sainte-terrer*, a saunterer – a holy-lander." They who never go to the holy land in their walks, as they pretend, are indeed mere idlers and vagabonds, but they who do go there are saunterers in the good sense, such as I mean. (597)

The second interpretation derives the word:

> from *sans terre*, without land or a home, which in the good sense, will mean, having no particular home, but equally at home everywhere. For this is the secret of successful sauntering. [. . .] every walk is a sort of crusade, preached by some Peter the Hermit in us, to go

forth and reconquer this holy land from the hands of the Infidels. (597)

It is clear to which category of saunterer Mr. Vane belongs. When he saunters into the parallel world of seven dimensions he does not want to be there. He is not a "*sainte terre*," a "holy-lander," but he is "*sans terre*," without a home; and definitely not in the sense which means he is "equally at home everywhere." Mr. Raven and Mr. Vane have a discussion about where home is and whether Mr. Vane will walk where he is told. Here is a part of their conversation:

> "Now we should be going!" said the raven, and stepped to the front of the porch.
> "Going where?" I asked.
> "Going where we have to go," he answered. "You did not surely think you had got home? I told you there was no going out and in at pleasure until you were at home!"
> "I do not want to go," I said.
> "That does not make any difference - at least not much," he answered. "This is the way."
> "I am quite content where I am."
> "You think so, but you are not. Come along." He hopped from the porch on the grass, and turned, waiting.
> "I will not leave the house to-day," I said with obstinacy.
> "You will come into the garden!" rejoined the raven.
>
> (*Lilith* 30)

The English garden he steps into becomes a garden where he meets Adam and Eve – one may presume this is the Garden of Eden. However, Vane's experiences are not easy or comfortable and he does not find anything close to paradise. Mr. Vane finally concludes, "I must accept my fate" (36). He first wonders, "How was life to be lived in a world of which I had all the laws to learn?" (36). His thoughts then turn to his responsibility and honor. He becomes philosophical and reflects: "I had never done anything to justify my existence; my former world was no better for my sojourn in it: here, however, I must earn, or some way find, my bread" (37). Thoreau's essay provides a response to this line of thinking:

> No wealth can buy the requisite leisure, freedom, and independence, which are the capital in this profession [of walking]. It comes only by the grace of God. It requires a direct dispensation from heaven to become a walker. (598)

No, Mr. Vane is not destined for a leisurely walk in paradise. His worry is warranted, for he encounters ominous and dangerous situations. Although Mr. Raven tries to guide him though the bewildering experience, Mr. Vane does not listen, exhausting all his energy in an effort to do what he thinks is right. He faces despair and disillusionment when he discovers his best efforts are useless and those he loves he puts in danger's way. What is even worse, the one he loves most he foolishly causes to die. If Mr. Vane had known what his future held could he have taken comfort in these words from Thoreau's essay?

> It is remarkable how few events or crises there are in our histories; how little exercised we have been in our minds; how few experiences we have had. [. . .] It would be well if all our lives were a divine tragedy even, instead of this trivial comedy or farce. Christ, Dante, Bunyan, and others, appear to have been exercised in their minds more than we; – they were subjected to a kind of culture such as our district schools and colleges do not contemplate. (627)

The Mythical Character of Sir Henry Vane

MacDonald very likely had a historic, crisis event in mind when he fashioned the character of Mr. Vane. In the seventeenth century, during the Great Rebellion in England, lived a noble and tragic figure, a Puritan like John Bunyan. He left England with other Pilgrims who sought in New England a place they expected to be a new Holy Land. It was meant to be a colony where all religious beliefs would be tolerated, where there would be liberty and justice for all. It would be different from Old England where Catholics in Ireland, or Presbyterians in Scotland, or the free-thinking Quakers would fear for their lives as the Monarchy sought to enforce a state religion. Such Puritan dissenters believed in a complete separation of church and state. When he departed for the New World, Henry Vane shared those beliefs.

Henry Vane was the sort of man MacDonald admired, a man of strong conviction and high ideals. Like MacDonald's Mr. Vane, Henry Vane was a graduate of Oxford University. As a young man he became a Puritan although he was the son of a courtier of the King and would have had an easy and privileged career in government service. He traveled to New England in 1635 at the age of twenty-two. Here he made an impression because of his learning and social rank which led to his election as the first governor of Massachusetts. As governor, by virtue of his belief in toleration of religion and freedom of conscience, he supported Anne Hutchinson against charges of heresy. However, Mrs. Hutchinson was banished from the colony, Vane was voted out of office, and he returned to England two years later. Due to his talents and upbringing, he was to find a useful place in government service after all. Vane was knighted by Charles I in 1640, appointed treasurer of the navy, and elected as a member of the Short and Long Parliaments.

As a politician, he was instrumental in getting a charter for the colony of Rhode Island, where founder Roger Williams offered religious freedom to Christians and Jews. Vane also opposed the proposal to force Irish Catholics to attend Protestant worship. Vane supported overthrowing Charles I but not executing him. He was valued by Cromwell and served in many capacities in government until the two clashed over Cromwell's dissolution of Parliament. He wrote an essay called "A Healing Question" in 1656 outlining principles of civil and religious freedom, and proposed a convention to write a national constitution. Vane's ideas provided a blueprint for the principles of constitutional government in America. After Cromwell's death, Vane returned to lead the republicans in Parliament. He was falsely suspected of conspiring to establish a military dictatorship and, after the Restoration, was imprisoned by Charles II, found guilty of high treason, and beheaded in 1662.

Vane immediately became a hero of the English people. John Milton composed a famous sonnet to his memory. Sir Walter Scott, in the historical romance *A Legend of Montrose* (1819), calls him "the celebrated Sir Henry Vane" (48). A few years later, Thomas De Quincey in *Confessions of an English Opium Eater* (1821) assumes his readers will be familiar with Vane and even that they would have access to his theological writings. De Quincey offers a humorous defense of his own writing when he says: "I shall be charged with mysticism, [. . .] but THAT shall not alarm me. Sir Henry Vane, the younger, was one of our wisest men; and let my reader see if he, in his philosophical works, be half as unmystical as I am" (from the chapter "The Pleasures of Opium." This 1821 essay was altered in 1856 and most modern editions use the later edition instead of the 1821 London Magazine edition. The George Rutledge & Sons edition (1886) uses the earlier version and can be located at the University of Adelaide site http://etext.library.adelaide.edu.au/q/quincey/thomas/opium/).

Along with basic history books available to MacDonald, there were four biographies of Vane – the first was written in 1662 by George Sikes, a follower of Vane. Of the three biographies written during MacDonald's lifetime, the first was published in 1835 when MacDonald was eleven years old and the second in 1838. The last was written in 1888 when MacDonald was sixty-four years old. The 1835 biographer, Charles Upham, thought Vane was the best historical link between American and English ideals because he presents "in one character, those features and traits by which it is our pride to prove our lineage and descent from the British Isles" (qtd in Hosmer 568). The 1888 biographer, James Hosmer, wrote that Vane is: "Thorough Englishman, thorough American, his mind possessed by no obsolete ideas, but with ideas so vital at the present moment, the figure of this half-forgotten martyr of freedom can well be brought forward" (568). In the April 1889 *Atlantic Monthly* magazine, the book review of Hosmer's biography begins with this sentence: "With the single exception of Cromwell, the greatest statesman of the heroic age of Puritanism was unquestionably the younger Harry Vane" ("Young Sir Henry Vane" 562). These brief quotations are representative of the mythic value of Henry Vane in the national consciousness of the nineteenth-century. He was a person as mythically important to this period as George Washington is to American revolutionary history.

The New England Transcendentalists and Emerson's *Nature*

We know that Nathaniel Hawthorne read the 1835 biography because he mentions it by name in his history book for children, *Grandfather's Chair* (1840). Henry David Thoreau wrote one of his early essays on Henry Vane. Ralph Waldo Emerson's 1836 book *Nature*, a book that marked a shift in the intellectual climate of nineteenth-century America, has a chapter in which Henry Vane figures prominently.

But first, you may be thinking, what has MacDonald to do with these Yankee writers? And that is something that needs explaining. MacDonald studies are so young that they have barely begun to consider all the influences on MacDonald's life and writings. The intellectual crosscurrents between the American Transcendentalists and English writers need to be introduced because there are many commonalties. In America as in England and Europe, Romanticism in arts and letters challenged neoclassical Enlightenment values. The mechanistic, rational worldview was being replaced with a more organic, emotional, and imaginative culture. The Idealism of Kant and the adaptations of his thought by Schelling and Coleridge helped to justify the value of intuition and feeling. An increasing emphasis on the interior principles of the human mind suggested that our perceptions and interpretations of life experiences take priority over a materialistic view of reality. No book laid a greater groundwork for the New England Transcendental Movement than the 1829 American edition of Coleridge's *Aids to Reflection*.

During the years that Hindu and Buddhist scriptures were being translated and published, Emerson and other educated New Englanders were comparing the religious experiences of other cultures and religions with the current understanding of Christianity. In 1832, Emerson toured Europe and met S. T. Coleridge, Thomas Carlyle, William Wordsworth, and John Stewart Mill. The year 1836 was a watershed year for books that would profoundly influence others for many decades. That year Carlyle's *Sartor Resartus* and Emerson's *Nature* were published in America.

With this background, let's look at an excerpt from Emerson's third chapter entitled "Beauty." Beauty, according to Emerson, has three aspects – the natural, spiritual and intellectual. Emerson uses Sir Henry Vane as an example of the complementary relation between natural and spiritual beauty:

> When a noble act is done, – perchance in a scene of great beauty; [. . .] are not these heroes entitled to add the beauty of the scene to the beauty of their deed? [. . .] When Sir Harry Vane was dragged up the Tower Hill, sitting on a sled, to suffer death, as the Champion of the English Laws ... his biographer says, "The multitude imagined they saw liberty and virtue sitting by his side." (15) Nature stretcheth out her arms to embrace man, only let his thoughts be of equal greatness. [. . .] whoever has seen a person of powerful character and happy genius, will have remarked how easily he took all things along with him, – the persons, the opinions, and the day, and nature became ancillary to a man. (16)

"To reconstruct a life of an individual"

MacDonald and Emerson both see the virtue of a man such as Sir Henry Vane through the eyes of an artist and a symbolist. The scene of Vane's execution presents a prophetic view caused by "the light of imagination . . . cast upon the facts of experience," to borrow words from MacDonald's essay "The Imagination: Its Culture and Function" (*A Dish of Orts* 17). The life of Sir Henry Vane suggested itself to Emerson to illustrate the historical imagination, where "nature becomes ancillary to a man" (*Nature* 15). If, as Kenneth Roemer writes, "half the utopian authors . . . hoped for the appearance of an Everyman-Superman who was a 'Scholar, Sage, Humanitarian, Reformer, Patriot, Author, Orator, and Statesman'," then MacDonald chose one of the few men in history who fit each of those rare qualities (69).

MacDonald writes that when Shakespeare describes characters at the point of death, their words are prophetic because their imagination "cleared of all distorting dimness by the vanishing of earthly hopes and desires [is], cast upon the facts of experience. Such prophecy is the perfect working of the historical imagination" (*A Dish of Orts* 17-18). He goes on to say: "In the interpretation of individual life, the same principle holds, and nowhere can the imagination be more healthily and rewardingly occupied than in endeavoring to reconstruct a life of an individual out of the fragments which are all that can reach us of the history of even the noblest of our race" (17-18).

It is not necessary to think that Mr. Vane possessed all the characteristics of the real Sir Henry Vane. Indeed, the ironic comparison between myth and reality is actually the point if *Lilith* is to be viewed as an anti-utopian book. The motivating factor for MacDonald may be what the symbol does to stimulate his imagination as an artist, and trusting that if the symbol is potent enough to his own mind, the associations will draw out images that communicate to his readers on other levels.

Mr. Fane and Mr. Vane

One obvious objection to my theory that MacDonald held Sir Henry Vane in his imagination when constructing Mr. Vane is that in manuscript "A" the character is named Mr. Fane. The introduction to the variorum edition of *Lilith* mentions a name change between manuscript "A" and manuscript "B" as being from "Henry Fane" to "Mr. Vane" (*Lilith*, vi) – but the writer of the introduction, Elizabeth McDonald Weinrich, is mistaken since there is no "Henry Fane" mentioned in manuscript "A." It remains a mystery why the name "Henry" suggested itself to the researcher, (I contacted her and she did not recall why she had included the name "Henry.") and I wonder if the name might exist in marginal notes in the text that were not transcribed into the Johannesen variorum editions.

Even without the first name of Henry as supporting evidence, I believe the change of surname from Fane to Vane actually supports my theory. In the second paragraph of chapter one Mr. Vane says, "I had made little acquaintance with the history of my ancestors" (7). But if I am correct, MacDonald knew considerably more than his character knew. Sir Henry Vane traces his ancestry to Henry Fane, an English commoner who was knighted in 1356 at the famous and important Battle of Poitiers during the hundred years war between the French and the English.

Henry Fane was an archer in the English army when he traveled with Edward the Black Prince to do battle against the French King John II. The French, who outnumbered the English four to one, were defeated and as a sign of surrender the Monarch removed his glove or gauntlet to have it presented to the English Prince who was not currently on the scene. The English soldiers and archers had a free-for-all struggling to be the one to retrieve the glove and bring it to the Prince. As you have guessed, Henry Fane emerged with the glove and presented it to the Prince. He was knighted on the spot - for shear dumb luck (Adamson 4-6).

This story suggests to me, and perhaps to MacDonald, a parallel in *Lilith*. That the act of surrender by the Monarch Lilith is not just the removal of her glove, but also the removal of her entire hand may not be coincidental. That by sheer dumb luck, and not by heroic prowess, the alleged many-times great-grandson of Henry Fane should be given the hand of an enemy Monarch to restore proper order to the Kingdom may have been in MacDonald's mind. Whether MacDonald knew of this part of Henry Vane's ancestry and incorporated it as another layer of meaning into his story remains conjecture and will likely remain so. But this family story is so important and well known that the image of three gloves is painted on the Vane family coat-of-arms. (see coat-of-arms illustration on page 44)

A "fane divine"

The appropriateness of the name Fane, as pointed out by John Docherty, is as a homonym to "fain" (a powerful desire expressed) and "feign" (which is to put a false appearance on something so as to deceive). Docherty suggests the primary meaning of "fane" is in the sense of a religious temple, which is "most often met with the romantic phrase, 'a ruined fane,' employed to describe the visible remains of a lost religion" (Docherty 375). The use of the word "fane" to represent a person is found in several places in MacDonald's writings, not as a "ruined fane," but in one of his poems "a fane divine." In *Robert Falconer* he writes, "He looked at her, inquiring of her whole person what numen abode in the fane." MacDonald associates the word fane with a person as a temple of the Holy Spirit (*Falconer* 448).

MacDonald wrote in his essay on the imagination: "God sits in that chamber of our being in which the candle of our consciousness goes out in darkness, and sends forth from these wonderful gifts into the light of that understanding which is His candle" (*A Dish of Orts* 25). This image of the candle reflects the idea of an "inner light" and the related Scripture verse from Proverbs 20:17 – "the spirit of man is the candle of the Lord," a phrase popular with Christian Platonists from the seventeenth to the nineteenth centuries. This seventeenth century image is explained in context in the chapters on "Cambridge Platonists" in Basil Wiley's books *The Seventeenth Century Background* and *The English Moralists*.

I have mentioned the symbol of the gloves on the Vane coat-of-arms. There is also a motto on the Vane family coat-of-arms that reflects the insight of man being a holy temple. Their motto in Latin, *"ne vile fano,"* can mean either "bring nothing base to the temple" or "desire nothing vile" (the Fane coat-of -arms illustration on page 44 does not include this motto, but others do). Fane is recognized as the original family surname, and Neville is a frequently used Christian name in the family and a link to their association with the Neville family lineage.

The Fanes, the Vanes, and the Lost Estate

MacDonald's decision to change from "Fane" to "Vane" could reflect a combination of reasons: 1) that "Vane" was not as obvious a historical reference as he originally thought, and, 2) that he prefered the multiple meanings of the second choice. The most straightforward explanation for MacDonald's changing of a single letter (*F* to *V*) is the historical linguistic consonant change affecting the Vane family name. Thus, the name change could be evidence that MacDonald means to reference the family who is both Fane and Vane.

Another possible textual link between the fictional and the historical Vane appears in a comment from the first sentence of manuscript "B." MacDonald writes that Vane returned to manage his family estate "which my father had lost his hold upon while I was yet a child" (*Lilith*, Variorum 7). Actually, the Vane estate of Raby Castle was seized by the Crown in 1569 because Vane's ancestors were part of the rebellion against Elizabeth the First and supporters of the Catholic, Mary Queen of Scots. It was Sir Henry Vane, the elder, who purchased the Castle back from the crown in 1626 when his son was 13 years old.

MacDonald's interest in Puritan History

We have several examples of MacDonald's interest in Puritan history. The plot of his novel *St. George and St. Michael* takes place in the 1640s, a story of the conflicts between the Roundheads and the Cavaliers and the Protestants and Catholics. In an article in the 2004 issue of *North Wind*, Miho Yamaguchi makes a strong case that several characters in MacDonald's *Wingfold Trilogy* are based on historical Puritan characters. In *Thomas Wingfold, Curate*, she believes that Magistrate Hooker is named for the nonconformist minister Thomas Hooker, who immigrated to Massachusetts in 1633 (two years before Henry Vane) and who, in 1629 wrote *Poor Doubting Christian*, which responds to the spiritual distress by Mrs. Joan Drake, who believed God had forsaken her. In *Paul Faber, Surgeon* Minister Drake may be named after Joan Drake because he also believed God had forsaken him (Yamaguchi 1-12).

The theological book *The Kingdom of Christ* by F. D. Maurice, which Stephen Prickett considers "the greatest nineteenth century attempt at reconstructing a universal Christian narrative," includes a very favorable mention of Sir Henry Vane (Prickett 7). Maurice was one of MacDonald's most influential mentors and it is virtually certain that MacDonald had read this important book. Greville MacDonald wrote in the biography of his parents: "In doctrine I do not think there was any sort of difference between F. D. Maurice and George MacDonald, and but little in opinion" (*GMD&W* 400). F. D. Maurice writes: "In the writings of Sir Harry Vane . . . we may detect very deep principles and remarkable distinctions indeed, which need only the acknowledgment that they were embodied ages before in the Catholic Church, to make them as practically important as they are profound" (*Kingdom*, Ch. 5, Section II, p. 239-40).

A Final Testimony *"before he fell asleep"*

In the 333 years since Vane's death, the only book written specifically on the topic of Vane's theology and language is *Sir Henry Vane, Theologian: A Study in Seventeenth Century Religious and Political Discourse* by David Parnham (1997). No serious study of Henry Vane's writings should be undertaken without first reading this book. It will be helpful to describe Henry Vane's theological position as outlined by Parnham. This will shed light on what Maurice appreciated in his writings and what MacDonald would have appreciated, assuming he also read Vane's theological works.

After the execution of King Charles I, during the period of the Restoration, Sir Henry Vane was sent to Bedford Prison. This was the same prison where John Bunyan wrote *The Pilgrim's Progress*. In fact, Vane's time of imprisonment overlapped with that of John Bunyan. Vane also used his time in prison to write symbolic theological books. Two years after his beheading, his final book was published, entitled *A Pilgrimage into the Land of Promise*, with the wonderfully long subtitle which serves almost as an introduction to the book itself: *A Pilgrimage into the Land of Promise: By the light of the vision of Jabob's ladder and faith; or A serious search and prospect into eternal life, pointing out the way and discovering the passage out of man's mutable state of life, into a state of immutable righteousness and glory, through the knowledge of Christ in Spirit. Written in the year 1662, by Henry Vane, Knight, towards the latter end of his prison-state; by himself reviewed and perfected, some few days before his suffering, and left as his testimony and service to this present generation, according to the will of God, before he fell asleep.*

A pilgrimage into the land of promife.

By *the light of the vifion*

OF

Jacobs ladder and faith;

OR

A ferious fearch and profpect into life eternal, pointing out the way and difcovering the paffage out of mans mutable ftate of life, into a ftate of immutable righteoufnes and glory, through the knowledg of Chrift in Spirit.

Written in the year 1662, by HENRY VANE, Knight, towards the latter end of his prifon-ftate; by himfelf fully reviewed and perfected, fome few dayes before his fuffering, and left as his laft Teftimony and fervice to this prefent generation, according to the wil of God, before he fell afleep.

HOSEA 12. 3. 4. and 6. verfes.

He took his brother by the heel in the womb, and by his ftrength behaved himfelf princely with God.
Yea, he had power over the angel and prevailed: he wept and made fupplication unto him: he found him in Beth-El, and there he fpake with us.
Therefore turn thou to thy God: keep mercy and judgment, and wait on thy God continually.

Printed in the yeare 1664.

You may notice that this book title, alluded to in the title of my chapter, applies equally to Henry Thoreau's essay and Vane's book. Just as *Pilgrimage into the Land of Promise* is Vane's "last testimonial and service to this present generation . . . before he fell asleep," so is *Lilith* to MacDonald his "last testimonial and service . . . before he fell asleep."

As we have seen already, Vane was a mediator between opposing religious views and a champion of freedom of conscience. According to Parnham, Vane positioned himself between the rationalistic Calvinists and the experiential Spiritualists such as the Quakers. Using the terminology of seventeenth-century federalist theology Vane "erected a counter-theology based on a counter-hermeneutic" (29). His goal was to confront "both the defective wisdom of the Spirit-suppressing biblicists and the outright heresy of the Antinomian extremists" (21). Regarding Calvinist doctrine Vane wrote that a man "is no further profited by the doctrine of another, [unless] he receives it in the light of his own conscious, and is made one with it by inward experience" (25).

As to the Quakers, Vane cautioned them "for their neglect of the scriptures, but he saw their diligence and moral strength – he was not an enemy of the Quakers, but of the Antinomian monists" (82). The problem with the monist position is that it ends in a pantheistic continuum where union with Christ leads either to debasing Divinity or improperly elevating humanity (86). Vane believed that God's grace enabled certain Christians to "operate as spiritual linguists to transmit Christ's spiritually apprehended 'heavenly voice'" (31). However, while "the Spirit revealed the mystery of the letter, it did not antiquate it" (81). Sikes, a disciple of Vane and author of the first biography in 1662, described Vane's writings as "a biblically based typology of Christian experience" (qtd in Parnham 57).

While walking his theological tightrope, Vane did nothing to endear himself to the Reformed Churches when he criticized them equally with the Catholic Church. He believed "neither Church desired the wisdom of the Spirit, and both used the power of the law and sword to persecute the spiritualists" (143).

Opinions of Henry Vane's Theology

It is little wonder that Vane accumulated his share of critics. The criticism formed itself along two lines. The first was that Vane was an obscurantist in his language and that his vague biblically based typology precluded investigation (58). He was accused of "claiming a blasphemous proximity to God and knowledge of God's purposes" (61). In using traditional imagery in an untraditional manner Vane was seen as an "exploiter, even a spoiler of established modes of inquiry" (61).

The second criticism moved beyond the accusation of Vane as a conspirator against plain language. It condemned Vane's judgment as being speculative, presumptive, and unwarranted. The first person to oppose Vane in writing was Martin Finch who thought Vane's view of scripture was suspect. According to

Finch, for Vane to believe that "the scriptures are not the word of God, but only Christ, it is as much to say, the scriptures are not what the Lord hath spoken" (152). Richard Baxter, known by many today only as the Puritan minister who inspired C. S. Lewis' title for *Mere Christianity*, considered Vane's writings to be unintelligible, but he apparently thought he understood enough to denounce Vane as being a Papist sympathizer (58).

Considering the almost universally negative opinions about Vane's theology from the time of his death until Parnham's appreciative study in 1997, it was bold of F. D. Maurice to describe Vane's theology as exhibiting "deep principles," "remarkable distinctions," and to say that it was "practically important," and "profound." (*Kingdom*, Ch. 5, Part II, p. 239-40) The extent to which Sir Henry Vane's theology influenced Maurice's book would make an interesting study. It seems more than coincidental that Maurice's book, which discusses Church and State relations by combining the Quaker idea of "the inner light" with Reformed insights about covenant theology, runs along a similar path as Vane's.

The extent to which MacDonald would have empathized with Vane is clear. Both were accused of being over-speculative in their theology. Both were accused of showing insufficient reverence toward scripture. Both were accused of being obscurantist and vague in their meanings. Both were accused of making too much of freedom of conscience and not enough of particular doctrines. Both attempted to communicate Christian experience through a symbolic use of language.

The influence of utopian and anti-utopian literature

Understanding *Lilith* as an apocalyptic anti-utopian romance introduces a socio-political perspective and commentary on the American/English myth of hope and freedom, especially in its Victorian context. It provides a new historical lens through which to explore MacDonald's artistic vision. Setting aside the usual modern and vague classification of "fantasy" also gives English departments the opportunity to include *Lilith* in utopian literature courses. This should help students avoid confusions arising from modern expectations of what constitutes the genre of fantasy.

The 1880s and 1890s are considered the Golden Age of utopian literature. Although there are earlier examples of nineteenth century utopias, the most famous utopian novel appeared in 1888 – Edward Bellamy's *Looking Backward*. This book was translated into over a dozen languages and was an international blockbuster, outselling every book except the Bible through the end of the century. Mark Twain's contribution to this literary trend was his 1889 book: *A Connecticut Yankee in King Arthur's Court*. William Morris was so upset by Bellamy's liberal enthusiasm for progress that he wrote his own utopian book in response called *News from Nowhere* in 1890 – the same year MacDonald began writing *Lilith*.

Another indication of MacDonald's backward glance toward a utopian mythology is the original title given to manuscript "B" – *Anacosm: A Tale of the Seventh Dimension*. The word "anacosm" is a composite of "ana" a Greek prefix meaning, according to the Oxford English Dictionary, "up, in place or time, back, again, anew." The root of the word is "cosm" from the word "cosmic" meaning "of the world or universe" and in its more original meaning (reflected in the word "cosmetic") – "relating to adornment, arrange, order." MacDonald encapsulates in a single word, the idea of going back in place and time to a world where nature was understood as the adornment and well-ordered revelation of God's creation. The world MacDonald is creating is not only a microcosm and a macrocosm, but also an "anacosm" which allows him to return to authors and ideas that best represent his worldview.

Nathaniel Hawthorn's *The Blithdale Romance* (1852) provides another imaginative template for us to evaluate the structure and meaning of *Lilith*. In a paper presented at Taylor University, *The Season for the Hawthorn To Blossom*, I list fifteen distinctive parallels between *Lilith* and Hawthorne's anti-utopian romance (Trexler 34-40). Both romances demonstrate the futility of man's attempts to create paradise on his own terms. MacDonald's kinship to Hawthorne is evident in a thank you letter sent to an unknown man who gifted him with some valuable Hawthorne books three years after Hawthorne's death. He wrote: "I believe I understand and sympathize with our lamented Hawthorne as much as any man" (Sadler 158).

The prefaces to Hawthorne's romances are the best places for us to discover quickly his similarity to MacDonald's artistic imagination. However, a selection from Hawthorne's book *Mosses From an Old Manse* provides a unique parallel to the Eden Myth as it appears in *Lilith*. To understand the transcendentalist interconnections between Hawthorne's *Old Manse*, Emerson's book, *Nature*, Thoreau's essay, "Walking", and MacDonald's *Lilith*, a few explanations may be helpful:

1) "The Old Manse" is Hawthorne's name for the former parsonage where the Hawthornes lived in Concord, Massachusetts,
2) the house was previously owned by Emerson and it is where he wrote *Nature*,
3) Nathaniel and Mrs. Hawthorne were neighbors of Henry Thoreau, and
4) Nathaniel and Mrs. Hawthorne nicknamed themselves "Adam" and "Eve."

Hawthorne writes:

> In one respect, our precincts were like the Enchanted Ground through which the pilgrim traveled on the way to the Celestial City! The guests, each and all, felt a slumberous influence upon them [...] what better could be done for anyone who came within our magic circle than to throw the spell of a tranquil spirit over him? And when it had wrought its full effect, then we dismissed him, but with misty reminiscences, as if he had been dreaming of us."
>
> (Mosses 39-40)

Lilith's Adam, Mr. Raven, could say the same about his enchanted grounds and his guest Mr. Vane.

Victorian Views of the Past

We have looked at MacDonald's view of the "historic imagination" and how the life of an individual might be constructed from the fragments of history. But this view of the "historic imagination" is not unique to MacDonald. The Victorians generally romanticized the past. Which historic period is romanticized depends on which Victorian you are examining. The early Romantics, Robert Burns and Sir Walter Scott, romanticized the Middle Ages, and this idealization of the middle ages continued among the Pre-Raphaelite writers and artists and others with, for example, the attention to Arthurian legend. Other Victorians identified with the Renaissance due to the huge influx of ideas, new languages, and an awareness of other cultures and religions. In 1941, F. O. Matthiessen coined the term "American Renaissance" to refer to the writings of Emerson, Whitman, Thoreau, Melville, and Hawthorne. However, as the Victorian literary scholar Vida Scudder points out: "The Elizabethans translated the past into terms of their own present; we of the later days seek to translate our present into terms of the unvarying past" (*Life* 150).

A third historic period revered especially by Victorian social reformers was the age of the Puritans. As Edward Bellamy wrote: "We look to the great Revolution as a . . . second creation of man" (qtd in Roemer, *The Obsolete Necessity* 15). In the Puritan struggle against the hardships imposed by government sponsored religion, reformers identified with similar complaints of Church-State relations, clericalism, and class distinctions. Elisha Mulford, an Episcopalian scholar who endorsed the ideas of Coleridge and Maurice, wrote in September of 1872 that no period of history attracted Maurice more than the Puritan Age. He quotes a comment Maurice made regarding John Milton:

[Milton] knew through the failure of his own age that freedom did not depend on these human agents. Every step in his painful discoveries had led him more to see that it belongs to the spirit of man; that parliaments and protectors can give it as little as kings – preachers as little as prelates; that all may do something to crush or weaken the hearts in which it should dwell and grow; that all may do something to strengthen it in those hearts, if they will confess a God who demands obedience of his creatures as a condition of their freedom. (qtd in Mulford 537)

Conclusion

When MacDonald wrote *Lilith* in the 1890s, the men who shaped his thinking in the 1840s – fifty years ago when he was a young man – were either dead or retired. The influence of men like Tennyson and Browning, Ruskin and Carlyle, Newman and Maurice, Thackery and Dickens, whose writing careers began in "the decade of origins," as Vida Scudder called the 1840s, had passed (*Introduction* 464). Their voices were already weak by the 1880s, the "decade of aestheticism," and were hardly audible in the 1890s, "the decade of decadence" (Buckley 207-246). MacDonald knew this was his last opportunity to combine the lessons of his lifetime and the values he had learned from others – into one last great story – his own last testament, but also a testament to the ideas of all the faded heroes of his dying world.

Greville MacDonald once called *Lilith* "the revelation of St. George the Divine" thus comparing it to the Apocalypse of St. John the Divine (*Reminiscences* 321). When you consider the double meaning of apocalypse as the ending of a world and apocalypse as a revelation, I think this a profoundly accurate summation of *Lilith*. After Mr. Vane's apocalypse – that is, after the ending of his otherworldly experience – there remains hope. However, it is not the humanitarian hope of the over-optimistic Emerson, nor the political hope of the naturalist Thoreau, nor the hope-against-hope of the melancholy Hawthorne. Just as each of these transcendentalists provided his own version of the American Dream – so MacDonald's vision is unique. His apocalyptic anti-utopian hope is reflected in a sentence on the last page of *Lilith*: "When a man dreams his own dream, he is the sport of his dream; when Another gives it him, that other is able to fulfill it" (396).

Works Cited

Adamson, J. H. and H. F. Folland. *Sir Harry Vane: His Life and Times 1613-1662*. Boston: Gambit, 1973.

Buckley, Jerome Hamilton. *The Victorian Temper: A Study in Victorian Culture*. New York: Random House, 1951.

Docherty, John. *The Literary Products of the Lewis Carroll–George MacDonald Friendship*, 2nd edition. Lewiston, N. Y.: Mellen, 1997.

Emerson, Ralph Waldo. *The Collected Works of Ralph Waldo Emerson. Vol. 1 Nature, Addresses, and Lectures*. Cambridge, MA: Harvard UP, 1971.

Hawthorne, Nathaniel. *Legends of the Province House, Howe's Masquerade, from The Novels and Tales of Nathaniel Hawthorne*. New York: The Modern Library, Random House, 1937.

---. "The Old Manse" in *Mosses from an Old Manse*. [1854] New York: Arno Press, 1970.

Hosmer, James K. *The Life of Sir Henry Vane, Governor of Massachusetts Bay, and Leader of the Long Parliament. With a Consideration of the English Commonwealth as a Forecast of America*. Boston: Houghton, Mifflin, 1888.

MacDonald, George. *Lilith: First and Final*. Whitethorn, CA: Johannesen, 1994. Reprint of 1896 Chatto & Windus edition.

---. *Lilith: A Variorum Edition Vol. 1*. Edited by Rolland Hein. Whitethorn, CA: Johannesen, 1997.

---. *Robert Falconer*. Boston: Loring, nd. (The quotation from this book appears in the chapter "The Neophyte," located between the chapters "The Brothers" and "The Suicide" in earlier editions of *Robert Falconer*, but removed from the 1880 Hurst and Blacket edition reprinted by Johannesen Publishers.)

---. "The Imagination: Its Culture and Function," *A Dish of Orts*. Whitethorn, CA: Johannesen, 1997. Essay originally published 1867.

MacDonald, Greville. *George MacDonald and His Wife*. Whitethorn, CA: Johannesen, 1998. Reprint of 1924 edition.

---. *Reminiscences of a Specialist*. London: Allen and Unwin, 1924.

Matthiessen, F. O. *American Renaissance: Art and Expression in the Age of Emerson and Whitman*. New York: Oxford UP, 1941.

Maurice, Frederick Denison. *The Kingdom of Christ*. Vol. I, London: J. M. Dent, nd. (This edition includes the dedication from 1938)

Maurice, Frederick Denison. *The Kingdom of Christ*. Vol. I & II, London: SCM Press, Ltd., 1958. (This edition omits the dedication from 1938)

Mulford, Elsiha. "F. D. Maurice". *Scribner's Monthly Magazine*, Volume 4, Issue 5. 1872. 529-546.

Parnham, David. *Sir Henry Vane, Theologian: A Study in Seventeenth Century Religious and Political Discourse.* Cranbury, NJ: Associated University Presses, 1997.

Prickett, Stephen. "Frederick Denison Maurice: The Man Who Wrote the Book," *North Wind* 21 (2002): 1-14.

Roemer, Kenneth M.. "Utopia and Victorian Culture," *America as Utopia.* Ed. Kenneth M. Roemer. New York: Burt Franklin, 1981.

---. *The Obsolete Necessity: America in Utopian Writings, 1888-1900.* Kent State UP, 1976.

Sadler, Glenn Edward, ed. *An Expression of Character: The Letters of George MacDonald.* Grand Rapids, MI: William B. Eerdman, 1994.

Scott, Sir Walter. *A Legend of Montrose.* New York: Harper & Brothers, 1901.

Scudder, Vida D. *The Life of the Spirit in the Modern English Poets.* New York: Houghton, Mifflin, 1896.

---. *Introduction to the Study of English Literature.* Yonkers-on-Hudson, NY: World Book Company, 1901.

Thoreau, Henry David. "Walking" in *Walden and Other Writings.* Ed. Brooks Atkinson. New York: The Modern Library, Random House, 1937.

---. "Sir Henry Vane," in *The Writings of Henry David Thoreau: Early Essays and Miscellanies.* Ed. Joseph J. Moldenhauer and Edwin Moser. Princeton UP, 1976.

Trexler, Robert. "The Season for the Hawthorn to Blossom," *Inklings Forever*, Vol. 4. Upland, IN: Taylor University Press. (2004): 34-40.

"Young Sir Henry Vane," *Atlantic Monthly Magazine.* Vol. 63. Issue 78. April 1889. 562-566.

Ward, Maise. *Robert Browning and His World: The Private Face 1812-1861.* London: Cassell, 1967.

Wiley, Basil. *The English Moralists.* Garden City, NJ: Doubleday Anchor, 1964.

---. *The Seventeenth Century Background: The Thought of the Age in Relation to Religion and Poetry.* Garden City, NJ: Doubleday Anchor, 1933.

Yamaguchi, Miho. "Poor Doubting Christian: An Exploration of Salvation, Love and Eternity in MacDonald's Wingfold Trilogy," *North Wind* 23 (2004): 1-12.

Chapter 4

Kore Motifs in the *Princess* Books:
Mythic Threads Between Irenes and Eirinys

Fernando Soto

Core, Persephone, and Hecate were, clearly, the Goddesses in Triad as Maiden, Nymph, and Crone, at a time when only women practiced the mysteries of agriculture....But Demeter was the goddess's general title, and Persephone's name has been given to Core, which confuses the story. (Graves, Greek, 24: 1) [1]

George MacDonald was interested in Greek mythology and religion. In one of his early letters (1855) to his wife, he mentions "Erebus," "the Sky God," "the Green Earth God," alongside "our own God" (Sadler 88). References to these other gods also find their way into his fantasy writings. His allusions to Greek myths and religion range from superficial references to full-blown creative reinterpretations of some very obscure, ancient stories (see Patterson; Willard; Soto 2004). MacDonald seamlessly merges the well known with the obscure, oftentimes including commonly known myths and religious practices alongside very archaic material (Soto 2000). My object here is to trace MacDonald's use of some implicit facets of the ancient Kore mythology and the related Greek religion in both his *Princess* books, particularly in *The Princess and Curdie*.

In "Kore Motifs in *The Princess and the Goblin*," Nancy-Lou Patterson presents a convincing case for MacDonald's use of a Greek myth - the Rape of Persephone - in his fairy tale. MacDonald continues to use parts of this same myth in the sequel, *The Princess and Curdie*. In what follows, I continue Patterson's original line of inquiry, by presenting MacDonald's inclusion of several other aspects of the Kore myth in *The Princess and the Goblin*, and showing how he expanded upon this same rich mythology in *The Princess and Curdie*.

Patterson is well aware of MacDonad's use of *The Homeric Hymn to Demeter* in *The Princess and the Goblin*. For instance, she links directly the grandmother's purifying rose fire to Demeter's purification of Prince Demophoon over similar flames (173). However, in *The Princess and Curdie* MacDonald includes a more direct reference to exactly this segment of the myth. In chapter XXXI, "The Sacrifice," we find a description of a ritual derived from the mid part of the Kore myth:

> The curtain to the king's door, a dull red ever before, was glowing a gorgeous, a radiant purple; and the crown wrought upon it in silks and gems was flashing as if it burned! What could it mean? Was the king's chamber on fire? He darted to the door and lifted the curtain. Glorious, terrible sight!
>
> A long and broad marble table, that stood at one end of the room, had been drawn into the middle of it, and thereon burned a great fire, of a sort that Curdie knew – a fire of glowing, flaming roses, red and white. In the midst of the roses lay the king, moaning, but motionless. Every rose that fell from the table to the floor, someone, whom Curdie could not plainly see for the brightness, lifted and laid burning upon the king's face, until at length his face too was covered with the live roses, and he lay all within the fire, moaning still, with now and then a shuddering sob. (293-5)

Once this "sacrifice" is over, MacDonald gives the reader additional information, further grounding some of the above rites in the Kore myth, found in *The Homeric Hymn to Demeter*:

> Then Curdie, no longer dazzled, saw and knew the old princess. The room was lighted with the splendour of her face, of her blue eyes, of her sapphire crown. Her golden hair went streaming out from her through the air till it went off in mist and light. She was large and strong as a Titaness. She stooped over the table-altar, put her mighty arms under the living sacrifice, lifted the king, as if he were but a little child, to her bosom, walked with him up the floor, and laid him in his bed. (295-6).

The sacrifice on the table-altar has many elements directly borrowed from the Kore myth, particularly elements dealing with the "sacrifice" found in *The Homeric Hymn to Demeter*. In the *Hymn*, while Demeter, Kore's mother, searches dejectedly for her abducted daughter, she is convinced to take up residence in Eleusis, at the royal palace. While there, she is assigned the duty of nursing a small child, prince Demophoon. Demeter performs part of her duty in the following unorthodox fashion:

> Thus she nursed in the house the splendid son of wise Celeus, Demophoon, whom beautiful robed Metaneira bore. And he grew like a god, not nourished on mortal food but anointed by Demeter

with ambrosia, just as though sprung from the gods, and she breathed sweetness upon him as she held him to her bosom. At night she would hide him in the might of the fire, like a brand, without the knowledge of his dear parents. (234)

Because of the strange metamorphosis and precocious growth of her son, Metaneira decides to spy on Demeter. One night she sees her child in the fire and she is shocked: "Great was her dismay and she gave a shriek and struck both her thighs, terrified for her child" (234). This unwarranted intrusion and interruption of the sacrifice causes Demeter to lose her temper and the spell to break: "with her immortal hands she snatched from the fire the dear son whom Metaneira had borne in her house, blessing beyond all hope, and threw him down on the floor" (234). The ancient sources are divided about Demophoon's ultimate fate. However, most agree that the interruption of the ritual leads to his death, either caused by Demeter's violent actions or by his natural demise as a common mortal. One important ancient source – Apollodorus – claims that the baby was consumed in the flames, after Demophoon's mother interrupted the rite (1: 5.1).

Curdie and the narrator seem aware of not only the main aspects of the rites, but also of some of the additional, implicit contingencies involved. For instance, when Curdie undergoes his own trial by fire, he and the narrator are aware that death follows the interruption of these rites:

> He rushed to the fire, and thrust both his hands right into the middle of the heap of flaming roses, and his arms halfway up to the elbows. And it did hurt! But he did not draw them back. He held the pain as if it were a thing that would kill him if he let it go – as indeed it would have done (93-4).

MacDonald makes sure that his protagonist and the narrator, unlike Metaneira, are aware of the dire repercussions that follow the interruption of these rites.

MacDonald borrows further aspects related to his elder Irene from the myths above. The grandmother Irene, like Demeter, uses something resembling ambrosia, along with the fire, to heal or purify. She twice resorts to a type of rose-smelling ointment to anoint and heal Irene and Curdie (*Goblin*, 119, 268). In addition, Demeter, as Demeter Louisa, is also associated with purifying baths, an attribute she shares with the elder Irene.[2] The purifying bath is apparent when the grandmother, who owns a magical bathtub, makes this aspect of herself explicit to the younger Irene: "Anytime you want a bath, come to me. I know you have a bath every morning, but sometimes you want one at night too" (149). Near the end of Chapter 23, Irene takes a bath that not only cleanses, but also heals and rejuvenates her (232). In *The Princess and Curdie*, the elder Irene performs a similar purification and healing of the King, Irene's father. As the King wakes refreshed after his purification, the reader learns that the rites he has undergone healed and cleansed him. After his ordeal by fire, he tells Curdie, "'No, I need no bath. I am clean'" (298), underscoring the grandmother's purifying and bathing attributes.

MacDonald's references to the Kore myths extend to other more obscure and related ancient stories and characters. However, before I approach these other implicit, complicated references, some background is necessary. As Patterson makes clear, the Kore myth cannot be understood without reference to the double and triple nature of the goddess(es) involved (175). The Kore myth incorporates the Greek conception of woman as daughter-mother-grandmother; maid, woman, and crone; or Persephone, Demeter, and the Titaness Hecate, respectively. While these goddesses possess individual identities, they also partake of something akin to the later Christian conception of the Trinity: simultaneous unity and plurality.[3] Moreover, each goddess could take on very different attributes given her state, role, or locality of worship. For example, Demeter could become Demeter Eirinyes ("Raging Mother"), Demeter Subterrene, or Eleusinian Demeter. Curdie and his father meet the goddess in the mine in her role as underground Hecate (closely related to Demeter Subterrene); the mine is her natural dwelling place (Kerenyi 37).

MacDonald, if he did not learn of the goddess' attributes from the original myths, could have found information on Hecate in a variety of sources, for instance in *Lempriere's Classical Dictionary* of 1788. Another possible source of information about Hecate is Alexander Murray's *Who's Who in Mythology* (Second Edition 1874). Murray notes that "her chief function" was "that of goddess of the nether world, of night and darkness....her festivals were held at night, worship was paid her by torchlight...Her presence was mostly felt at lonely cross roads, whence she derived the name of Trivia" (Murray 71). Hecate Trivia is associated directly with caves and lonely, dark tri-ways.

Torch-bearing Curdie and Peter first perceive signs of the grandmother in her underground persona exactly at an underground tri-way: "Father and son had seated themselves on a projecting piece of the rock at a corner where three galleries met.... They had just risen and were turning to the right, when a gleam caught their eyes, and made them look along the whole gangue. Far up they saw a pale green light" (63).

Soon after this, they find that the light belongs to "the old princess, Irene's great-great grandmother" (67). The grandmother also carries her Trivia nature above ground, just as the ancient Hecate had dominion in the three realms of the ancient universe: the earthly, the oceanic, and the heavenly (Hesiod 36-7). Thus it is no surprise that the younger Irene first hears her grandmother's voice in a three-way landing, "in a little square place, with three doors, two opposite each other, and one opposite the top of the stair" (20). Once the two Irenes meet, the younger is told of the queenly identity of the grandmother, another attribute of Hecate – the queen of the underworld.

In her aboveground guise, Hecate was directly associated with the moon (Kerenyi 36). MacDonald underscores the layout of the elder Irene's residence, and her dominion over, or her direct association with, the moon in his second book. He names Chapter III, "Mistress of the Silver Moon," and describes her habitation almost exactly as he had done in *The Princess and the Goblin*. As Curdie climbs the same steep stairs Irene had climbed in the earlier book prior to meeting the grandmother, the reader is told that: "he reached the top at last – a little landing, with a door in front and one on each side" (32). Once he meets the grandmother, the elder Irene implies that Curdie is in the interior of the moon, or in the presence of the moon herself (34-5). Curdie, at least, cannot separate this Mistress of the Silver Moon and moonlight: "Her grey hair mixed with the moonlight so that he could not tell where the one began and the other ended" (36). That Curdie could not tell the difference between the moonlight and the grandmother's hair is natural enough, because the younger Irene had earlier claimed, in her first meeting with her grandmother, that this latter's "hair shone like silver" (*Goblin* 24). Here the words "hair" and "moon" are associated with silver and this color is directly linked with the grandmother. MacDonald uses "silver hair" and "silver moon" to directly describe the grandmother as "Mistress of the silver moon" and as one possessing silver hair, which hair intermingles with moonlight.

Hecate, queen of the underworld – who has much in common with Persephone and Demeter in their underground roles and identities (Lempriere 294; Monaghan 149) – is also related to MacDonald's other underground queen, Hairlip's stepmother (Patterson 179), and this latter's predecessor. Hecate and her daughter, Empusa, like Harelip's mother and stepmother, were known to wear extremely hard footwear, such as a brass shoe, or a pair of copper sandals (Aristophanes 567; Graves, *Greek* 55: 1). It seems hardly an accident that these four heavy-footed, underground queens should be found in MacDonald's work and in Greek mythology. What is more, MacDonald's obscure references to Greek mythology in his stories do not end with women who wear brazen or petrified footwear. The continual exploration of similar chthonic entities allows for major segments and characters of *The Princess* books to emerge as creatively modeled on the Kore myths.

MacDonald names Chapter VII of *The Princess and Curdie*, "What is in a Name," a title posing a central question for his book. The most crucial name in the book is "Irene," assigned to the two most important characters. MacDonald gives the name Irene to Princess Irene and to her grandmother, presenting the reader with two Irenes. Several commentators note that the name Irene – once pronounced in three syllables, as in the original Greek (Hanks and Hodges 785) – derives from the Greek Eirene, meaning "peace." This meaning, however, is not very helpful for our understanding of the general nature of *The Princess and Curdie*, because of the lack of peace in the book. Instead, the book, particularly the final chapters, deals almost exclusively with avengers, vengeance, judgment, and destruction. This emphasis on vengeance and violence probably derives from the overlap between MacDonald's two Irenes and the original Greek goddesses of vengeance, the Eirenyes. MacDonald's Irenes are linked with the Eirenyes not only by sharing similarly sounding names, but also by their respective attributes. For instance, the goddess Eirene/Irene is directly linked with Demeter: each was worshipped as "Mother" in Athens (Harrison 270), and each was thought to be the mother of the chthonic Ploutos/Pluto, Persephone's brother or husband (Hesiod 55; Murray 66 and 131; Lempriere 491 and 542). An equally crucial fact is that Demeter is directly linked with the Eirenyes, in her role as "Raging Mother," or as Demeter Eirenys (Graves, *Greek* 16: f). She becomes enraged after she takes the form of a mare, and subsequently is raped by Poseidon in the likeness of a stallion. Furthermore, Hecate is often accompanied by the Eirinyes (Graves, *Greek* 31: 8). These connections between the mythical Eirenyes and MacDonald's Irenes explain much of the general themes of Vengeance and More Vengeance near the end of *The Princess and Curdie*.

The theme of vengeance may be MacDonald's attempt to balance, or provide a counterpoint to the general theme of peace at the end of *The Princess and the Goblin*. On the other hand, because of the underlying Greek nature of both books, MacDonald may be tapping into the ever-present theme of vengeance and its ultimate dire results running through many of the ancient myths. Either way, the chthonic aspects of his Irenes/Eirinyes also help to elucidate other puzzling episodes in MacDonald's book.

Mythologically speaking, Demeter and the Eirenyes are sometimes confused with each other, since each is at times identified with the Gorgons or Medusa, because of their chthonic facets, their respective "husbands," and their winged horse offspring. Under the heading of Poseidon, Murray claims that in Arcadia, this god "was worshipped side by side with Demeter, with whom, it was believed, he begat that winged and wonderfully fleet horse Arion. In Boeotia, where he was also worshipped, the mother of Arion was said to have been Erinys, to whom he had appeared in the form of a horse. With Medusa he became the father of the winged horse Pegasos" (52). Apollodorus claims that "Demeter gave birth to it [Arion] after she had intercourse with Poseidon in the form of a Fury" (3: 6.8). Thus, there are strong mythological links between Demeter, Erynyes and Gorgons. None of this is very surprising, because all of the above goddesses, along with Persephone/Kore and Hecate, were usually described in very similar fashion, and each had a dark, chthonic role to play in their stories.

MacDonald seems aware of another aspect of the Eirenyes. In one story they are associated with protective threads, similar to the one linking MacDonald's two Irenes in *The Princess and the Goblin*. The elder Irene presents her granddaughter with a special ring and thread. Once Irene asks about the use of the ring, her grandmother tells her: "If ever you find yourself in any danger – such, for example, as you were in this same evening – you must take off your ring and put it under the pillow of your bed. Then you must lay your forefinger, the same that wore the ring, upon the thread, and follow the thread wherever it leads you" (155). The first time the younger Irene feels threatened (by what seem to be Cobs' creatures fighting in her bedroom), she follows her grandmother's directions, and thus finds her way to the imprisoned Curdie. After she helps to release Curdie, Irene tells the incredulous young miner that her grandmother is taking care of them via the string (214). Later on, when the young Irene is again in danger when the goblins invade the castle, the string leads her to the safety of Curdie's mother's cottage. Thus the thread's main purpose is to protect Irene, or to lead her to safety.

There is a story in Greek history that sheds light on the curious thread MacDonald assigns the grandmother. Herodotus, Thucidides, and Plutarch mention an episode involving the treasonous actions of Cylon in the history of Athenian democracy (Herodutus, V: 71; Thucidides I:126). This is how Plutarch, the more informative of the three historians, tells the story:

> The execrable proceedings against accomplices of Cylon had long occasioned great troubles in the Athenian state. The conspirators had taken sanctuary in Minerva's temple; but Megacles, then Archon, persuaded them to quit it, and stand trial, under the notion that if they tied a thread to the shrine of the goddess, and kept hold of it, they would still be under her protection. But when they came over

against the temple of the Furies, the thread broke of itself; upon which Megacles and his colleagues rushed upon them and seized them, as if they had lost their privilege. Such as were out of the temple were stoned; those that fled to the altars were cut in pieces. (96-7)

Harrison casts doubt on the string being attached to the shrine of the "goddess" (Athena), by implying that it was more likely that the luckless suppliants attached themselves to the shrine of the Semnae, goddesses synonymous with the Eirinyes/Furies. The nearby shrine of these goddesses was specifically associated with a famous protective sanctuary (Harrison 243).

Harrison proceeds to conjecture that originally the shrines of Athena and of the Samnae were one and the same (301). Thus, in a manner, it does not matter exactly to which shrine the thread was attached, because the Eirinys/Semnae were directly associated with the story of the protective thread, because Athena was herself sometimes associated with chthonic goddesses similar to the Eirinyes (Herodotus, VIII: 41; Murray 95), or because she was identified directly with the Eirinyes (Harrison 306-7), and their cousins, the Gorgons (Murray 91). Moreover, Athena, the Kore of Athens, was often linked directly with Persephone/Kore, in her darker aspects as queen of the underworld, and as Eiriny. There is a second reason why it does not matter to which of the two goddesses the conspirators attached themselves. MacDonald seems to be concentrating mainly on the historico-mythic thread, generally linking those in danger to protecting, related goddesses.

The ongoing study of some chthonic goddesses – Hecate, Erinyes, and Gorgons, particularly Medusa – sheds light on another part of *The Princess and Curdie*: the episode involving the wallet given to Curdie by his mother, who herself is compared with the (grand)mother in the two books (*Goblin* 123-4, 225; *Curdie* 108,).[4] In Greek traditional fashion, MacDonald's miners receive the overwhelming majority of their information about the grandmother (as witch/crone) from their wives, mothers and grandmothers (*Curdie* 55). Part of the reason for this appears in the epigraph by Graves, heading this paper. Some of the information about the grandmother includes the idea that this Greek-like old/young and ugly/beautiful witch, like the Gorgon Medusa, would strike her onlookers "stone blind" (*Curdie* 57). This, of course, is one of the ugly/beautiful Medusa's attributes, both while she is alive and after her death (Murray 191).

In the underworld, the head of Medusa, used by Persephone, was historically feared (Homer, *Odyssey* XI: 635; Kerenyi 49-50), while above ground its resting place is in the Athenian "Maid's" fear inspiring aegis. Athena's aegis has a curious history. In Demeter's role as Demeter-Eirinys, she was known to have a mask made of goatskin called a gorgoneion (Graves, *Greek* 9: 5). This gorgoneion was also identified with the wallet in which Perseus placed and kept the head of Medusa. Thus, this particular goatskin wallet, related to the head of the gorgon Medusa, was magical, and later came to form part of Athena's aegis, a word related to a "goat's hide with the hair on" (Rose 48).[5] Here is how Kerenyi describes the connection between this wallet/mask and Demeter-Erinys:

> The mask-like Gorgon's head, the gorgoneion, was thenceforth worn by Athene, either as a sign on her shield or attached to her breast-plate, which was her sacred goatskin named aegis. It was even supposed that the gorgon had been the original owner of this goatskin, and that she was a child of Gaia whom Athene had flayed. The goddess Artemis, and very probably also the scolding Demeter – Demeter-Erinys, as she was called – wore the mortally terrible countenance as if it were their own, set on their necks. (50)

This passage may remind us of one of Athena's surnames: Gorgonia (Lempriere 287). This Athena (or Athena Gorgophone) is credited with flaying Medusa (Graves, *Greek* 33: b). On the other hand, the above description of Demeter wearing the awful Gorgon's head on her neck, could easily apply to a number of the graphic depictions of Athena. For instance, her depiction on an Attic amphora (pictured above) in the Berlin Museum makes her connection to Demeter Eirinys – with the gorgoneion/aegis on her neck – very clear (Morford and Lenardon 110).

Thus, the goatskin wallet/mask, linked to Gorgons, can hardly be anything other than the curious goatskin wallet Curdie's "mother" gave him, and which came to be placed on the neck of Lina, the main "avenger of evil," or Erinyes, now described as a Gorgon.

It may be recalled that the Eirinyes were closely associated and identified with dogs and hounds (Aeschylus, *Choephoroe* 80, *Eumenides* 82; Euripides, *Electra* 338). Gruesome Lina is described continually as a type of dog, as well as a kind of partially flayed Gorgon in the story: "Her head was something between that of a polar bear and a snake.... Her under teeth came up like a fringe of icicles, only very white, outside of her upper lip. Her throat looked as if the hair had been plucked off" (101-2). The Gorgons are often depicted as snakes, while Medusa's head is generally covered with snakes (Harrison 235-6). Gorgons, flayed or otherwise, are also depicted with huge teeth or tusks almost always pointing upward, like a boar's (Harrison 187, 193; Kerenyi 49). To understand the lack of skin and hair on the Gorgon's and Lina's throat, however, more material is at hand.

Curdie's mother is closely related to the Princess' grandmother, who provides Curdie with his helper Lina. The connection between the two "mothers" becomes particularly apparent once Curdie, who has the tactile power to perceive the true nature of people and animals, holds his mother's hand and claims that it "feels just like that of the Princess" (108). Curdie recalls this other "mother" when he, in a reflective mood, wishes to cover up the flayed part of Lina's repulsiveness:

> Then he bethought him of the goatskin wallet his mother had given him, and taking it from his shoulders, tried whether it would do to make a collar for the poor animal. He found there was just enough, and the hair so similar in colour to Lina's, that no one could suspect it of having grown somewhere else. (125)

Thus, there are multiple links between the gorgoneion (wallet and mask) worn by Demeter Erinys and Athena on their necks, Athena's aegis — manufactured from a hairy goatskin, and Medusa's head — and MacDonald's Lina. In addition, the similarities continue to emerge when we consider the ancient depictions of the Gorgon's head and Lina's Gorgon-like, snaky head and her missing skin/hair, now so perfectly replaced by Curdie's mother's goatskin wallet. It seems that the goatskin neck collar that fits the gorgon-like Lina so well did not grow elsewhere other than on her own neck! This is probably the explanation for MacDonald calling the neck covering a "gorget," recalling the flayed Gorgon and "a piece of armour to protect the throat" (Skeat 240). This once again links the Eirinys,

Athena, and their close cousins, the Gorgons, to MacDonald's Irenes and their dog-like, snaky helper, Lina.

The fact that Athena is known as the slayer of Gorgons – as Athena Gorgophone – adds to the theory that the wallet given to Curdie is composed of none other than the piece taken from the Gorgon flayed by the Athenian Maid. Moreover, the merging of Demeter Eirinyes and the warrior Kore, Athena, explains two other attributes MacDonald assigns to grandmother Irene. Through Demeter, the grandmother's doves can be placed in a mythic context, while a concentration on Athena accounts for the elder Irene's spinning. Demeter was directly associated with doves (Graves, *White* 354; Harrison 263), while Athena, through her vanquishing of Arachne (Ovid 129-133), is linked with spinning and spiders, just as Irene's grandmother is in MacDonald's story.

Additional descriptions and episodes in *The Princess and Curdie* recall the myths of the ancient goddesses of Vengeance, the inexorable Eirinyes. For example, MacDonald's description of the avengers is reminiscent of the ancient goddesses whose purview was vengeance. The Uglies are called "the avengers of wickedness" (251-2), "inexorable avengers" (263), "demons" (277, 278), "demons of indescribable ugliness" (279), "evil spirits" (290-1), and "hounds" (311). Every one of these can easily be applied to the original Greek avengers, the Eirenys. The Eirinyes, like MacDonald's inexorable avengers, do not seem able to kill those deserving retribution, but must resort to more internal, psychological punishments. While the dread goddesses are pursuing Orestes, for the murder of his mother, one of the tools at their disposal is their ability to burden the wrongdoer's conscience and to drive him mad. This is exactly the type of torment brought to bear on most of the evildoers in *The Princess and Curdie*, particularly the secretary (267) and the preacher (276). The Eirinyes were also assigned the role of tormenting evildoers in Hades, after death. This is probably the reason for MacDonald's claim that Lina's roar can "terrify the dead" (260).

MacDonald appears to borrow and creatively change another part of the Orestes myth. While Eirinyes are hounding and psychologically torturing Orestes, he is driven to bite off one of his fingers. The blood Orestes draws seems to pacify the Eirinyes, at least for a short time. This part of the Orestes story is mirrored in the tale of Heracles, another madman who shed kindred blood. While Heracles is wrestling the Nemean Lion, this beast bites off one of his fingers. Graves, perhaps like MacDonald, connects both accounts of severed fingers, when he claims that it is probable "that he [Heracles] bit it off to placate the ghosts of his children – as Orestes did when pursued by his mother's Erinnyes" (123: e, 2). These mythological accounts of the biting of fingers are similar to what occurs to the footman, who loses his finger to the avenging Tapir in MacDonald's tale.

The Eirinyes were, for the most part, avengers of spilled blood, particularly that of a close relative. While the reader does not know how Irene's mother died, we do know that the elder Irene must first purify Curdie of a blood crime. It is only after the grandmother brings to life the dove Curdie killed that his conscience is cleared and his punishment averted. As Curdie is making his way home up the mountain, he has the following feelings exactly where the dove's blood was spilled:

> As he passed the rock from which the poor pigeon fell wounded with his arrow, a great joy filled his heart at the thought that he was delivered from the blood of the little bird, and he ran the next hundred yards at full speed up the hill. Some dark shadows passed him: he did not even care to think what they were, but let them run. (46-7)

Because the grandmother had delivered Curdie from his bloodguilt, the "dark shadows" let him run! In the myths, at the very spot where the crime took place (where blood seeps into the earth, and pollutes it), the blood awakens and calls forth the dark, shadowy Eirinys to the scene of the crime and to their duty as avengers. It seems that in MacDonald's tale the avengers of evil, mirroring the original avengers (themselves formed from the blood Zeus spilled when he castrated his father Cronos), arrive too late at the scene of the pseudo-crime, a transgression no longer requiring retribution.

The "maid" who helps in the administering of vengeance near the end of the book is not only directly linked by MacDonald with the elder Irene (310, 313), but this "maid" also recalls additional aspects of Kore. Calling this woman the "maid," MacDonald links her to Persephone, the original maid, or to Athena, the warrior "Maid." This latter connection to Athena fits the narrative very well, particularly when MacDonald's warrior "maid" assumes the role of general over the avian forces during the war.

It becomes clear at the end of *The Princess and Curdie* that the Uglies, like the Eirinyes, also have the role of directing evildoers to their natural home, the underworld.[6] After the worst seven miscreants are bound to the backs of the Uglies, these latter are dispatched by the king with these informative words: "I thank you, my good beasts; and I hope to visit you ere long. Take these evil men with you, and go to your place" (314). MacDonald's last description of the seven Uglies, bearing off the horrified evildoers, is worthy of comparison to some of the ancient accounts: "Like a whirlwind they were in the crowd, scattering it like dust. Like hounds they rushed from the city, their burdens howling and raving" (315). When the old king refers to the Uglies as "good beasts," MacDonald seems to follow the ancient Greeks who, out of fear, called their own ugly goddesses of vengeance, Eumenides, or "The Benevolent." That these "good beasts'" place of residence is naturally located in the underworld may be concluded from the fact that the king does indeed visit them ere long. In the very next chapter of the narrative, MacDonald informs the reader that the old king died (319), thus making his journey to the beasts' "place," the underworld.[7]

Conclusion

> I wish I knew half you do about the conditions of former generations, but neither my tastes nor opportunities have ever led me into those regions – except where they bordered on the interests of literature and the history of religious development. (George MacDonald quoted in Greville MacDonald 518)

MacDonald's two books, *The Princess and the Goblin* and *The Princess and Curdie*, draw much of their content and depth from Greek mythology and religion. Particularly in the latter of the two books, MacDonald uses many chthonic strands of myths and a variety of similar chthonic goddesses (and motifs associated with them) to furnish material for his story. In the above quotation (from MacDonald's letter to C. Edmund Maurice), he states directly that he had been interested in and had studied literature and the history of religious development. It seems that parts of this interest and aspects of his studies dealt with Greek myths and religious thought, and that some of this material found its way to MacDonald's fantasy writings, though now creatively re-worked and re-applied. In the Kore myth there is much of interest to students of literature and religious development, particularly that relating to the identification of the soul with the sown seed, and the idea of the immortality of the soul.

MacDonald also presents the reader with the idea that the ancient Greek goddesses' characters partook of a large range of action - from the benevolent to the destructive. His goddesses, like their ancient predecessors, have real personalities and cannot be fully understood in a merely superficial manner. Perhaps it is this deep mystery usually surrounding them that draws MacDonald to present them continually to his readership in an effort to convince us to reflect upon our ideas of Deity.

Endnotes

1. Because of the varied spelling of the Greek names, in the original sources, commentaries, and translations, there may some minor inconsistencies in this aspect of the chapter. The various spelling of names such as Core and Kore; Irene and Eirene; Eirinyes, Erinyes, and Erinys; etc. will be used throughout.
2. It is very likely that the surname, Louisa – of the bath – used to describe a "mother," would have proved important to a writer married to a woman named Louisa, who herself seems to be MacDonald's ideal of motherhood.
3. The struggle between polytheism and monotheism seems to reach its peak in Lucius' *The Golden Ass*. Here the goddess claims to incorporate into herself most of the other general and particular deities, when she claims, "I am nature, the universal Mother, mistress of the elements, primordial child of time, sovereign of all things spiritual, queen of the dead, queen also of the immortals, the single manifestation of all gods and goddesses that are" (228). Directly following this, the goddess enumerates eleven different names by which she is known, including Demeter, Persephone and Hecate.
4. The very fact that both "mothers" are directly involved with the two respective strings/threads speaks volumes for their affinity within the story. This affinity is made more explicit in *The Princess and Curdie*.
5. It is very likely that MacDonald was as meticulous with his study of the original language of the myths as he was with the myths themselves. MacDonald very likely read the ancient Greek myths in their original language, or, at the very least, studied the words in question in Liddell and Scott's *Greek English Lexicon*. I base this assertion mainly on two arguments: MacDonald, like most university students of his time, studied Greek; and because of the close connection between some Greek words and their respective meanings in relation to MacDonald's "translation" of similar words and meanings in his stories. To show this latter, I provide the following evidence. According to Liddell and Scott the word for pigeon/dove, *perister-a* - has only two possible meanings: "pigeon/dove" and "a woman's ornament" (1388). This latter – "a woman's ornament" is undoubtedly connected with the next entry in the Lexicon *peristern-idion*, which, with the ending izw, means, "put around the breast." The same word, with the ending ton, probably meaning "a breast-band," rounds out the possible meanings of the word in question. Thus the word *peristera* has two meanings: 1) "a pigeon/dove," and 2) "a woman's ornament worn on the breast" or a "breast-band." MacDonald uses

exactly these two meanings in *The Princess and Curdie*. The former hardly needs an exposition; however, the latter meaning may be found by considering that MacDonald writes this about the wounded pigeon: "the wounded bird had now spread out both its wings across her bosom, like some great mystical ornament of frosted silver" (45).

6. The forty-nine Uglies are very likely related to the forty-nine Danaids, underground dwellers closely linked with the Erinys, and with Danae, Perseus' mother. These forty-nine maidens were punished in Hades for decapitating their husbands on their wedding night. For this grave transgression, they were forced to perpetually carry water in sieves or broken pots (Monaghan 89).

7. MacDonald appears to associate this king with the male seasonal deities of Greek religion and mythology. Because the younger Irene is identified with Kore, this "king" may be linked with some of the male gods of fertility, for example "king" Dionysus. This is particularly apparent in *The Princess and the Goblin*, in the chapter titled "Spring-time," which MacDonald begins with: "The spring, so dear to all creatures, young and old, came at last, and before the first few days of it had gone, the king rode through its budding valleys to see his little daughter. He had been in a distant part of his dominions all the winter" (164). It is exactly in this chapter that Patterson identifies Irene with Persephone in terms of their flower "picking."

Works Cited

Aeschylus. *Choephoroe*, in G. M. Cookson, trans., *The Plays of Aeschylus* in R. M. Hutchings, ed., *The Great Books of the Western World: Aeschylus, Sophocles, Euripides, Aristophanes*, 70-80.

---. *Eumenides*, in G. M. Cookson, trans., *The Plays of Aeschylus* in R. M. Hutchings, ed., *The Great Books of the Western World: Aeschylus, Sophocles, Euripides, Aristophanes*, 81-91.

Apollodorus. The Library, in Michael Simpson, trans., *Gods and Heroes of the Greeks: The Library of Apollodorus*. Amherst: University of Massachusetts Press, 1976.

Apuleius, Lucius. *The Golden Ass*. Robert Graves, trans., Harmondsworth: Penguin, 1985.

Aristophanes. *The Frogs*, in B. B. Rogers, trans., *The Plays of Aristophanes*, in R.M. Hutchings, ed., *The Great Books of the Western World: Aeschylus, Sophocles, Euripides, Aristophanes*, 564-582.

Euripides. *Electra*, in E. P. Coleridge, trans., *The Plays of Euripides*, in R. M. Hutchings, ed., *The Great Books of the Western World: Aeschylus, Sophocles, Euripides, Aristophanes*, 327-339.

Graves, Robert. *The White Goddess*. (1948) New York: Farrar, Straus and Giroux, 1991.

---. *The Greek Myths*. (1955) New York: George Braziller, 1957.

Hanks, Patrick and Hodges, Flavia. *A Dictionary of First Names*, in P. Hanks, F. Hodges, A. D. Mills, A. Room, *The Oxford Names Companion*, Oxford: Oxford UP, 2002.

Harrison, Jane. *Prolegomena to the Study of Greek Religion*. (1903) New York: Meridian, 1955.

Hesiod. *Theogony*, in Dorothea Wender, trans. *Hesiod and Theognis*. London: Penguin, 1973.

Homer. *The Odyssey*. Richond Lattimore, trans. London: Harper and Row, 1967.

Hutchings, R. M., ed. *The Great Books of the Western World: Aeschylus, Sophocles, Euripides, Aristophanes*. Chicago, London, Toronto: William Benton, 1952.

Kerenyi, Carl. *The Gods of the Greeks*. (1951) London: Thames and Hudson, 1985.

Lempriere, J., *Classical Dictionary* (1788). F. A. Wright, ed. *Lempriere's Classical Dictionary*. London: Bracken Books, 1984

MacDonald, George, *The Princess and the Goblin*. (1872) Whitethorn, CA: Johannesen, 1997.

---. *The Princess and the Goblin*. (1883) Whitethorn, CA: Johannesen, 2000.

MacDonald, Greville, *George MacDonald and His Wife*. (1924) Whitethorn, CA: Johannesen, 1998.
McGillis, Roderick, ed. *For the Childlike*. Metuchen & London: Scarecrow Press, 1992.
Monaghan, Patricia. *The Book of Goddesses & Heroines*. St. Paul: Llewellyn Publications, 1990.
Morford M. P. O. and Lenardon, R. J. *Classical Mythology*. New York & London: Longman, 1985.
Murray, Alexander. *Who's Who in Mythology*. (second ed. 1874). New York: Bonanza Books, 1989.
Ovid. *The Metamorphoses*. Rolfe Humphries, trans. Bloomington: Indiana UP, 1983.
Patterson, Nancy-Lou. "Kore Motifs in *The Princess and the Goblin*," in Roderick McGillis, ed., *For the Childlike*, 169-182.
Plutarch. *Lives of Illustrious Men*, in John and William Langhorne, trans. *Plutarch's Lives of Illustrious Men*. London: Chatto and Windus, 1878.
Sadler, Glenn, ed. *An Expression of Character: The Letters of George MacDonald*. Grand Rapids: William B. Eerdmans, 1994.
Skeat, Walter. *An Etymological Dictionary of the English Language*, Oxford: Clarendon Press, 1882.
Sophocles. Electra, in R. C. Jebb, trans., *The Plays of Sophocles* in R. M. Hutchings, ed., *The Great Books of the Western World: Aeschylus, Sophocles, Euripides, Aristophanes*, 156-169.
Soto, Fernando, "Chthonic Aspects of *Phantastes*: From the Rising of the Goddess to the Anodos of Anodos." *North Wind: Journal of the George MacDonald Society*, 19 (2000), 19-49.
---. "The Two-World Consciousness of North Wind: Unity and Dichotomy in MacDonald's Fairy Tale." *Studies in Scottish Literature*, 34 (2004), 150 - 168.
Willard, Nancy, "The Goddess in the Bellfry: Grandmothers and Wise Women in George MacDonald's Books for Children," Roderick McGillis, ed., *For the Childlike*, 67-74.

ADELA CATHCART.

He had spent his years like a weary dream through a long night, — a strange, dismal, unkindly dream, — and now the morning was at hand. Often in his dream he listened with dreamy senses to the ringing of the bell, but that bell would awake him at last. He was like a seed buried too deep in the soil, to which the light has never penetrated, and which, therefore, has never forced itself upwards to the open air, never experienced the resurrection of the dead. But seeds grow ages after they have fallen into the earth; and, indeed, with many kinds, and within some limits, the older the seed before it germinates, the more plentiful the fruit. And may it not be believed of many human beings, that, the great Husbandsman having sown them like seeds sown in the soil of human affairs, there they lie buried a life long; and, only after the upturning of the soil by death, reach a position in which the awakening of their aspiration and the consequent growth become possible. Surely he has made nothing in vain.

from "The Bell," Chapter 6 in Adela Cathcart

Chapter 5

George MacDonald and Universalism

David L. Neuhouseer

Is it true that George MacDonald believed that all would eventually be saved? What form did his belief in universalism take? The term "universalism" covers many shades of belief. What influences contributed to this belief? And finally, what justification, including biblical, did he have for this belief? These are the questions I address here. This is not an attempt to determine whether or not universalism is true. It is only an exposition of MacDonald's views on the subject. Because he had so much to say about universalism, it seems only fair to give him a thoughtful hearing.

A major theme in all of MacDonald's writing was his belief that a loving Father is our best image of God. He believed that a corollary to that belief was that God would not send any of his children to an eternal punishment. No earthly loving father would send a son or daughter to such a punishment and therefore neither would God. Now, words like "loving" and "father" when used about humans may not have quite the same meaning when used of God. However, as C. S. Lewis has pointed out, if the meanings of the words we use about God have no relation to their ordinary meaning, then we are really not saying anything at all about God (*The Problem of Pain* 28). Or, as John Greenleaf Whittier put it in "The Eternal Goodness,"

> But nothing can be good in Him
> Which evil is in me. (Whittier 231).

A sermon on "Justice," published in *Unspoken Sermons, Series 3*, is MacDonald's most clearly developed statement on this subject. In it he claims that the prevalent view that God would condemn or even allow a person to suffer eternal torment is one that, if attributed to any human would bring almost universal condemnation. In reality, God's punishment is always remedial and destroys sin by saving people from their sin. MacDonald believed that God's love is a tough love. He did not believe that God would not care what we did and just wants us to be happy. He did believe that God would keep working and do whatever was necessary to get us to repent no matter how long it would take for us to repent. This belief will be developed later in the paper, but first I examine the origins of and influences on the belief in universalism.

In his novel *Robert Falconer*, the hero as a young boy experiences the same difficulty that I believe MacDonald himself experienced as a boy.

> And he must believe, too, that God was just, awfully just, punishing with fearful pains those who did not go through a certain process of mind which it was utterly impossible they should go through without a help which he would give to some and withhold from others, the reason of the difference not being such, to say the least of it, as to come within the reach of the persons concerned. And this God they said was love. It was logically absurd, of course, yet, thank God, they did say that God was love; and many of them succeeded in believing it, too, and in ordering their ways... accordingly. (77).

In *Weighed and Wanting*, a character says: "I well remember feeling as a child that I did not care for God to love me if he did not love everybody: the kind of love I needed was ... the love ... that all men needed, the love that belonged to their nature as the children of the Father, a love he could not give me except he gave it to all men" (37). I believe that MacDonald, even as a boy, was troubled by the then prevalent view of hell as a place of eternal suffering. His early sense of justice and his own father as an earthly example of the loving heavenly Father were the early beginnings of his later beliefs. That MacDonald's idea of God as a loving father is the basis for his belief in universalism is shown by the following passage from the novel *Adela Cathcart*.

> And the man was telling them, sir, that God had picked out so many men, women, and children, to go right away to glory, and left the rest to be damned for ever and ever in hell. And I up and spoke to him; and "sir," says I, "if I was tould as how I was to pick out so many o' my childeren, and take 'em with me to a fine house, and leave the rest to be burnt up... which o' them would I choose?" "How can I tell?" says he. "No doubt," says I; "they aint your sons and darters. But I can. I wouldn't move afoot, sir, but I'd take my chance wi' the poor things. And, sir," says I, "we're all God's children; and which o' us is he to choose, and which is he to leave out? I don't believe he'd know a bit better how to choose one and leave another than I should, sir – that is, his heart wouldn't let him lose e'er a one o' us, or he'd be miserable for ever, as I should be, if I left one o' mine i' the fire." (220)

However, as well as his own sense of divine justice, outside influences affected his belief in universal salvation. In 1843, a split occurred in the Church of Scotland; nearly a third of the members and clergy left to start the Free Church of Scotland. Although a number of issues were involved, one was "the doctrine of universal redemption, with ministers being expelled and churches disendowed because of it" (Hein, *George MacDonald* 18). MacDonald was a college student at this time and this conflict in the church would have reinforced his doubts about the orthodox theology of his day. "In Glasgow, students were expelled from the Congregational Theological Seminary for adhering to the doctrine of Universal Redemption" (Greville MacDonald 79). Just a few years after the split in the Church of Scotland, MacDonald was a student at the Congregational seminary in London. Even earlier, in 1831, John MacCleod Campbell, who later became a friend of MacDonald, was driven out of the Established Church for his views on atonement.

Some friends of MacDonald also influenced him. One of them was Thomas Erskine who "had a reputation for genuine godliness of spirit and attitude, together with a sense of justice and compassion that served to exclude him from the institutionalized church. He believed in the universality of the Atonement and the eventual restoration of all people to the unsullied divine image" (Hein, *George MacDonald* 174). Erskine's work was "read at the Broadlands conferences" (Parry and Partridge 229). These conferences were held from 1874 until 1888 at the estate of Lord and Lady Mount Temple, two of MacDonald's most intimate friends. One of the major organizers of the conferences was another friend, Russell Gurney. MacDonald was a major speaker at many of these meetings.

A more important influence was the preacher Alexander John Scott who was disfranchised from the Presbyterian ministry for preaching universalism. As a young seminary student in London, MacDonald attended many of Scott's lectures. At various difficult times Scott was a friend and counselor to MacDonald. MacDonald's first daughter, Lilia Scott was named after him, and MacDonald's novel *Robert Falconer* was dedicated to Scott. In a letter to Scott's daughter, MacDonald wrote: "I looked up to your father more than to any man except my own father" (Sadler 335). MacDonald wrote a poem in tribute to this friend. In it he described the darkness and confusion he experienced until

>Thy [Scott's] voice, Truth's herald,
>Calm and distinct, powerful and sweet and fine:
>I loved and listened, listened and loved more.
>(*Poetical Works*, Vol. I 272).

According to Rolland Hein,

> [T]he most prominent Victorian theologian to influence MacDonald's thought was [Frederick Denison] Maurice... A man whose deep practical spirituality lent a moral beauty to his life... MacDonald became a disciple of his in the late 1850's. Among the ideas that MacDonald clearly shared with him were his stress upon the Fatherhood of God and the conviction that Christ is absolutely at one with the Father ... Both rejected the idea that sin would be eternally punished, emphasized the "Inner Light" with the possibility of revelation to the individual apart from Scripture (but not inharmonious with it.) (Hein, *The Harmony Within* 32-33).

However, Maurice stated, "I have said distinctly that I am not a Universalist, that I have deliberately rejected the theory of Universalism, knowing what it is; and that I should as much refuse an Article which dogmatized in favour of that theory as one that dogmatized in favour of the opposite" (Vidler 59). Although not a Universalist, his sympathy to universalism is apparent in the following quotations:

> Within the last ten years the Scotch Church has ejected from its bosom some of the most devout, laborious, and able of its preachers. These men may have had offensive opinions, but that which was put forward as the reason for their expulsion, was their belief in the universal redemption of mankind by Christ, and their repeated declarations in their sermons that all whom they addressed were the objects of God's love. (Maurice, *The Kingdom of Christ Vol. 1* 152).

and

> I ask no one to pronounce, for I dare not pronounce myself, what are the possibilities of resistance in a human will to the loving will of God. There are times when they seem to me – thinking of myself more than of others – almost infinite... I am obliged to believe in an abyss of love which is deeper than the abyss of death: I dare not lose faith in that love. I sink into death, eternal death, if I do. I must feel that this love is compassing the universe. More about it I cannot know. But God knows. I leave myself and all to Him." (Maurice, *Theological Essays* 323).

MacDonald attended Maurice's London church and named one of his sons Maurice in his honor. In a poem, "A Thanksgiving For F. D. Maurice," MacDonald praised him for his "prophet's calm commanding voice," "obedient, wise, clear listening care," "learning," and "humility." According to Greville MacDonald the following verse of that poem was omitted from the printed version.

> He [Maurice] taught that hell itself is yet within
> The confines of thy kingdom; and its fires
> The endless conflict of thy love with sin,
> That even by horror works its pure desires.
> (Greville MacDonald 398).

Another of MacDonald's friends, Charles Dodgson (Lewis Carroll) wrote an interesting essay, "Eternal Punishment." In it he identified what he believed were three contradictory statements.

I. God is perfectly good.
II. To inflict Eternal Punishment on certain human beings, and in certain circumstances would be wrong.
III. God is capable of acting thus.
(Collingwood 345).

These are somewhat similar to the three inconsistent propositions that Thomas Talbot uses to defend universalism in *Universal Salvation? The Current Debate* (see Parry and Partridge 7). In his essay, Dodgson stated that "My object has been throughout, not to indicate one course rather than another, but to help the Reader to see clearly what the possible courses are, and what he is virtually accepting, or denying, in choosing any one of them" (Collingwood 355).

Although Dodgson uses his training as a mathematician and logician to attempt to identify the logical possibilities without advocating any one, it seems to me that the position that rejects the Eternal Punishment proposition is shown in a favorable light. He does not indicate whether dropping the second one leads to universalism or annihilationism. As close as MacDonald and Dodgson were it seems likely that they would have discussed this issue with each other.

MacDonald was influenced by authors as well as personal friends. He admired Tennyson's poetry. According to MacDonald, "In Memoriam," "was the poem of the hoping doubters, the poem of our age" (*England's Antiphon* 329). He must have especially loved the following lines,

> Behold we know not anything;
> I can but trust that good shall fall
> At last — far off —at last, to all.
> And every winter change to spring. (Hill 237).

It is true that Tennyson follows this verse with one expressing doubt about this trust in universal salvation:

> So runs my dreams; but what am I?
> An infant crying in the night;
> An infant crying for the light;
> And with no language but a cry.
> (Hill 237)

However, this stanza is, in turn, followed by the claim that the wish for universal salvation comes from that within us that is most like God, a belief that MacDonald held as well. In fact, MacDonald quotes this stanza in *England's Antiphon*.

> The wish, that of the living whole
> No life may fail beyond the grave,
> Derives it not from what we have
> The likest God within the soul.
> (Hill 237; also MacDonald, *England's Antiphon* 330.)

Even Martin Luther must have been of some help to MacDonald as the following hymn by Luther suggests that even in hell we can turn to Christ. Here is MacDonald's translation.

> When amidst the pains of hell
>   Us our sins are baiting;
> Whither shall we flee away
>   Where relief is waiting?
> To thee, Lord Christ, thee only
>   Who didst outpour thy precious blood
> For our sins sufficing good:
>   (Luther's Song-Book in *Rampolli* 172).

MacDonald admired and was influenced in many ways by the German poet, Georg Friedrich Philipp von Hardenberg who wrote under the pen name, Novalis. He translated and published privately many of Novalis' poems into English.

Support for universalism is evident in the following lines from MacDonald's translation of Novalis's *Spiritual Songs*:

> Thou stand'st with love unshaken
>   Ever by every man;
> And if by all forsaken,
>   Art still the faithful one.
> Such love must win the wrestle;
>   At last thy love they'll see,
> Weep bitterly, and nestle
>   Like children to thy knee.
>   (*Rampolli* 25. Italics added)

On MacDonald's lecture tour of the United States in 1872, he met the Quaker poet John Greenleaf Whittier as well as most of the other major literary figures of the day. Mrs. MacDonald wrote to her children about their visit with Whittier and commented, "He is a most lovable, holy man, but full of fire and enjoyment of all things good. He is very wide in his beliefs" (Greville MacDonald 426). MacDonald probably read "The Eternal Goodness" by Whittier, and if he did, I am sure he would have found welcome support for his views, especially in the lines,

> I only know I cannot drift
> Beyond His love and care.
>   (Whittier 231)

Also, MacDonald must have been aware that some of the earlier Christian leaders believed in universalism. MacDonald refers to Origen of Alexandria (c. 185-254) in *The Seaboard Parish* (314) and in his lectures. Origen was one whose beliefs were remarkably similar to MacDonald's. According to Kenneth Scott Latourette,

> Origen taught that ultimately all the spirits who have fallen away from God will be restored to full harmony with Him. This can come about only with their cooperation, for they have freedom to accept or to reject the redemption wrought in Christ. Before their full restoration they will suffer punishment, but the punishment is intended to be educative, to purge them from the imperfections brought by their sin. After the end of the present age and its world another age and world will come, so Origen believed, in which those

who have been born again will continue to grow and the unrepentant will be given further opportunity for repentance. Eventually all, even the devils, through repentance, learning, and growth, will be fully saved. Origen's conception of the drama of creation and redemption was breath-taking in its vast sweep and in its confident hope. (151)

In *Lilith*, MacDonald suggests that even Satan may be saved eventually. Hans Denck (c. 1495-1527), an Anabaptist leader, had similar views. Denck believed that "A God of love could not punish the sinner vindictively and eternally. His love would find a way to overcome evil by correctives that would not coerce the individual's free will" (Goertz 69). This is an important point, one that MacDonald also believed, that evil would be overcome without coercing the individual's free will.

Although MacDonald was aware of earlier and contemporary advocates of universal salvation and he certainly was influenced by his friends and mentors, he seems to have had confidence in his own understanding of the implications of God's love and power. According to Barbara Amell who has researched numerous contemporary accounts of his lectures, "It is a peculiar feature of MacDonald's lectures that he does not refer to others who share his belief in the triumph of God's mercy or even quote Scriptures in behalf of his case; he simply states it as an absolute, a certainty of moral fact" (email from Barbara Amell, June 25, 2005).

In his book, *Universal Reconciliation*, Michael Phillips quotes ten early church fathers who suggest a belief in universal salvation or at least the possibility of salvation after a time of punishment in hell (41-3). They are, Theophilus of Antioch, Iranaeus of Lyons, Clement of Alexandria, Origen of Alexandria, Eusebius of Caesarea, Gregory of Nazianzus, Gregory of Nyssa, Ambrose Bishop of Milan, Jerome, and Theodoret of Antioch. Morvenna Ludlow, a Cambridge and Oxford scholar whose specialty is a study of the historical development of universalist ideas in Christianity, states that the intention in her chapter in *Universal Salvation? The Current Debate* was "neither to provide an exhaustive account of all those people who have advocated universal salvation nor to defend any particular belief... [but] rather... to show ... that there has been a more or less continuous tradition of universalism within (and on the penumbra of) Christianity." She adds, "[W]hat is ... striking is that most of the writers I have examined, despite their many speculations have ultimately based their convictions on the biblical promises that God wills all to be saved and that in the end, God will be all in all" (in Parry and Partridge 215). [Examples of biblical references for universalism are given below.] Barbara Amell's book, *Triumph*, contains references to many books published in the nineteenth century supporting universalism.

The remainder of this chapter will illustrate and further develop MacDonald's views on universalism. In many of his novels, he expressed his belief in universalism and clarified his views and his reasons for that belief. *There and Back* contains the description of a dream that MacDonald said was almost word for word the account that one of his friends gave of an actual dream of his own.

> But this part of my dream, the most lovely of all, I can find no words to describe; nor can I even recall to my own mind the half of what I felt. I only know that something was given me then, some spiritual apprehension, to be again withdrawn, but to be given to us all, I believe, some day, out of his infinite love, and withdrawn no more. Every heart that had ever ached, or longed, or wandered, I knew was there, folded warm and soft, safe and glad. And it seemed in my dream that to know this was the crown of all my bliss - yes, even more than to be myself in my Father's arms. (392)

Another evidence of his belief in universalism appears in the following conversation in *Donal Grant*.

> "But some are lost after all!" she said.
> "Doubtless; there are sheep that will keep running away. But he goes after them again."
> "He will not do that for ever!"
> "He will."
> "I do not believe it."
> "Then you do not believe that God is infinite!"
> "I do." ...
> "But if his mercy and his graciousness are not infinite, then he is not infinite!"
> "There are other attributes in which he is infinite."
> "But he is not infinite in all his attributes? He is partly infinite, and partly finite! — infinite in knowledge and power, but in love, in forgiveness, in all those things which are the most beautiful, the most divine, the most Christ-like, he is finite, measurable, bounded, small!" (221)

Although the following are the thoughts of a character in *The Elect Lady* following her father's death, they certainly agree with MacDonald's own ideas:

> She pondered much about her father, and would find herself praying for him, careless of what she had been taught. She could not blind herself to what she knew. He had not been a bad man, as men count badness, but could she in common sense think him a glorified saint, shining in white robes? The polite, kind old man! Her own father! – could she, on the other hand, believe him in flames forever: If so, what a religion was that which required her to believe it, and at the same time to rejoice in the Lord always! (154).

In *Robert Falconer*, Robert's grandmother believed that her son had just died and was unsaved.

> She was, of course, greatly distressed.
> But in a few weeks she was more cheerful. It is one of the mysteries of humanity that mothers in her circumstances, and holding her creed, do regain not merely the faculty of going on with the business of life, but, in most cases, even cheerfulness. The infinite Truth, the Love of the universe, supports them beyond their consciousness, coming to them like sleep from the roots of their being, and having nothing to do with their opinions or beliefs. And hence spring those comforting subterfuges of hope to which they all fly. Not being able to trust the Father entirely, they yet say: 'Who can tell whether God did not please to grant them saving faith at the eleventh hour?" – that so they might pass from the very gates of hell, the only place for which their life had fitted them, into the bosom of love and purity: This God could do for all: this for the son beloved of his mother perhaps he might do? (91-2).

I believe that many people have thoughts like these, "How can this good person that I love suffer in hell forever?" Or, "Surely it is possible that at the last minute this beloved friend or relative may have accepted Christ." Thoughts like these were the beginnings of MacDonald's universalism.

In *David Elginbrod*, the following was said about one of the characters and could be said of MacDonald himself:

> He believes entirely that God loves, yea, is love; and therefore, that hell itself must be subservient to that love, and but an embodiment of it; that the grand work of Justice is to make way for a Love which will give to every man that which is right, and ten times more, even if it should be by means of awful suffering, – a suffering which the Love of the Father will not shun, either for himself or his children, but will eagerly meet for their sakes, that he may give them all that is in his heart. (371-2)

MacDonald was concerned that people might believe that if universalism were true, nothing really matters. After all, if we are all saved eventually, why not do as we please in this life. In 1885, he wrote: "... thousands of half thinkers imagine that since it is declared with such authority that hell is not everlasting, there is then no hell at all" (*Letters From Hell*, viii).

According to Greville MacDonald, *Lilith* "was written, I do think, in view of the increasingly easy tendencies in universalists, who, because they had now discarded everlasting retribution as a popular superstition, were dismissing hell-fire altogether, and with it the need for repentance as the way back into the Kingdom" (552). In *Lilith*, the salvation of Lilith was not a simple or painless operation.

So MacDonald's universalism was not an easy out for the sinner and certainly not a doctrine that would make Christians less likely to want to evangelize. Who would want a friend to have to suffer for any length of time and possibly for a long time? The following conversation appears in *The Elect Lady*.

> "Time is plentiful for his misery, if he will not, repent; plentiful for the mercy of God that would lead him to repentance. There is plenty of time for labor and hope; none for indifference and delay. God will have his creatures good. They can not escape Him."
>
> "Then a man may put off repentance as long as he pleases!"
>
> "Certainly he may – at least as long as he can – but it is a fearful thing to try issues with God." (55-6)

In *Robert Falconer* a character says, "I believe that you will be compelled to repent some day, and that now is the best time. Then, you will not only have to repent, but to repent that you did not repent now" (407).

The following statement from the sermon "Justice" shows his belief that suffering may be necessary.

> Justice then requires that sin should be put an end to; and not that only, but that it should be atoned for; and where punishment can do anything to this end, where it can help the sinner to know what he has been guilty of, where it can soften his heart to see his pride and wrong and cruelty, justice requires that punishment shall not be spared. And the more we believe in God, the surer we shall be that he will spare nothing that suffering can do to deliver his child from death. If suffering cannot serve this end, we need look for no more hell, but for the destruction of sin by the destruction of the sinner. That, however, would, it appears to me, be for God to suffer defeat, blameless indeed, but defeat. (*Unspoken Sermons, Series I, II, and III.* 515-6).

This passage from MacDonald's sermon opposes C. S. Lewis' beliefs about hell. Lewis believed that hell is not a place of conscious eternal suffering; for Lewis, what is in hell forever is the remains of a person. As he put it in *The Great Divorce*, a grumbler may at some point become only a grumble (Lewis, *The Great Divorce* 77). To put it more plainly, although a person may be in hell forever, he is not continually conscious of pain. This would be one answer for anyone who has a problem with the idea that God would punish a finite creation of his (therefore one whose sin must be finite) with an infinite punishment. The preceding quotation from MacDonald's sermon shows that MacDonald rejects this position. He believes that the destruction of the sinner would be a defeat of God's love. The quotation also clearly shows that he believed that God must do whatever it takes to destroy the sin. One of his sermons is entitled "Our God is a Consuming Fire."

MacDonald thought that some biblical verses supported his belief in universalism. He found support for his views in Psalms 22:27-28, "All the ends of the world shall remember and turn unto the LORD: and all the kindreds of the nations shall worship before thee. For the kingdom is the Lord's: and he is the governor among the nations." (This and all subsequent biblical quotations are from the *King James Version*.) Also, Romans 14:11 says, "For it is written, 'As I live, saith the Lord, every knee shall bow to me, and every tongue shall confess to God.'" Every knee will bow is also claimed in Phil. 2:10, and Isaiah 45:23. John 12:32 says that Jesus will draw all men unto Him. I Cor. 15:22, says that all men will be made alive in Christ. Acts 3:21 in the *New English Bible* speaks of "universal restoration." Titus 2:11 says that the grace of God brings salvation to all men. There are more biblical texts I could cite, but one that I think is especially interesting is I Tim. 4:10 which says that God "is the Savior of all men, specially of those that believe."

Of course, there are many biblical passages that seem to refute universalism. One such verse is Matthew 25:46, "And these shall go away into everlasting punishment: but the righteous into life eternal." Matthew's words seem to be a strong refutation of universalism. However, William Barclay said that the Greek word translated here as "punishment" is *kolasis* and he avers,

> I think it is true to say that in all of Greek secular literature *kolasis* is never used of anything but remedial punishment. The word for eternal is *aionois*... The simplest way to put it is that *ainios* cannot be used properly of anyone but God... Eternal punishment is then literally that kind of remedial punishment which it befits God to give and which only God can give" (Barclay 66).

Barclay's suggestion is in accord with MacDonald's views. In the sermon 'Creation in Christ," MacDonald said, "If God would not punish sin, or if he did it for anything but love, he would not be the father of Jesus Christ" (*Unspoken Sermons, Series I, II, and III* 421). He believed that God's love would punish, not for the sake of punishment, but for the destruction of sin and the restoration of the sinner.

In one way, MacDonald may be the ultimate Calvinist. He believes so much in the sovereignty of God that he argues God will not be defeated but will accomplish what He desires, namely that all men will be saved (I Tim. 2:4). However, he may also be the ultimate Arminian. He believes in free will, namely, that we can resist God as long as we want. His reconciliation between predestination (he believed that all were predestined to be saved) and free will was that eventually God's love would convince everyone even though it may take a prolonged effort to convince some. Suppose that I had resisted the love of the woman who became my wife (this is a big supposition since I definitely did not resist!). Nevertheless, her love and her beauty of form and character would, without doubt, have conquered my resistance eventually. According to MacDonald, "People are not coerced into choosing God; they will all one day simply be allowed a clear-sighted choice" (Hein, *The Harmony Within* 121).

To summarize: MacDonald believed that God's love would be a consuming fire that would eventually rid the world of sin by convincing everyone to accept their rightful place as obedient children and worship their heavenly Father. He came to these beliefs from his firm faith that God is love and that His love will never fail. He was influenced by his friends and contemporaries as well as by books. In particular, he believed that universalism is what the Bible taught. I think that he would like to leave us with this question. "When shall a man dare to say that God has done all He can?" (*Robert Falconer* 410).

[1] For a more complete study of universalism, one excellent source is *Universal Salvation? The Current Debate* edited by Robin A. Parry and Christopher H. Partridge.

Works Cited

Amell, Barbara. *Triumph*. Portland, OR: Wingfold Books, 2005.
Barclay, William. *A Spiritual Autobiography*. Grand Rapids, MI: Eerdmans, 1975.
Collingwood, Stuart Dodgson, ed. *Diversions and Digressions of Lewis Carroll*. New York:Dover Publications, 1961.
Goertz, Hans-Jurgen, ed. *Profiles of Radical Reformers*. Kitchener, Ontario: Herald Press, 1982.
Hein, Rolland. *George MacDonald: Victorian Mythmaker*. Nashville, TN: Star Song Publishing Group, 1993.
---. *The Harmony Within*, Chicago: Cornerstone Press , 1982.
Hill, Jr., Robert W., ed. *Tennyson's Poetry*, 2nd edition. New York: W. W. Norton, 1999.
Latourette, Kenneth Scott. *A History of Christianity*. New York: Harper & Brothers, 1953.
Lewis, C. S. *The Great Divorce*, San Francisco: Harper Collins, 2001.
---. *The Problem of Pain*, San Francisco: Harper Collins, 2001.
MacDonald, George. *Adela Cathcart*, London: Hurst & Blackett, 1864.
---. *David Elginbrod*. Philadelphia: Mackay, 1900.
---. *Donal Grant*. London: Kegan Paul, Trench,Trubner, 1900.
---. *The Elect Lady*. Kegan Paul, New York: George Munro's & Sons, 1900.
---. *England's Antiphon*. New York: Macmillan, 1890.
---. *Poetical Works, Vol I*. London: Chatto & Windus, 1893.

---. *Rampolli*. London: Longmans, Green, 1897.
---. *Robert Falconer*. London: Hurst & Blackett, 1880.
---. *There and Back*. London: Kegan Paul, Trench,Trubner,1900-1910.
---. *The Seaboard Parish*. London: Strahan, 1869.
---. *Unspoken Sermons: Series I, II, and III*. Whitethorn, CA. 1997.
---. *Weighed and Wanting*. Boston: Lothrop, 1882.
MacDonald, Greville, *George MacDonald and his Wife*. 2nd edition. London: George Allen & Unwin, 1924. (This is also the Johannesen edition.)
Maurice, Frederick Denison. *The Kingdom of Christ, Vol. 1*. London: SCM Press, 1958.
---. *Theological Essays*. London: James Clarke, 1957.
Parry, Robin A. and Christopher H. Partridge, eds. *Universal Salvation? The Current Debate*. Grand Rapids, MI.: Wm. B. Eerdmans, 2004.
Sadler, Glenn Edward. *The Letters of George MacDonald*. Grand Rapids, MI: Wm. B. Eerdmans, 1994.

The little princess was handed down by the tongs
Illustration by F. D. Bedford

Part 2: His Master's Voice

Chapter 6

"More is Meant Than Meets the Ear":
Narrative Framing in the Three Versions of
George MacDonald's *The Light Princess*

Jan Susina

"To ask me to explain, is to say, 'Roses! Boil them, or we won't have them!'
My tales may not be roses, but I will not boil them."
(George MacDonald, "The Fantastic Imagination" 321)

George MacDonald's *The Light Princess* is one of his earliest and most successful literary fairy tales. Over the years, he created three distinctive versions of the fairy tale, each using a slightly different framing technique to better address the intended or specific audience. In this chapter, I will examine how MacDonald situated and modified the *The Light Princess* in these three versions. The story appeared first in print as an interpolated fairy tale within *Adela Cathcart* (1863), one of MacDonald's novels for adults. Then MacDonald published it as the introductory fairy tale in the illustrated children's collection, *Dealings with the Fairies* (1867). Finally, MacDonald handwrote it on a scroll that functioned both as script and prop for a performance piece that he read aloud, often to a college-aged audience.

Composition History of The Light Princess

Lewis Carroll recorded in his diary on 9 July 1862 that he accompanied MacDonald on his way "to a publisher with the MS. of his fairy tale *The Light Princess* in which he showed me some exquisite drawings by Hughes" (Carroll, I: 184). The date of this passage suggests that MacDonald had composed *The Light Princess* sometime in 1862, or perhaps earlier. Carroll's admiration of Arthur Hughes' drawings must have instigated his interest in meeting the artist. Through his friendship with MacDonald, Carroll met Arthur Hughes and his family. Carroll first visited Hughes in his studio on 21 July 1863 accompanied by Alexander Munro, the sculptor who used Greville MacDonald as the model for his statue, "Boy with a Dolphin," which still stands in Hyde Park. Later,

Carroll photographed Hughes with some of his four children, and subsequently shot images of Hughes' daughter Agnes on 12 October 1863. In 1863, Carroll purchased Hughes' painting "Lady with the Lilacs" from the artist, which he kept in his rooms at Oxford. Jeffery Stern has argued that Hughes' "Lady with the Lilacs" was the model for Carroll's drawings of Alice that appear in *Alice's Adventures Under Ground* (1863), the early version of *Alice's Adventures in Wonderland* that Mrs. MacDonald read to her children, prior to its 1865 publication (174). This is the version of Carroll's book that the six-year-old Greville MacDonald announced, after hearing it read aloud by his mother: "there ought to be sixty thousand volumes of it" (342).

Despite Carroll's admiration of Hughes' drawings, the artwork that accompanied the manuscript of *The Light Princess* failed to secure a publisher for the illustrated version of the literary fairy tale. MacDonald subsequently used "The Light Princess," without Hughes' five illustrations, as one of the twelve interpolated tales told within *Adela Cathcart* (1864), in which the telling of stories has a therapeutic effect on the listless twenty-one-year old protagonist.

MacDonald would republish *The Light Princess* as the lead fairy tale in *Dealings with the Fairies* (1867), his collection of literary fairy tales published after the popularity of Lewis Carroll's *Alice's Adventures in Wonderland* (1865). This volume was published five years after he had shared the illustrated manuscript with Carroll. In compiling his first book for children, MacDonald added Hughes' illustrations for *The Light Princess*, but removed the narrative frame of John Smith reading the story to Adela Cathcart and her companions. Hughes' black-and-white pen-and-ink illustrations for *The Light Princess* dominate the illustrations for *Dealings with the Fairies*. Five of the volume's twelve illustrations feature this fairy tale, including the frontispiece, "The Christening." The frontispiece features Princess Makemnoit casting a spell on the infant princess so that she loses her senses of gravity. This image helps to situate *The Light Princess* as part of the tradition of Victorian literary fairy tales in which characters and events from traditional folk tales, such as "Sleeping Beauty," were revised and gently mocked. MacDonald takes the opportunity to use the christening scene in *The Light Princess* to humorously warn of the dangers of overlooking poor relations when hosting family events.

The Moral at the End, or the Lack of It

In the discussion that ensues after John Smith completes his reading of "The Light Princess" to his adult audience in *Adela Cathcart*, he is pointedly asked by Adela's protective aunt, Mrs. Cathcart: "'What is the moral of it?' drawled Mrs.

Cathcart, with the first syllable of moral very long and very gentle" (98). To which John Smith replies with his tongue set very firmly in his cheek, "It is, that you need not mind forgetting your poor relations. No harm will come of it in the end" (98). Lewis Carroll would borrow Mrs. Cathcart's insistence that fairy tales, and everything else for that matter, ought to have a moral and place this insistence in the figure of the Duchess who, in *Alice's Adventures in Wonderland*, reminds Alice that, "Every thing's got a moral, if only you can find it" (78). It is worth noting that the Duchess and her moralizing are a late  addition to Carroll's *Wonderland*. This character and episode did not appear in Alice's *Adventures Under Ground*, suggesting that Carroll was influenced by his reading of *Adela Cathcart*.

What is curious about MacDonald's three versions of "The Light Princess" is that the two versions intended for adults feature a moral at the conclusion of the story, but the children's version, in *Dealings with the Fairies*, drops the moral. When asked about the appropriateness of fairy tales by Mrs. Cathcart, John Smith insists that such stories are "Not for children alone, madam; for everybody that can relish them" (53), but he adds in reference to "The Light Princess," "I confess I think it fitter for grown than for young children" (*Adela Cathcart* 53). Smith provides a comic moral, which is similar to the one that concludes the scroll version of "The Light Princess": "This story teaches us never to mind offending our poor relations because no harm will come of it in the end" (Manuscript). Harry Armstrong, who by the conclusion of the novel will be engaged to Adela Cathcart, rightly observes, "I think the moral is," said the doctor, "that no girl is worth anything till she has cried a little" (*Adela Cathcart* 98).

The children's version of "The Light Princess," published in *Dealings with the Fairies*, better conforms to recommendations that MacDonald proposed in his 1893 essay "The Fantastic Imagination" concerning whether a writer ought to provide the reader with an explicit moral or meaning of the text. MacDonald writes: "But indeed your children are not likely to trouble you about the meaning. They find what they are capable of finding, and more would be too much" ("Fantastic" 317). While the first published version of "The Light Princess" in *Adela Cathcart* features the second title, "A Fairy-Tale without Fairies" (54), this second title does not appear in the two other versions of the story. The title, *Dealings with the Fairies*, focuses attention on supernatural creatures. In *Adela Cathcart* the focus is on the telling of fairy tales and the effects the stories have on individuals. Each of the five stories in the collection includes at least one supernatural being, if not a fairy. The other four fairy tales that appear in *Dealings with the Fairies* are: "The Shadows" (fairies), "The Giant's Heart" (giant), "Cross Purposes" (fairies), and, "The Golden Key" (fairies). Either MacDonald or his publisher, Alexander Strahan, was consciously trying to place the collection of stories within the Victorian boom of literary fairy tales that resulted after the publication of Carroll's *Alice's Adventures in Wonderland*.

Princess Makemnoit is described, even in *Adela Cathcart*, as both witch and fairy:

> In fact, she was a witch; and when she bewitched anybody, he very soon had enough of it; for she beat all the wicked fairies in wickedness, and all the clever ones in cleverness. She despised all the modes we read of in history, in which offended fairies and witches have taken their revenge. (14-15)

What is missing from "The Light Princess" are the less powerful fairies to counteract this fairy's curse, as is the case in "Sleeping Beauty." The scroll version of "The Light Princess" makes this distinction more obvious when Princess Makemnoit is referred to as follows: "In fact she was a wicked fairy, or witch, or something of that sort" (Manuscript). MacDonald's dedication to *Dealings with the Fairies* emphasizes that these stories are to be read as literary fairy tales for children, in the manner of Carroll's *Alice's Adventures in Wonderland* or John Ruskin's *The King of the Golden River* (1861). The dedication reads:

> My Children,
> You know I do not tell you stories as some papas do. Therefore, I give you a book of stories. You have read them all before, except the last. But you have not seen Mr. Hughes' drawings before.
> If plenty of children like this volume, you shall have another soon.
> Your Papa. (*Dealings* iii)

The Artistic Frame of the Hughes Illustrations

The partnership between MacDonald and Hughes was long and complementary. William Raeper has suggested the matching of the illustrations to text was as apt as that of Tenniel and Carroll (166). Hughes illustrated more of MacDonald's children's books including *At the Back of the North Wind* (1870), *The*

Princess and the Goblin (1872), and *The Princess and Curdie* (1883), but none of these is another volume of fairy stories, which is promised in the dedication of *Dealings with the Fairies*. The twelve illustrations for *Dealings with the Fairies* do not seem clearly linked in tone to the other illustrations Hughes did for MacDonald's books. Rather, they more closely resemble the set of twelve illustrations that Hughes would later create for Christina Rossetti's *Speaking Likenesses* (1874), a collection of three literary fairy tales that was also created to take advantage of the success of Carroll's *Alice's Adventures in Wonderland*. I want briefly to address the manner in which Hughes' illustrations work so effectively with MacDonald's prose.

In "The Fantastic Imagination," MacDonald wrote:

> A genuine work of art must mean many things; the truer its art, the more things it will mean. If my drawing, on the other hand, is so far from being a work of art that it needs THIS IS A HORSE written under it, what can it matter that neither you nor your child should know what it means? . . . If, again you do not know a horse when you see it, the name written under it will not serve you much. At all events, the business of the painter is not to teach zoology. (317)

Even the captions for the illustrations in "The Light Princess" support this belief. For instance, "The Prince Lost in the Forest" is not labeled "THIS IS A HORSE." While the horse may dominate the space of Hughes' illustration, the significance of the illustration lies in the Prince gradually blending into the forest background. Hughes is not a realist or a zoologist in his illustrations, but a fellow traveler of the Pre-Raphaelite Brotherhood as is suggested in his illustrations to *Dealings with the Fairies*. As George Bodmer has observed: "Following the tenets of Pre-Raphaelitism, Hughes' pictures stress a certain medievalism in portraying MacDonald's fairy tales" (126).

Hughes marked his reading in 1850 of the short-lived Pre-Raphaelite journal *The Germ* as the pivotal artistic inspiration in his life. Hughes subsequently told William Michael Rossetti in 1908 of the impact that the Pre-Raphaelites had on his own work:

> It wld. be impossible and dreadful to conceive what I might have been without it all, and I shudder to think it. From the cover of the "Germ" to this last books [Rossetti 1908], the pictures, poems and history have encouraged, helped, and tried their best to teach me, and if the result in my case is but poor, yet to me it has been [one] of the most welcome of gifts that have for these long years sustained me. (Wildman 9)

As Lorraine Janzen Kooistra has observed, Hughes participated in two of the most important Pre-Raphaelite-related projects that took place after the dissolution of the Brotherhood in 1854; the illustration of William Allingham's *The Music Master* (1855) which featured Hughes' drawing as well as those of Dante Gabriel Rossetti and John Millais and the ill-fated painting of the Oxford Union Murals in 1857 (98). According to Stephen Wildman, Hughes' "The Long Engagement" (1854-9) became "a much-loved icon" of Pre-Raphaelite painting (18). Hughes' book illustrations to Christina Rossetti's *Sing-Song: A Nursery Rhyme Book* (1872) and *Speaking Likenesses* (1874) reflect both the artistic style and collaboration that is keeping with Pre-Raphaelite spirit. Indeed these two children's books combined together the artistic and poetic talents of the two of the most significant, but unofficial members, of the Pre-Raphaelite Brotherhood.

In Hughes' illustration of the Prince in "The Light Princess," the Prince becomes another element of the mysterious forest landscape. This is also true of the caption for "On the Water," the final illustration of "The Light Princess." Here the Princess looks intently as the water covers the prince's face; what we see is the transformational moment of the fairy tale captured effectively in Hughes' illustration.

John Smith provides the motto, "where more is meant than meets the ear" (*Adela Cathcart* 55), for "The Light Princess," borrowed from John Milton's discussion of Edmund Spenser. Smith uses this motto to explain the purpose of his tale. In other words, he would, "scorn to write anything that only spoke to the ear, which signifies the surface understanding" (*Adela Cathcart* 55). In "On the Water," the key element of Hughes' illustration is not actually on the water – the princess in the swan boat – but what lies just below the water's surface, the prince who gives up his life for the princess. With its overt use of swan imagery in both text and illustration, "The Light Princess" is reminiscent of Hans Christian Andersen's "The Ugly Ducking." However, the transformation of the ugly ducking into a beautiful swan functions on the physical surface of Andersen's protagonist, while the major transformation of MacDonald's Light Princess rests internally with her attitude and behavior.

It seems odd that MacDonald did not share Hughes' illustrations to the stories of *Dealings with the Fairies* with his own children, as he suggests in the book's dedication. It is also curious that Lewis Carroll should comment only on the illustrations of "The Light Princess," but not the text, while John Ruskin, the major art critic of the Victorian age, commented on the text, but not the illustrations. Rather than using Hughes' illustrations to frame the story when it appears in *Adela Cathcart*, MacDonald uses the text to frame "The Light Princess" and provide metatextual commentary on the story. The purpose of telling stories is to rouse Adela Cathcart out of her depression. It is an example of the transformative power of storytelling that MacDonald explores in "The Fantastic Imagination": "The best thing you can do for your fellow, next to rousing his conscience, is – not to give him things to think about, but to wake things up that are in him; or say, to make him think things for himself" (319). The actions and feelings of Adela Cathcart and Harry Armstrong resemble those of the prince and the princess in "The Light Princess." Adela must learn to think about others, if she is to regain her health. The home of Colonel Cathcart, Adela's father, is "The Swanspond" (*Adela Cathcart* 9), a name that reinforces the links between Adela and the Light Princess who swims like a swan and becomes graceful in the lake. The connection to swans is also apparent in Hughes' "The Princess Swimming," the third illustration of the story. Hughes' illustrations in *Dealings with the Fairies* are rich with swan imagery. Visual details begin with "The Christening" where the priest holds a swan-like staff, and continues to the final illustration, "On the Water," where the princess grasps the swan head of her boat as she gazes at the prince.

Audience Reactions in *Adela Cathcart*

The audience response to and discussion of "The Light Princess" was removed from the children's version that appeared in *Dealings with the Fairies*, but MacDonald would reuse parts of this commentary in "The Fantastic Imagination" (1893), his analysis on the meaning and function of fairy tales. Mrs. Cathcart is the most vocal critic of the fairy tales in *Adela Cathcart*. She particularly objects to the swimming scenes between the prince and princess in "The Light Princess" which she deems: "very improper, – to my mind" (*Adela Cathcart* 79).

Her niece, Adela, is less troubled by these romantic encounters and suggests:

> "You must remember all this is in Fairyland, aunt," said Adela, with a smile. "Nobody does what papa and mamma would not like here. We must not judge the people in fairy tales by precisely the same conventionalities we have. They must be good after their own fashion." (79).

Both William Raeper and U. C. Knoepflmacher have observed that MacDonald had playfully used John Ruskin's objections to "The Light Princess" in the character of Mrs. Cathcart. MacDonald had shared the manuscript of "The Light Princes" in 1863 with John Ruskin as well as with Lewis Carroll. Ruskin felt that the fairy tale "will not do for the public in its present form" (Unpublished letter reprinted in Knoepflmacher 138). Ruskin noted two key problems with the fairy tale: MacDonald's excessive attempts at humor – "the parts which are intended to be laughable are weak" (Unpublished letter reprinted in Knoepflmacher 138) and perhaps more troubling, the erotic nature of the children's text. Ruskin warned MacDonald:

> Then lastly, it is too amorous throughout – and to some temperaments would be quite mischievous. You are too pure-minded yourself to

feel this — but I assure you the swimming scenes and the love scenes would be to many children seriously harmful — Not that they would have to be cut — but to be done in a simpler and less telling way. (Unpublished letter quoted in Knoepflmacher 138-9)

After the publication of *Adela Cathcart*, Ruskin strongly objected to MacDonald in another letter:

You did make me into Mrs. Cathcart. She says the very thing I said about the fairy tale. It's the only time she's right in the book — you turned me into her and then invented all the wrongs to choke my poor little right with. I never knew another thing so horrid.
(Ruskin 487)

Variations in the Public Reading Version

The third important, but unpublished, version of "The Light Princess," is the scroll version that MacDonald devised to be used as a script and prop for his dramatic readings of the tale. Greville MacDonald remembers that "The Light Princess" was "written on a long scroll, perhaps with some idea of making it's form accord with vocal delivery, should be defined rather as *jeu d'esprit*" (324). This manuscript is now located at the Houghton Library of Harvard University. It is catalogued as a manuscript composed of one continuous scroll of sheets of paper pasted together into a single strip by the author.

Having spent several weeks transcribing the heavily edited manuscript of the scroll version of "The Light Princess," I doubt that MacDonald could have actually read the text of the fairy tale and kept his place while unscrolling the manuscript in front of an audience. He must have had the story memorized and improvised as he performed, using the scroll both as a prop and a script to jog his memory. According to Greville MacDonald, "now and again, in place of a lecture, he would read or recite a fairy-tale — particularly "The Light Princess" (325). Greville MacDonald also mentions that the family's homeopathic physician, Dr. Hale, arranged for his father to give a performance of one of his own fairy tales and selections from Spenser's *The Faerie Queene* on two occasions in 1862 (327). Greville's recollections of "The Giant's Heart" were based more on his memories of his father's dramatic presentations rather than reading the text (325). Knoepflmacher also suggested that MacDonald occasionally read "The Light Princess" to his own children and to the undergraduates at Bedford College who had come prepared for a lecture on Spenser's *The Faerie Queene* (119). During the period that he was writing *Adela Cathcart*, MacDonald was a professor of Literature and Philosophy at Bedford College, which was an all-women's institution during the period.

While the scroll version of "The Light Princess" is not the original manuscript of the fairy tale, it is clearly an early reading copy that MacDonald used for public and family performances. From differences in the text of the manuscript, I would argue that the scroll version is the earliest of the three versions of "The Light Princess," or at least based on an earlier version of the fairy tale. The scroll for "The Light Princess" resembles the manuscript of "The Cruel Painter," the vampire story that Harry Armstrong reads to Adela and company in *Adela Cathcart*. The scroll, like Harry's manuscript, is "gummed together in a continuous roll, so that he might not have to turn over any leaves" (*Adela Cathcart* 346). In some ways "The Cruel Painter" and "Light Princess" are tales that mirror one another, or at least have an uncanny resemblance. "The Light Princess" scroll version does contain some significant differences from the subsequent published versions of "The Light Princess." While the version of "The Light Princess" in *Dealings with Fairies* is framed by Arthur Hughes' illustrations and the *Adela Cathcart* version is for an the adult audience, this handwritten version was created specifically for MacDonald to perform.

It is significant that in *Adela Cathcart*, John Smith reads, rather than simply tells, the fairy tale. Yet, "The Light Princess" is a literary fairy tale, not an oral one. MacDonald created a text to read "The Light Princess" to his college-aged audience. The format of the scroll gives the impression that MacDonald was reading from an ancient text. Smith warns his listeners that "The Light Princess" is a story that "I have just scribbled off" (*Adela Cathcart* 53). He also informs the reader that, "The story, as I now give it, is not exactly as I read it, then, because, of course, I was more anxious that it should be correct when I prepared it for the press than when I merely read it before a few friends" (*Adela Cathcart* 53).

The scroll version is a more breezy, comic rendition of the tale. While the plot remains essentially the same, MacDonald provides many more humorous digressions in his oral presentation. For instance, a long paragraph suggests why families tend to overlook poor relations, such as Princess Makemnoit. In the other versions, this section is reduced to; "But poor relations don't do anything to keep you in mind of them. Why don't they?" (*Adela Cathcart* 56). In the scroll version, MacDonald uses ironic humor to justify why it is appropriate to forget poor relations when making out a will.

It is greatly to be feared that you will forget to leave them even a [brass farthing] shilling in your will and quite right too! For of course they haven't anything, and why should you give them anything? They couldn't make a good use of it, if you did, for they never had an opportunity of trying. [So Alas] Why haven't they saved [some] something? They would only [spend yours foolishly] waste it upon meat & drink & clothes. Whereas if you leave your money to your rich nephew, he will never spend it that way. He doesn't want it for such mean purposes. He'll lay it by and your dear [money will] family of sovereigns & notes will never be scattered abroad to the four corners of the earth, like the swarms of [brother] cousins fist fight boys & girls. They will – breed more notes and more sovereigns – and a few moths & some rust & a score or two of maggots that never die, and find out the hardest places in your heart and gnaw there to be sure. But that doesn't signify." (Manuscript)

Given MacDonald's constant search for funds to support his increasingly large family, the humor cuts close to home. What is perhaps even more interesting than this digression on difficulties of poor relations is the passage that follows which is crossed out, but is still readable: "[Here Falconer paused, and delivered a whole broadside of tobacco smoke from the pipe he had hither to been only nursing. Then he resumed:]" (Manuscript). So it appears at one point in the composition of "The Light Princess," the tale was to be narrated by Robert Falconer and not John Smith. MacDonald must have considered having Falconer tell the story in *David Elginbrod* (1863), his first novel, but waited until *Adela Cathcart* to publish it.

There are also details found in the scroll version of "The Light Princess" that suggest MacDonald created it for a presentation to his students at Bedford College. While Princess Makemnoit is identified as clever in the other versions of "The Light Princess," in the scroll version the narrator also notes, "she [too] had been to a ladies college [as well as the queen] and [if the queen could make a good use of her Latin, the Princess] could make a bad use of the [her] Physics she learned there" (Manuscript.). This humorous digression seems to suggest that the scroll version of the story was created with the Bedford College audience in mind. There is also a longer, pseudoscientific explanation of the process by which Princess Makemnoit was able to destroy gravitation:

For you know that gravitation is an inverse ratio as the square of the distance: [I] and that it operates in straight lines between centres. Now as the earth is a sphere and a sphere is a circle revolving upon one of its diameters, you have only to take your circle and square it to your purpose, and put in verse, and the charm is done.

(Manuscript)

One of the chief differences between the scroll "The Light Princess" and the published versions is how Princess Makemnoit drains the lake. Rather than unleashing the White Snake of Darkness, she locates in the cavern that forms the underside of the bottom of the lake:

a strange awful-looking complication of machinery, to which Princess Makemnoit hobbled up, muttering fearful words. She laid hold of some sort of a handle, which she turned vigorously with her skinny arms. Soon a sound like a cap of distant thunder was heard, followed by the rushing of distant torrents. (Manuscript)

Finally the punishment of Princess Makemnoit in the scroll version is much less severe than in the published texts. As in the other versions, the scroll version has the Light Princess treading hard on her aunt's gouty toe the first time that she saw her after she recovered her sense of gravity. But the published versions go on to describe the death of Princess Makemnoit as the result of water from the lake undermining her house and burying her in the ruins, and since "no one ever ventured to dig her up her body. There she lies to this day" (*Adela Cathcart* 97).

MacDonald's Continuous Revisions

Raeper has observed that MacDonald "wrote quickly, but later agonized over his manuscripts, which are filled with cross-outs" (195). This is certainly the case of the scroll version of "The Light Princess." Raeper also mentioned that MacDonald frequently changed his text from edition to edition. He noted that the 1882 edition of *Adela Cathcart* removed three of the interpolated stories, but added "The Snow Fight' and that *Robert Falconer* was completely rewritten from the serialization in Argosy to a novel version published 1868 (195). MacDonald's impulse to revise is present in his three versions of "The Light Princess." In *Adela Cathcart*, John Smith says in presenting "The Light Princess" that he hopes to provide a fairy tale in which "more is meant than meets the ear" (55). Quoting John Milton as his authority, Smith articulates MacDonald's credo that will be further developed in "The Fantastic Imagination," that a story ought to move beyond surface meaning. Using Smith as his spokesman, MacDonald writes, "I am no bard, I should scorn to write anything that only spoke to ear, which signifies the surface understanding" (*Adela Cathcart* 55). While MacDonald achieves this deeper meaning in each of the three versions of "The Light Princess," he also chooses to frame the telling of the story using a slightly different and distinctive frame. As a performance piece intended to be the script for a dramatic reading, the scroll version emphasizes auditory elements. The version that appears in *Dealings with the Fairies* accompanied by Hughes' illustrations is intended to appeal to the eye. The version in *Adela Cathcart*, surrounded and interrupted at four different points by the audience, is the most literary and complex version in that it provides its own commentary on the story itself. These different narrative techniques suggest that while MacDonald might have famously declared in "The Fantastic Imagination" that, "For my part, I do not write for children, but for the childlike, whether five, or fifty, or seventy-five" (317), the three versions of "The Light Princess" were carefully created for three distinctive audiences.

Works Cited

Bodmer, George. "Arthur Hughes, Walter Crane, and Maurice Sendak: The Picture as Literary Fairy Tale." *Marvels & Tales* 17.1 (2003): 120-137.

Carroll, Lewis. *Alice's Adventure in Wonderland and Through the Looking Glass*. 1865, 1872. The Centenary Edition. Ed. Hugh Haughton. New York: Penguin, 1998.

---. *The Diaries of Lewis Carroll*. 2 vols. Ed. Roger Lancelyn Green. New York: Oxford UP, 1954.

Knoepflmacher, U. C. *Ventures into Childland: Victorians, Fairy Tales, and Femininity*. Chicago: U of Chicago P, 1998.

Kooistra, Lorraine Janzen. *Christina Rossetti and Illustration: A Publishing History*. Athens: Ohio UP, 2002.

MacDonald, George. *Adela Cathcart*. 1864. New York: Routledge, 1891.

---."The Fantastic Imagination." *A Dish of Orts*. 1893. Whitethorn, CA: Johannesen, 1966. 313-322.

---. "The Light Princess." *Dealings with the Fairies*. London: Alexander Strahan, 1867. 1-93.

--- Manuscript of "The Light Princess," undated. George MacDonald Papers. MS Eng 1112.2. Houghton Library, Harvard University.

MacDonald, Greville. *George MacDonald and His Wife*. London: George Allen & Unwin, 1924.

Raeper, William. *George MacDonald.* Batavia, IL: Lion Publishing, 1987.
Ruskin. John. *The Wimmington Letters: John Ruskin's Correspondence with Margaret Alexis Bell and the Children at Wimmington Hall.* Ed. Van Akin Burd. Cambridge: Harvard UP, 1969. 486-87.
Stern, Jeffery. "Lewis Carroll the Pre-Raphaelite: 'Fainting in Coils.'" *Lewis Carroll Observed: A Collection of Unpublished Photographs, Drawings, Poetry, and New Essays.* Ed. Edward Guiliano. New York: Clarkson N. Potter, 1976. 161-180.
Wildman, Stephen. "Biographical Introduction." *Arthur Hughes: His Life & Works, A Catalogue Raisonne.* Compiled by Leonard Roberts. Woodbridge, Suffolk: Antique Collector's Club, 1997. 9-43.

Captions for Illustrations:

Arthur Hughes' "The Christening" from George MacDonald's *Dealings with the Fairies* (1867).
John Tenniel's "Alice and Duchess" from Lewis Carroll's *Alice's Adventures in Wonderland* (1865).
Arthur Hughes' "The Prince Lost in the Forest" from George MacDonald's *Dealings with the Fairies* (1867).
Arthur Hughes' "On the Water" from George MacDonald's *Dealings with the Fairies* (1867).
Arthur Hughes' "The Princess Swimming" from George MacDonald's *Dealings with the Fairies* (1867).

Chapter 7

An Ambivalent Marriage of Heaven and Hell: Some Aspects of Irony in *Lilith*

John Docherty

The Lewis Legacy

In the Eerdmans and Lion paperback edition of *Phantastes* and *Lilith* that for many years has flooded the Christian bookshops both in Britain and in America, the publishers have taken fragments of C. S. Lewis' Preface to his 1946 anthology of MacDonald's writings, and used them as an "Introduction by C.S. Lewis."[1] In a highly relevant passage from the original preface that Eerdmans omit from the "Introduction," Lewis states that his anthology "was designed not to revive MacDonald's literary reputation but to spread his religious teachings. Hence most of [the] extracts are taken from the three volumes of Unspoken Sermons" (18). There was therefore no need for Lewis to include in his Preface his scathing – and largely erroneous – attack upon MacDonald's other writings. And when this Preface is fragmented and used as a so-called "Introduction" to *Phantastes* and *Lilith*, error is compounded by absurdity. Lewis' theology differs radically from MacDonald's in some crucial aspects (Durie 169-76), and his genuine literary criticism of MacDonald is largely limited to comments in one letter to Arthur Greeves of September 1, 1933 (Prickett, "Death" 159-62).

The Eerdmans "Introduction" to *Phantastes and Lilith* cannot but greatly add to readers' difficulties in approaching these two books, which in some ways ignore all usual literary conventions. Hence the present need for sensitive exegesis that helps and encourages readers to explore these books further for themselves. In addition, extensive rewriting of MacDonald's novels (see note 12) creates the necessity for working towards much wider recognition and acknowledgement of the ways in which MacDonald attacks preachers who distort Christian truths, and some of his most powerful criticism of this practice occurs in *Lilith*.

"Nothing Very Obscure in It that Is Worth Finding Out."

MacDonald must have been aware that many Christian readers would want to think of his *Lilith* (1895) as the last and greatest "Revelation of St. George," as his son Greville called it (548). However, he apparently felt that his last major work must be devoted to spiritual warfare relevant to the evils of its time – the *fin de siècle*.

When MacDonald wrote *Lilith* he was living in the midst of the expatriate community of Bordighera, on the Italian Riviera, where he was inevitably taken up as its Christian sage. This was a situation where it would not have been possible for him overtly to expound a radical Christianity. It seems to have stimulated him in writing *Lilith* to be more radical, but at the same time more covert, in his Christian warfare than in any of his previous books. And this in turn favoured the use of more – and more elaborate – irony than he had previously employed. The irony, however, is essentially positive.[2]

Lewis accurately defines MacDonald's fantasy writing as "fantasy that hovers between the allegorical and the mythopoeic" (*MacDonald* 14). But, although it is usually closer to the allegorical pole,[3] neither *Lilith* nor *Phantastes* is allegorical in the usual sense of the term. In MacDonald's essay on "The Imagination: Its Functions and its Culture," he stresses that "its development is one of the main ends of the divine education of life" (36), and that the first and foremost task in this is to comprehend "the spiritual scaffolding or skeleton of any work of art being studied" (38). It should be no surprise, therefore, that his own works cannot be understood properly, if at all, by readers unwilling to approach each work, as far as is within their powers, with true Coleridgian Imagination, and to search carefully to determine the form of its spiritual skeleton. Any fruitful study of MacDonald's work needs to undertake these tasks and not be deterred by the pronouncements of materialists who deny all reality to the imagination, or of sentimentalists who disdain to comprehend any writing that has a consciously intended, articulated and symbolical skeleton and who maintain that the only way to read works of fantasy is to "throw yourself in."[4]

In *Lilith* (as in *Phantastes*, and in the great myths of antiquity) the principal characters are archetypal realities. They live within the soul of the narrator-protagonist and are antithetical to the cold idealized abstractions of most allegorical art in recent centuries. Mara is equivalent to the beneficial suffering that Vane experiences.[5] She is very close to MacDonald's Wise Woman figures (Prickett, "Death" 162), most obviously to the Wise Woman of "The Lost Princess." Lona is the asexual love (*agape*) Vane gradually comprehends. Both she and Mara are in themselves profoundly lovable characters. MacDonald, however, does not follow this scheme rigidly. Mara devolves to a conventional allegorical figure in the final chapter when Vane is back in this world (263), and Lona soon begins to be sexually attractive to Vane.

Lilith and Adam, if categorized in twentieth-century terminology, approximate to Vane's anima and his ego (or, better, his "egoism"). Both are in themselves profoundly unlovable characters. This is primarily because they are in most important respects like human beings living on Earth – yet they are immortal. MacDonald recognizes that material immortality for humanity at its present state of development would totally undermine morality. When Adam is involved with his cemetery, however, he can – up to a point – be trusted (34). His wife is almost wholly involved in this work, and thus is truly beautiful in soul and body, although with a deathly beauty.[6]

MacDonald's Adam is highly regarded by many authoritarian Christians. His Lilith is equally highly regarded by many militant feminists, who rightly point out that Adam, when manifesting as "Adam," is the archetypal unregenerate bourgeois male.[7] The reasons for this can perhaps be understood if we perceive the *fin de siècle* nuances of character that these figures incorporate. Lilith then appears as an image of the "New Woman" of the period as held by a conventional contemporary clergyman; Adam as this New Woman's ambiguous, but largely critical, view of him; and Eve as his ideal of woman as an "angel in the house."[8]

These attributions are straightforward enough. So MacDonald, commenting on *Lilith* to his old friend Henry Sutton, can in this respect legitimately claim that: "it seems to me there is nothing very obscure in it that is worth finding out" (Sadler 366-67).[9] MacDonald, however, underestimates the power of his characterization. Readers have found the characters in *Lilith* so fascinating in themselves that it is scarcely surprising this has distracted attention from their underlying allegorical status except in the case of Mara.

Readers, moreover, tend to identify with any protagonist-narrator, and Vane, experiencing his internal images as external, is not in a favorable position calmly to evaluate these images. He does acknowledge that he is bi-locally existing: "While without a doubt, for instance, that I was actually regarding a scene of activity, I might be, at the same moment, in my consciousness aware that I was pursuing a metaphysical argument" (46). But, if he did not foreground his imaginative anthropomorphizing, his story would, of course, collapse to these metaphysical arguments that are, in effect, the dynamic of its "spiritual skeleton." In practice, therefore, any critic of *Lilith* or *Phantastes* has to comment upon the characters as if they were exterior to Vane or Anodos while at the same time being aware of the implications of their actually being within these protagonists.

Vane's name, apparently given him by Raven, characterizes him well, both literally and in its homophones. So it is no surprise that his responses to Lilith and Adam are more often than not deplorable. Because these figures are within him, his most usual mistake is to yield to their pressure to obey them. But, inasmuch as he is able to differentiate and anthropomorphize these aspects of his personality, he should be held as accountable for his responses to them as if they were actual people in the external world.

Richard Reis perceptively puts Vane (and by implication Anodos) into the same category as the "ignorant/stupid" narrators commonly found in detective stories, such as Dr Watson in the *Sherlock Holmes* tales (25). As Reis points out: "MacDonald is using the ignorant-narrator point of view as a challenge to his reader, challenging us to get the point which Vane misses" (27).

However, as Adam/Raven is an aspect of Vane's own personality, it is not valid when Reis goes on to associate "the wise Adam/Raven" (26) with the actual detective figures such as Holmes — even though Raven is often much wiser than is Vane at his usual level of consciousness.

In some (possibly most) of MacDonald's works, covert subplots are present alongside the overt plot — for example, Joseph of Arimathea at Glastonbury in *Thomas Wingfold, Curate* (Docherty, "Reductionist" 64-66). They may, as in that case, attain to the level of myth, but more often — as with other subplots in *Thomas Wingfold* — they are better classed as high-quality imaginative allegory. These covert subplots are only to be discovered by what MacDonald's friend John Ruskin, exploring the great myths of antiquity, describes as "slow mining" for "a gift of unexpected truth" (*Queen* 1.17).[10] Lewis was applying essentially the same spiritual technique as Ruskin when he describes how he discovered gradually that: "The quality which had enchanted me in [MacDonald's] imaginative works was the quality of the real universe, the divine, magical, terrifying and ecstatic reality in which we all live" (*MacDonald* 21).

Lilith, however, seems to be unique in MacDonald's writing in that all the essential content — except in the frame chapters — is of this covert nature, to be discovered only by Ruskin's "slow mining."[11] This "slow mining" is easier with some aspects of the plot than with others. However, the frequent allusions to *Faust II* suggest that MacDonald may further intend *Lilith* to be like that play, which Goethe maintained he had made incommensurable so that people would ever and again be drawn back to it (*Conversations* 206).

Homage to William Blake's *Marriage of Heaven and Hell* [1790]

Most of MacDonald's biographers emphasize that, as a very intense person, he seems to have experienced periods of depression alternating with his periods of creativity. This would have made him particularly aware of humanity as poised between heaven and hell, which, in turn, seems to be the basis of his wish to align himself with very great writers such as Blake and Dante. As Stephen Prickett points out:

Behind the magical beings of MacDonald's universes lie the philosophical and theological principles of a scheme that is as carefully worked out as that of Dante – indeed, his references to Dante [...] make it clear that, almost unbelievably, he is inviting just such a comparison. [He] is seeking to establish himself within an existing literary tradition – a tradition not of folklore and primitive ritual, but of complex theological sophistication. ("Two Worlds" 18)

Lewis, in *The Great Divorce*, where MacDonald is Lewis' fictional guide, includes a preface that is highly critical of Blake's *Marriage*. His character "George MacDonald" also is critical of Blake. But Durie points out that the MacDonald depicted there by Lewis "is a ventriloquist's dummy. It is Lewis' voice which subverts the real MacDonald's belief in hell as a temporary, purifying force, and heaven as the home of every one of God's children" (175). Devotees of Lewis, after reading *The Great Divorce*, would be astonished if told how, in *Lilith*, MacDonald makes very important and exceptionally detailed covert allusions to Blake's *Marriage* that are far from critical in tone. These allusions, although accompanied by others that are critical of some of Blake's radical ideas, seem to affirm solidarity with key elements of Blake's book. Roderick McGillis, drawing upon other evidence, goes so far as to state that in *Lilith* "MacDonald wishes to marry hell and heaven, cycle and permanence" (*Lilith MSS*, 49).

The closest parallel between MacDonald and Blake is perhaps the way both attack church doctrines that set up authoritarianism as good and its rejection as evil. In *Lilith* this attitude is largely implicit and part of the overall covert plot that is left for readers to recognize. Readers accustomed to accepting the judgments of authoritarian preachers like MacDonald's Adam will be the least likely to achieve this recognition. Most American readers are particularly badly placed to recognise MacDonald's iconoclasm because any of his novels they have read will probably have been expurgated and rewritten editions where his iconoclasm is unrecognizable in the fragments that remain.[12]

MacDonald's important covert allusions to the *Marriage* in *Lilith* are to Blake's illustrations. Some allusions to the *Marriage* I have noted previously (Docherty, *Literary* 388-89). But in my earlier work, I did not recognise the most obvious and important ones. Nor had I recognized many of the details of the allusions.

Blake's main illustrations on Plates 10 and 11 of the *Marriage*[13] are very important for Chapters 5 and 6 of Lewis Carroll's *Alice's Adventures in Wonderland*, and this is likely to have been a major stimulus to his friend MacDonald to allude to the *Marriage* in a similar way. The tree stump resembling an old man in Blake's Plate 11 may have suggested the tree that is also an old man in *Lilith* (22).[14] But such imagery is not unusual, and MacDonald may initially not have noticed he was paralleling Blake here.

MacDonald's most striking covert allusions to the *Marriage* are to Blake's main illustrations on plates 2 and 5 and to his main illustration on Plate 20 with its accompanying text on plates 18 and 19. Plate 2 shows a deceitful woman, a prototype of the Vala figure of Blake's later writings; her deceit is indicated by her crossed legs, as is usual with Blake. She is standing clasping a tree and is apparently encouraging a person who has climbed the tree for her and who wears an off-white, oriental-looking, trousered garment embroidered at the neck and torn in long strips below the knee. These details resemble the passage where Lilith coaxes Vane to climb a tree in her palace courtyard (143-44). Vane is wearing a garment she has given him, although the strips that hang down below his feet have been torn by Lilith from her own garment. Individual copies of Blake's illuminated books show considerable variation. MacDonald's text seems to fit best the illustration in the "F" copy of the *Marriage* that originally belonged to Thomas Butts, where the tree climber seems to be a slim young man and strips and patches of torn bark are hanging from the tree.[15] Lilith utilizes fallen fragments of the bark, fastened with the strips of fabric, to improvise climbing sandals for Vane.

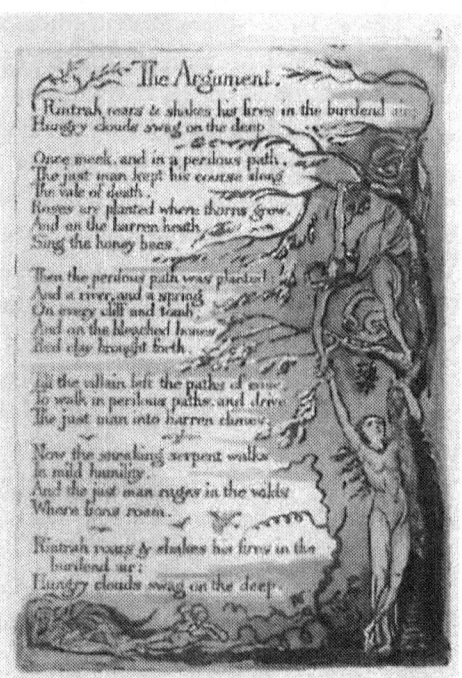

Plate 2

In Blake's Plate 5, a horse, rider and moon are falling out of the sky together.[16] This is paralleled in *Lilith* by the fall of Vane with Adam's dead horse, while a moon descends "rolling like the nave of Fortune's wheel bowled by the gods." Blake's illustration alludes to Ovid's account, in Books 1 and 2 of the *Metamorphoses*, of the fall of Phaethon when attempting to drive the chariot of his father Helios. Blake avoids crowding his picture by showing only one falling horse and only one half-wheel of the chariot.

MacDonald hints that he is alluding specifically to Blake's Phaethon picture by introducing the chariot wheel in a superfluous second metaphor for the descent of the moon, describing it as rolling "like an old chariot-wheel down the hill of heaven" (165-66). Vane's falling horse is probably white, like Phaethon's in Blake's picture, since Vane had earlier described him when standing still as like "a block of marble" (163).[17] A shaman's horse is normally white and Adam's horse certainly seems to fit this category. Mircea Eliade remarks that "the gallop and dizzying speed are traditional expressions of 'flight,' that is, of ecstasy" (154), which perfectly fits Vane's ride that leads to his fall.[18] Vane says: "Rejoicing in the power of my steed and the pride of my life, I sat like a king and rode" (165). In the "B" draft, the Raven summons this horse out of the swamp of monsters, a very surprising act were Raven/Adam the sort of spiritual guide most critics claim.

Plate 5 (top half)

MacDonald's text closely reflects Blake's illustration on Plate 20, and its accompanying text on plates 18 and 19. An angel claims he will show Blake the place of his (Swedenborgian) "eternal lot," and from this spot the terrible figure of Leviathan rushes towards them "with all the fury of a spiritual existence." [Plate 20 was too dark to reproduce here satisfactorily in black and white] But when Blake stays his ground "this appearance was no more." The monster's advance seems to be balked by Blake's disbelief. In Blake's picture it throws back its head in apparent exhaustion and all the details that make Blake's description of its advance so frightening become invisible: the "fiery crest [...] like a ridge of golden rocks," the eyes as "two globes of crimson fire," the "red gills," and the forehead "divided into streaks of green and purple like those on a tyger's forehead."

Vane, when crossing a "Bad Burrow," encounters a number of great monsters arising from beneath the ground, and the first of these is "an animal like a tiger."

Like Blake, Vane too stays his ground (he has no alternative), and the tiger disappears just before reaching him. This tiger, like the horse in the "B" draft mentioned above, is of more-or-less realistic shape. But most of the creatures Vane sees on this and subsequent visits to the Burrow (except for the wolves that can pursue their prey beyond the bounds of the Burrow) are grotesque monsters with serpent bodies. The next creature that struggles out of the ground, "a step or two" from Vane, displays the same exhaustion as does Blake's Leviathan in his illustration: "The moment its tail was free, it lay as if exhausted" (49). In the "A" and "B" drafts, however, it falls exhausted only after first coiling harmlessly round Vane (299; 48).

MacDonald's essential reason for alluding to these three images from the *Marriage* seems to be that he relates them to the Temptation, the Fall and Eternal Torment. Those are the three themes that dominated most Christian teaching throughout most of the nineteenth century in Britain – especially in Scotland in the earlier part of the century, as is abundantly testified in MacDonald's Scottish novels. This brand of Christianity had distressed the charismatic theologian Frederick Denison Maurice and those around him – including MacDonald (and Carroll) – who, while not neglecting the Old Testament, attempted to practice a redemptive New Testament Christianity.

Once we recognize this trio of themes in these three Blake illustrations, some further relevant parallels with MacDonald's text become evident. At the bottom left of Blake's Plate 2 illustration, a perplexed naked youth lies near two naked maidens.[19] This solitary youth has apparently been successfully taught by his church to resist temptation – with the churches' usual emphasis upon sexual temptation – because a gigantic leaf beside him, although pointing in the direction of the girls, is totally flaccid. But his expression shows that he is bewildered by this prohibition. He is like the vine beyond the girls, that attempts to grow up without twining around the tree (of knowledge of Good and Evil) near it and is totally sterile. On the right, Temptation is not resisted. Blake overtly alludes to Genesis Temptation imagery here. The deceitful maiden below has tempted the figure who climbs the tree for her. As the tempter, she represents the serpent and not Eve.[20] But the climb has apparently yielded nothing: their touching hands are empty.

MacDonald emphasizes the Genesis 3 imagery by describing the tree that Vane climbs as the central and "tallest" of the trees in Lilith's palace courtyard, and one "not quite like the rest" (143). Lilith's mention of the presence of a snake is also relevant here. Vane does not believe in it because he more than half believes that Lilith is the biblical snake. But MacDonald prevents this imagery from being too overt by having Lilith claim to want "a tiny blossom" from the tree rather than an apple that would acknowledge her as the innocent victim of Temptation that Vane tries to believe he sees in her. The way Vane climbs with the aid of dead bark from the Tree of Knowledge tied to his feet by strips from Lilith's garment is a very powerful metaphor. It is no wonder he climbs higher than his imagination can sustain and experiences a letdown – out of the Region of the Seven Dimensions – by the fountain of Imagination in the courtyard of his house.

Blake's Plate 5 illustration is followed by his textual comments on Milton's account in *Paradise Lost* of Satan and his angels being cast out of Heaven and falling into Hell. Milton, in his *Argument to Book 1*, describes this as "the prime cause of [man's] fall." Blake – sympathetic towards the spirit underlying Phaethon's passionate desire to drive the chariot of his father Helios – is famously critical of Milton here:

> Those who restrain desire, do so because theirs is weak enough to be restrained; and the restrainer or Reason usurps its place & governs the unwilling. [...] The history of this is written in Paradise Lost, and the Governor or Reason is call'd Messiah. [...] It indeed appeared to Reason as if Desire was cast out, but the Devils account is that the Messiah fell, & formed a heaven of what he stole from the Abyss.
>
> This is shewn in the Gospel, where he prays to the Father to send the comforter or Desire, that Reason may have Ideas to build on. (5-6)

MacDonald seems to equate the "Ideas" Blake mentions here with the products of Coleridgian "Imagination," which he advocates so passionately in his essay "The Imagination: Its Function and Its Culture" (MacDonald, *Dish*, 1-42). Vane's obsession to ride the huge horse that Adam claims as his is very like Phaethon's obsession. There are further parallels here in that Adam is ultimately called "father" by Vane and is a sky-god. Helios feels bound by a rash promise to grant Phaethon his wish. Vane breaks his promise to Raven-Uranus, and in taking his horse acts wholly against Raven's instructions grounded in 'commonsense' Reason. But in the "B" draft, Vane, even before he has seen the horse from hell, argues: "Surely reason was the same in any world. And what reason could there be, when action was calling aloud for her man[,] to go to sleep like one of the very dead?" (147). The flaw in Vane's argument is, of course, that any action without knowledge could only harm the Little Ones for a second time.

Blake's Plate 20 illustration of Leviathan is at the end of his Memorable Fancy describing the contrasting metaphysical conceptions of hell held by Blake and by a Swedenborgian angel. Hell is not an event, closely restricted in duration, so MacDonald can insert his Hell allusion before his Temptation and Fall allusions. Vane at first assumes that the monsters who assault him in the "Bad Burrow" (Hell) are frustrated by his disbelief in them, as seems to be the case with Leviathan's rush upon Blake. But he soon discovers he is protected from the monsters only when a moon shines on him.

MacDonald in his "A" draft associates the "Bad Burrow" with "Dante's Malbolge" (299), deep in Hell. But MacDonald, in many places in his writings, rejects the doctrine of eternal torment in a macrocosmic Hell as emphatically as does Blake. However, he fully accepts the reality of the microcosmic hell as symbolized by the Bad Burrow. Vane remarks in the "A" draft that when, much later, he "speculated on what, vision or reality, the thing might mean, I thought I knew that the ground of that moor outside the house of death was but the out-issue of my own soul [...] in which, unknown to myself, lay such nameless horrors" (299). Near the end of the final version, however, after he has learnt much of questionable value from Adam, he has lost all this humility. Passing the Burrow (become a lake) for the last time on his pilgrimage to the New Jerusalem, he describes the monsters in even more lurid terms than previously and concludes with the truism: "So long as exist men and women of unwholesome mind, that lake will still be peopled with loathsomenesses" (256).

> Adam versus Lilith –
> Opposition to any Marriage of Perceived Heaven and Hell

In *Lilith*, MacDonald, like Blake, recognizes that the outlook popularly termed 'Heaven' is misguided. But he depicts 'Hell' (as asserted by Lilith) as even more misguided, although in very different fashion from Adam's 'Heaven.'

Many modern readers of *Lilith* respond to Lilith's resistance to Mara's inquisition in Chapter 39 in the same way as many people (including Blake) respond to Satan's defiant resistance to God's crushing might in John Milton's *Paradise Lost*. In both cases the resistance is seen as heroic. And there is a powerful tradition of regarding the heroic as noble, even when this is self-evidently not the case. Lilith's stance in Mara's presence is absurd and ought to prevent any reader from regarding her as heroic. In 1895, Lilith's defiance could no longer be considered to be "noble defiance" of "God's Laws" because it was directly contrary to what by then had come to be regarded as natural laws everyone has to accept, and thus as absurd as Don Quixote's tilting at windmills. But the bourgeois male of the *fin de siècle* tended to equate *himself* with God,[21] and Lilith opposes an Adam who, as noted above, is an archetypal example of just such a bourgeois male. Thus many of Lilith's present-day supporters see Mara as acting merely as Adam's surrogate.

Lilith would be content with the beauty of the Earth (entirely focused for her in her own beauty) but for its impermanence. In this she seems to derive from Blake's Vala, who *is* the beauty of the Earth. Like the Alder maiden of *Phantastes*, she strives to retain forever her earthly body in all its beauty, and this obsession obliges her to be wholly indifferent to the needs of any other beings. Wholly bereft of *agape* she murders many.

Lilith's aspect as Anima is described in her fragmentary, but lucid and revealing, account of herself (150-53). The first verse of this account that Adam reads is particularly revealing:

> But if I found a man that could believe
> In what he saw not, felt not, and yet knew,
> From him I should take substance, and receive
> Firmness and form, relate to touch and view;
> Then should I clothe me in the likeness true
> Of that idea where his soul did cleave!

Prickett observes that this verse confirms Lilith as "a projection not of [Vane's] worst desires but of his highest aspirations. [...] [S]he takes the form of her victim's most cherished and noblest desires. Yet in the end she stands for Death" ("Death" 164-65). A man's highest aspirations, however, need not necessarily be wholly, or even solely, appropriated by Lilith. Vane, in this respect, is sycophantic equally to both Lilith and Adam.

Adam parallels Lilith, as Prickett defines her, in standing for traditionally noble desires and for Death – most notably in the episode when he cuts off Lilith's hand so that she may "sleep." But the primary dictionary definition of "Adam" should not be ignored. It is: "**Adam 1.** The name given in the bible to the first man, the father of the human race; *the unregenerate condition or character.*" (OED., my italics).[22]

When Vane first encounters the figure he ultimately recognizes as "Adam," this figure is in the form of a Raven who claims to have recently lived on the planet Uranus. But when he subsequently remarks of his wife's house: "She is very good to let me live with her, and call it 'the sexton's cottage!'" (25), it is clear that he himself (at this stage at least) is the sky-god who married Gaia. That Raven-Uranus regards his wife's "cottage" (Earth) as "the sexton's cottage" can seem to parallel Blake's Neoplatonic view of the descending soul dying to Earth existence, where its task becomes that of "exploring the recesses of the grave."[23] Yet when Raven is together with his wife they have the opposite opinion: that a person's task on Earth is not to explore but to sleep. As his wife says of Vane: "He has not yet learned that the day begins with sleep!" (27). Raven-Adam seems to equate this "sleep" with "death," and "death" in turn with the killing of a person's lower impulses. Blake would not have quarrelled with that – although he might well have regarded it as an absurdly contorted way of expressing a simple (albeit unfashionable) fact.

However – extrapolating from the dead whom Vane specifically notices – it would seem that most, and possibly all, of the people in this cemetery are already dead in the everyday sense of the term (32; 44).[24] Adam implies that everyone, when ultimately awakening from "sleep," directly makes a pilgrimage to heaven. The pilgrimage could be a metaphor for living thereafter on Earth with purified vision, but that does not fit Vane's account. Vane ponders this problem in the final chapter of *Lilith* but reaches no conclusion.

The nature of "death" in *Lilith* is one of a number of important concepts that are least obscurely expressed in the "A" draft. MacDonald, in removing many helps to understanding in subsequent drafts, apparently wants readers to wrestle to draw out meanings appropriate to themselves, as he implies in his essay "The Fantastic Imagination" of 1891. Faced with this challenge, however, most people in the *fin de siècle* were more likely to manufacture meanings congenial to themselves.

Adam's Initiation Stages

As perceived by Vane, Adam is passing up (and often down) through the series of stages of an initiation process of a traditional pre-Christian mystery religion of the Mediterranean region. Most Mediterranean mystery religions shared more or less the same seven initiation stages, but MacDonald seems to draw specifically upon the late form termed Mithraism. This is the best known of the mystery religions because the Roman army took it to all parts of the Empire. An initiate passing the first stage was called Raven (Corax) in all the cults. The next stage was called Nymphus, or Occultist. The third was Warrior (Miles). The fourth was Lion (Leo). The fifth was Representative of the Race (Perses in Mithraism). The sixth was Courier of the Sun (Heliodromus). The seventh was Father (Pater).[25]

A "Raven" became fully alert to the world around him and to the needs of his fellow men. I Kings 17.6 allegorizes this well. In the second stage, the initiate became able to communicate with the dead. Mr. Raven, as sexton, communicates with Vane as a representative of the spiritually dead and looks after the dead of ambiguous status in his cemetery. At the third stage, represented in *Lilith* by Mr. Raven as librarian, the initiate became able to mediate knowledge from the supersensory to the sensory world, which is precisely what a librarian should do.

At the fourth (central) stage, the task of the initiate was to establish new communities. Adam apparently omits this stage, with very serious consequences for the way he develops at the fifth level. But fortunately his daughters Lona and Mara compensate for him. Mara began and maintains the community of Little Ones by bringing new babies from Bulika and also protects it from Lilith; Lona nurtures it with loving care. Adam tells Vane what he should have done for the Little Ones (145-48), and he sends a message to Mara when they are in danger (160). But to be a Leo he would have had to do very much more than this.[26]

At the fifth stage, Adam ought to become a representative of *his own* race and thus an "Israelite" (cf. John 1:47). But he presumes to become "Representative of the Whole Human Race" and thus "Adam." Adam manifests the sixth level of initiation, as "Courier of the Sun," when he heralds what Jacob Boehme calls the Aurora: the dawning of the eternal day (251). Vane at this point calls him an Angel of the Resurrection (252). But this appears to be extreme vanity on Vane's part, related to the way he perceives his own resurrection as the first where "the golden cock," "[s]ilent and motionless for millions of years," "begin[s] to crow!" (252). This resurrection contrasts utterly with the humble simplicity of Fane's resurrection in the "A" draft (359-60). After Vane has lain down to "sleep" he calls Adam by the universal name for the highest initiation stage – "Father."

In linking all Adam's different personas with a pre-Christian initiation sequence, MacDonald, amongst other things, appears to associate him with the Old Testament theology focused upon the Fall. This would seem to relate to the way he covertly alludes to Blake's images of the Temptation, Fall and Eternal Torment noted above in section 2. It is perhaps because Uranus/Adam associated himself so completely with the Earth as Gaia (whom he now calls Eve) that he resembles Lilith in being unable to comprehend spiritual matters in other than Earthly terms.

When Adam reverts to his "Raven" stage he usually speaks more wisely than in his authoritarian "Adam" stage. Raven can (literally) reverse forward to the second and third initiation stages and appear as "Mr. Raven."[27] When this first happens and Vane comments, "I have seen you before," Mr. Raven responds: "How can you say so from seeing me behind?" (11). When this transition happens in the opposite direction, back to Raven, it permits seeing a thing – in Blake's words – "in its infernal or diabolical sense" (*Marriage* 24). In this way, Mr. Raven's eschatology becomes the Raven's scatology when the latter leads Vane "to a little door that gave upon a grasspatch in a nook between two portions of the rambling old house. I made haste to open it for him. He stepped out into its creeper-covered porch. [...] 'Fine weather for worms, Mr. Raven!' 'Yes', he answered [...] 'It must be a grand time on the steppes of Uranus!'" (15-16)

This "rambling old house" at one level corresponds to Vane's physical body, as he has already made clear (13). So the equivalence of the "little door" out of Vane's house with the *Port Esquiline* of Spenser's House of Alma (*F.Q.* 2.9.32) is self-evident. The thunder claps and the "cataract" also seem related to the scatological imagery. Vane here is at a point of entry to the "region of the seven dimensions." When he is finally about to leave it there is again dramatic rain and lightning and a cataract, but no thunder (259-60).

Adam progresses to the "Father" stage only late in the book. Vane talks to him then both before his death-sleep and when prematurely awaking from it. We might have expected Adam to manifest as Sexton again here, but MacDonald would not then have had an opportunity of depicting him in his highest state. Adam here is again wise, although in a noticeably different way from when in his "Raven" persona (245-46). He explains what it means to "see through a glass darkly" (I Cor. 13:12). But it is perhaps noteworthy that he does *not* mention II Corinthians 3:18: "But we all, with open face beholding as in a glass the glory of the Lord, are changed into the same image from glory to glory, even as by the Spirit of the Lord." The verse previous to this ends: "where the Spirit of the Lord is, there is liberty"; and there is no true liberty in Adam's authoritarian world-view.

A *Phantastes* Parallel to the Adam and Lilith of *Lilith*

MacDonald seems to draw in part for his depictions of both Adam and Lilith upon details of the "garden of love" episode that is the climax of *Phantastes* (308-11).[28] Anodos is squire to the knight at this point, and the knight has been overawed by the solemnity of the elaborate ceremony there. "[F]ull of reverence and awe," he bows "his spirit to the belief that in [it] lay some great mystical meaning" (308-09). This shocks Anodos, who, being without armor (a rigid faith), has, by contrast, developed his sight so that it has become "much more keen than that of other people" (307). He can thus discern much of what is going on in the gathering dusk and strongly suspects it is evil. Understandably, he resolves to defend his ideal man: to ensure that his "master should not be deceived" as he puts it (309). And we soon realize why it is essential that Anodos does have a genuine ideal to defend, even though this ideal is so trusting and naïve .

Anodos strides up to the throne in the center of the garden, discovers that the "majestic-looking," proud yet benign figure seated there is mere rotting wood, and tears the effigy down, leaving a great hole in its pedestal.[29] A great wolf rushes up out of the hole, like a genie from an opened bottle, but Anodos is able to strangle it.

Until this point, Anodos has held naively to a faith that divides the self, with these two parts of a profane self-image continuously and inevitably reinforcing each other. His 'werewolf' caused him to picture his inherited ideals as a 'father king' who (although Anodos, of course, did not notice this) was a hollow decaying figure with affinities to Blake's Nobodaddy. Conversely, this hollow image of a father-king made his natural appetites appear as a werewolf.

Without his knightly ideal to defend, Anodos might well have joined the worshippers idolizing the hollow king and, like some of them, fallen prey to the werewolf. This does happen to Vane in *Lilith*, where his 'hollow king' is Adam and his 'werewolf' is the lycanthropic Lilith. [30] The psychological mutual dependence of the protagonist's "king" and "werewolf" is exactly the same in both cases.

Anodos, by destroying these two distorted halves of his personality, apparently causes his own death in Fairy Land. But the vows he subsequently makes to succor mankind, although high-flown and not grounded (he is floating in the air at the time), are undoubtedly sincere.

Lilith Lends a Hand

The climax of *Lilith* occurs where Lilith yields up her hand. Her genuine repentance is achieved by Mara independently of Adam. But Mara then, to Vane's surprise, helps bring Lilith to Adam, so critics tend to associate her with Adam's authoritarianism. This authoritarianism, while arguably apt for the fifth stage of initiatory development in the ancient world (provided that the fourth stage was *not* omitted), is inappropriate for the modern world.[31]

Extremely powerful pagan and Christian imagery is counter-pointed in Adam's act of figurative castration. In Chapters 38-40 that lead up to the amputation of the hand, MacDonald makes a sequence of semicovert allusions to Mark 9. 33-50 (Docherty, in Pennington 64-67). Jesus, after trying to make his disciples aware that the Kingdom is related to childlikeness and love (36-42), goes on to stress how obsession with the material world is fatal to any life of the spirit. He exhorts them that "if thy hand [representing possessiveness towards material things] offend thee, cut it off" (43).

MacDonald apparently chose to begin his *Unspoken Sermons* with Mark 9 and the concept of "childlikeness" because he believed that failure to understand this concept was at the heart of the popular Victorian (mis)conception of the Atonement that he so abominated.³² According to this misconception, Christ, in freewill, took all the sin of the world upon himself to appease his wrathful sky-god Father. Adam alludes to the ancient legends that depict how Lilith – likewise in freewill (albeit of a very different sort) – took all the evil of the world upon herself. But after her conversion by Mara (206-217) she becomes prepared to 'lend a hand' in appeasing another tyrannical sky-god.³³ Here this sky-god (as noted above) is Adam-Uranus. (And MacDonald would have been well aware that, in Greek myth, Uranus himself was castrated by his successor Cronos.)³⁴ MacDonald's ironic replacement of Christ here by the figure of Lilith is the culmination of all his attacks upon the misrepresentations prevalent in the religious establishment of his time (Docherty, "Ruskin" 110).

Checkmate?

Vane has now wholly submitted himself to Adam's law, and Adam-Uranus believes he has the authority to make his disciple a zombie.³⁵ Vane's actions in his burial of Lilith's hand in Chapters 41 and 42 exactly follow Adam's orders. *Lilith* Chapter 41 is titled "I am sent" and Vane says: "I had not set myself the task, and the minute I started I learned I was left to no chance."

Vane's burial of the hand is directly antithetical to Gluck's resurrection of the desiccated Treasure Valley as described in Ruskin's *The King of the Golden River* (Docherty, "Ruskin" 107-112). Equally, it is antithetical to that of the prince who is the hero of MacDonald's early story "The Light Princess." That prince, in a *free* choice arising from love, 'buries' *his* body so that the waters of life flow again and the heroine and her country are saved (46-50). In each of these three contrasting stories the hero causes the Water of Life to recommence its flow. But no logical reader could approve of all three.

To what extent similar irony continues in the resurrection chapters 44-46 of *Lilith* – the sequence MacDonald was careful to describe in the "B" draft as "only a dream" (217) – is a question that cannot be explored properly here. Irony in these three chapters in the "A" draft, although reduced in subsequent drafts, is intensified again in the final version. Adam's outlook is not wholly misguided, so some of what his disciple Vane perceives on his pilgrimage is true vision: most notably the nature of the stones of one of the gates of the city. But other elements are horrifying, especially in the "A" draft. There the captain of the guard is named Cacourgos Heteros, and the guardian of the city is Vala as Blake depicts her in Plate

53 of *Jerusalem* where she is guardian of the false (i.e., material) New Jerusalem and obscures the true light behind her (387). In the colored copy of *Jerusalem* often reproduced today Vala is not of "dark visage" and "as like Albrecht Dürer's *Melancolia* as she could look" ("A" 387). But this feature is extremely striking in Blake's black-and-white version, of which MacDonald possessed a facsimile.

At first he is in despair, but ultimately he comes to accept that the hand which sent him back was benign. Then, in a beautiful closing passage, he is able to become conscious of the wind of the spirit and to associate his experiences, as did MacDonald himself, "with the much wider mysticism of Plato that has found echoes in the intuitions of a minority in every age of our literature" (Prickett, *Victorian* 170).

Endnotes

1. Eerdmans claim that their Introduction is "a slightly abbreviated version of Dr Lewis' Preface" (v), but it is actually cut by more than a quarter. The text of the initial Eerdmans 1964 edition was reproduced by photo-lithography from the 1962 Gollancz edition. Victor Gollancz included a copy of his proposed modification of Lewis' Preface along with his letter of April 3rd 1962 to Lewis requesting permission to use the Preface. Lewis' agents Curtis, Brown, to whom Victor Gollancz was referred by Lewis, apparently approved the proposed cuts. Wm. B Eerdmans Jr applied for permission for Eerdmans to photograph the Gollancz edition on July 18th 1963, suggesting that the Lewis 'Introduction' could be used unchanged. Permission to photograph (excluding, of course, the Lewis 'Introduction') was given by Gollancz Ltd. on November 14th 1963, after an initial refusal. This was eight days before Lewis' death. Eerdmans, like Gollancz, combined the two titles, and they used (and continue to use) a much longer fragment of Lewis' Preface for their 'Introduction' than that used by Gollancz.

I would like to thank Southampton Book Services and their archivist James Palma for access to this correspondence.

2. The irony in *Lilith* derives from Romantic Irony, which Frederick Schlegel defines as "a mode of poetic reflection" that can "raise this reflection to higher and higher powers and can multiply it, as it were, in an endless array of mirrors" (qtd in Behler 45).

3. This was stressed to me by Lewis' close friend Owen Barfield when we were discussing his paper "Some Reflections on *The Great Divorce* of C.S. Lewis," *Mythlore* 13 (1976): 7-8.

4. The quotation is from W. H. Auden's "Afterword" to the Farrar centenary edition of "The Golden Key." To "throw oneself in" is nevertheless the only sensible approach for the initial reading or readings of any important 'fantasy' work.

5. The suffering associated with Mara, when not recognized as beneficial, is usually termed "Care" or "cares," and MacDonald makes covert play with the (apparently) contrasting meanings of "Care." In this he seems to draw upon the "Midnight" scene in Goethe's *Faust* II Act 5 where Care (*Sorge*) comes to dwell with Faust. In the "A" and "B" drafts of *Lilith* it is Hope who is Fane's ultimate comforter.

6. In the "A" draft of *Lilith*, Eve is very far from being a conventional retiring "angel in the house." As a white dove she works actively with her raven husband, to the extent that at one point they between them carry the dead panther Astarte (353-54).

7. Greville MacDonald in his autobiography demonstrates that his father was an active supporter of the feminist movement. So it is not surprising that *Lilith* should so savagely parody the typical bourgeois male outlook of the nineteenth century, which reached a hideous nadir in the *fin de siècle*.

8. The Victorian obsession (particularly in the mid-Victorian period) with the image of a wife as an "angel in the house" is explored in detail by Bram Dijkstra (11-24 etc).

9. On page 1 of the "B" draft of *Lilith*, Fane/Vane states that "the only one I have reason to care about as a reader is my one college-friend, who will himself know whom I mean, and that is enough, for there can be no mistake." This is repeated on page 2 of the "C" draft in nearly the same words. The comment would have no meaning unless MacDonald himself intended the book for a specific reader. His "one college-friend" was Carroll, and there is a comparable allusion to Carroll in a footnote in *A Dish of Orts* (1893) where MacDonald refers to "a mathematical friend, a lecturer at one of the universities" (13).

10. Ruskin's whole passage here is:

> all pieces of [great] art are didactic in the purest way, indirectly and occultly, so that, first, you shall only be bettered by them if you are already hard at work in bettering yourself; and when you are bettered by them it shall be partly with a general acceptance of their influence, so constant and subtle that you shall be no more conscious of it than of the healthy digestion of food; and partly by a gift of unexpected truth, which you shall only find by slow mining for it; – which is withheld on purpose [...] that you may not get it till you have forged the key of it in a furnace of your own heating. (1.17)

11. In *Phantastes*, nearly all the essential content requires "slow mining" to be discovered. But the outside world is darkly present from when Anodos encounters his shadow to where he finds the stream that leads him to the Fairy Palace. Also, MacDonald includes a great deal of autobiographical material from where Vane ventures out of the different doors of the old woman's cottage to the end of the story. For reading *The Portent*, "slow mining" is essential from chapter 4 onwards, although a few key events in later chapters, such as Duncan's serious head wounds, belong to both the external world and Duncan's imagination. (Docherty, Thubron 19-23). At the opposite extreme, the beautiful parable underlying Belorba's story of her life in *The Flight of the Shadow* is undoubtedly intended to be grasped subconsciously without any "slow mining."

12. Massive cutting and revising of most of MacDonald's novels has been undertaken in America, ostensibly to make them acceptable to churchgoers sharing an essentially "fundamentalist" outlook. Through large-scale marketing, these rewrites outsell unexpurgated editions many times over.

13. The term "main illustrations" is used to distinguish them from Blake's numerous tiny interlinear illustrations.

14. Raven comments of this "gnarled old man with a great white head" that is also a hawthorn: "The season for the hawthorn to blossom is when the hawthorn blossoms" (22). Robert Trexler has suggested that MacDonald may be giving a hint to readers here that Lilith contains borrowings from Nathaniel Hawthorne (36-38). Trexler points out that the MacDonalds knew the Hawthornes, and he lists interesting parallels between Hawthorne's *The Blithedale Romance* (1852) and *Lilith*, although not the very striking ones between Hawthorne's character Hollingsworth and Adam (see note 31 below). MacDonald certainly seems to

be thinking of the twice-blooming Glastonbury Hawthorn here because, of all his characters, this tree-man most closely resembles Joseph Polwarth in *Thomas Wingfold, Curate*, who has a huge white head and twisted body; lives in Glaston, the old name for Glastonbury; and, moreover, is an 'avatar' of the Joseph who, according to legend, came from the Eastern Mediterranean, via Cornwall, to Glastonbury bringing the staff that became the original Hawthorn (Docherty, "The Limitations" 65-66). Why Polwarth should obliquely be alluded to here is not obvious – although he would have been a better guide for Vane than Raven-Adam.

15. This is thick rough dead bark, not the thin smooth bark shed naturally each year by some trees such as the Eucalyptus.

16. Erdman (102) and Keynes (n. pag.) identify the central orb as a falling moon.

17. Elsewhere when MacDonald alludes (metaphorically or allegorically) to marble he always seems to be thinking of white marble. Examples in *Phantastes* are the marble lady and marble palace.

18. William Raeper told me of a men's secret society associated with horse-lore formerly existing in Huntly of which MacDonald would have been aware in his youth. As Raeper described it, the cult seems to have derived from traditional Indo-European horse cults mentioned by Eliade.

19. The sex of the central figure lying on the ground and of the climbing figure is not clearly defined in Blake's picture. However, the posture and expression of the male figure lying on the far left makes most sense if both figures lying near him are female. And MacDonald reads the climbing figure as male.

20. Vala is the great tempter figure throughout Blake's *Jerusalem*.

21. The epoch's hideous perversions of the Lilith legend are documented by Dijkstra (374-79).

22. These are not two separate meanings, numbered 1 and 2. The one is integral with the other. In several papers, Fernando Soto has shown how important unexpected dictionary definitions often are for MacDonald's plots. For example see "Some Linguistic Moves in the Carroll-MacDonald 'Literary Game,'" *North Wind* 18 (1999): 45-53.

23. "The Soul Exploring the Recesses of the Grave" is the title of one of Blake's engravings, a print of which always hung in MacDonald's study (Greville MacDonald 554).

24. The dead whom Vane specifically notices seem to be MacDonald's own dead relatives. This suggests that MacDonald probably is recalling one or more early experiences of his own, when – despite his favorite phrase at that time being "I wis

we war a' deid" – he fought against death when it came close to him.
25. See R.J. Vermaseren, *Mithras, the Secret God* (London: Chatto & Windus, 1963.)
26. In total contrast, in Lewis' Narnia stories, which draw heavily upon MacDonald, Aslan, although a god, is an archetypal Leo but the other six initiation stages are not differentiated.
27. At whichever of these three levels Adam is manifesting, Vane has little option but to address him indiscriminately as Mr. Raven. But MacDonald takes care that confusion never arises through this.
28. MacDonald's friend Garth Wilkinson had published an unillustrated edition of Blake's *Songs of Innocence and Experience* that MacDonald would undoubtedly have seen. It seems Wilkinson must have told MacDonald that in Blake's illustration for "The Garden of Love" a priest looks as if he might be about to push a boy and girl in an open grave. But Wilkinson cannot have given many more details about the illustration or MacDonald would not have alluded to the high hedge and the king on a high throne that are traditional elements of mediaeval "Garden of Love" imagery but are not used by Blake. Carroll obviously had seen Blake's illustration. The illustration in *Wonderland* of Alice in the Queen of Hearts' "Garden of Love" closely parodies many key elements of Blake's illustration (Docherty, "Easter Bunny" 24).
29. Anodos' anxious haste to tear down the idol and the response of the armed priests to this are both described with exaggerated alliteration. With the idol Anodos says, "I failed at first, for I found it firmly fixed" (310). The sound of the numerous priests drawing their swords is described as "a universal hiss of steel, as every sword was swept from its scabbard" (311).
30. MacDonald's short story "The Gray Wolf," *The Portent and Other Stories* (London: Adelphi-Fisher Unwin 1909) 295-303, demonstrates his knowledge of lycanthrophy. Eliade notes that in Africa the equivalent animal to the wolf in this respect is normally a leopard or leopardess (467). This may be related to the way, in Vane's journey to Lilith's city, the climate becomes increasingly African and the plain before the city is full of African animals.
31. Trexler's correlations between *Lilith* and Hawthorne's *The Blithedale Romance* have been noted above. Most of the important negative aspects of MacDonald's Adam as "Adam" seem likely to be borrowed from Hawthorne's vivid descriptions of the character Hollingsworth in his story. Hollingsworth is a skillfully manipulative and intensely religious person (36). His one fixed idea is to establish

idealist curative communities — but they would be communities where he had absolute authority over every detail. Furthermore, he is prepared to manipulate the emotions of anyone and everyone whom he meets in furtherance of this 'ideal' (53). Probably because "Adam" omitted the "Leo," community-building stage of his spiritual development, he perceives everything in the same religio-materialistic, authoritarian-philanthropic fashion as does Hollingsworth.

32. This misconception still persists in some Christian churches today. When the first edition of Michael Phillips' biography of MacDonald, *George MacDonald: Scotland's Beloved Storyteller* (Minneapolis: Bethany, 1987) was published, his publishers insisted on inserting a prominent disclaimer of MacDonald's view of the Atonement at the beginning of the book.

33. Mara is quick to reassure Vane that a "true, lovely hand is already growing" in its place (229). So Lilith's yielding up her hand *is* only a loan (Docherty, "Ruskin" 110).

34. Carroll covertly makes the most important consequence of this castration — The Birth of Venus — the central event in *Through the Looking-Glass* (Docherty, *Literary* 286-88).

35. Vane's submission to authoritarianism can perhaps be understood from some of MacDonald's letters. When, as very frequently happened, he had to console people after a bereavement, it seems he found he could not do so effectively in most cases without creating a very earthly picture of heaven. Additionally, as he grew older, he apparently sometimes felt when preaching that there was no way of saving the souls of many people other than by browbeating them to obedience to God by authoritarian teaching. With such traits in his own character he could realistically depict Adam's authoritarianism. What in these circumstances is remarkable is how, in *Lilith*, he is able to see his own authoritarianism so objectively and employ such consummate irony in depicting it.

Works Cited

Behler, Ernest. "The Theory of Irony in German Romanticism". In Garber 43-81.

Bindman, David, ed. *The Complete Illuminated Works.* London: Thames and Hudson, 2000.

Blake, William. *The Gates of Paradise.* 2nd ed. [1818]. In Erdman 268-79.

---. *Jerusalem: The Emanation of the Giant Albion.* In Erdman 280-379.

---. *The Marriage of Heaven and Hell.* [1790]. Ed. Geoffrey Keynes. London: Oxford UP, 1975.

Bunyan, John. *The Pilgrim's Progress.* 1677-85. Ed. Ernest Rhys. London: Everyman-Dent, 1907.

Carroll, Lewis. *Alice's Adventures in Wonderland* and *Through the Looking-Glass.* (1865 and 1872). Oxford: World Classics-Oxford UP, 1982.

Coleridge, Samuel Taylor. *Biographia Literaria.* 1817. London: Everyman-Dent, 1956.

Dijkstra, Bram. *Idols of Perversity: Fantasies of Feminine Evil in Fin de Siècle Culture.* New York: Oxford UP, 1988.

Docherty, John. "Carroll's Easter Bunny." *Reflections on Lewis Carroll.* Ed. Fernando J. Soto. Shelburne, Ontario: Lewis Carroll Society of Canada, 2000, 5-34.

---. "Fantasy Animals versus Fantasy About Animals: George MacDonald's *A Rough Shaking* and Maurice Sendak's *We Are All in The Dumps with Jack and Guy.*" *Inklings* 20 (2002): 45-69.

---. "The Limitations of Reductionist Approaches to *Thomas Wingfold, Curate.*" *North Wind* 19 (2000): 50-69.

---. *Literary Products of the Lewis Carroll – George MacDonald Friendship.* 2nd ed. Lewiston, NY: Mellen, 1997.

---. "The Water of Life in John Ruskin's *The King of the Golden River* and in Some of the Writings of George MacDonald". *Inklings* 23 (2005): 87-116.

---. "Worlds Beyond the Looking-Glass: Charles Dodgson's Second Alice Book and the Structural Elements of George MacDonald's *Lilith*". *Inklings* 13 (1995): 61-72.

Durie, Catherine. "George MacDonald and C.S. Lewis." *The Gold Thread: Essays on George MacDonald.* Ed. William Raeper. Edinburgh: Edinburgh UP, 1990, 163-85.

Eckermann, Johann Peter. *Conversations with Goethe.* 1836, 1848. Trs John Oxenford, Ed. J.K. Morehead. London: Everyman-Dent, 1930.

Eliade. Mircea. *Shamanism: Archaic Techniques of Ecstasy.* Trs. William R. Trask. London: Arkana-Penguin, 1989.

Erdman, David V. ed. *The Illuminated Blake.* London: Oxford UP, 1975.

Garber, Frederick ed. *Romantic Irony.* Budapest: Akadémia Kiado, 1988.

Guénon, Réne. *Symbolism of the Cross.* 1931. Trs. Angus Macnab. London: Luzac, 1996.

Hein, Rolland. *The Harmony Within: The Spiritual Vision of George MacDonald.* 2nd ed. Chicago: Cornerstone, 1999.

Hawthorne, Nathaniel. *The Blithedale Romance.* 1852. New York: Norton, 1978.

Knoepflmacher, U.C. ed. *George MacDonald: The Complete Fairy Tales.* New York: Penguin, 1999.

Lewis, Clive Staples. *George MacDonald: An Anthology.* London: Bles, 1946.

---. *The Great Divorce.* 1946. London: Collins-Fount, 1977.

MacDonald, George. *A Dish of Orts.* 1893. Whitethorn CA: Johannesen, 1996.

---. "The Golden Key. (1867). New York: Farrar, 1967.

---. "The Light Princess". 1864. In Knoepflmacher 15-53.

---. *Lilith.* 1895. In *Lilith: First and Final.* Whitethorn, CA: Johannesen, 1994.

---. *Lilith: A Variorum Edition.* Vols.1 & II. Ed. Rolland Hein. Whitethorn, CA: Johannesen, 1997.

---. *Phantastes.* 1858. Whitethorn, CA: Johannesen, 1994.

---. *The Princess and Curdie.* 1872. In McGillis, Princesses, 168-342.

---. *The Princess and the Goblin.* 1883. In McGillis, Princesses, 32-167.

---. *A Rough Shaking.* 1891. Whitethorn, CA: Johannesen, 1991.

---. *Thomas Wingfold, Curate.* 1876. Whitethorn, CA: Johannesen, 1997.

---. "The Wise Woman or The Lost Princess." In Knoepflmacher. 225-303.

MacDonald, Greville. *George MacDonald and his Wife.* 1924. Whitethorn CA: Johannesen, 1998.

---. *Reminiscences of a Specialist.* London: Allen, 1932.

McGillis, Roderick. "George MacDonald – The Lilith Manuscripts". *Scottish Literary Journal* 4 (2) (1970): 40-57.

---. ed. *The Princess and the Goblin; The Princess and Curdie.* Oxford: Oxford UP-World Classics, 1990.

Ovid [Publius Ovidus Naso]. *Metamorphoses.* Ed. Mary Innes. London: Penguin Classics-Penguin, n.d.

Pennington, John. "Of 'Frustrate Desire': Feminist Self-postponement in George MacDonald's *Lilith*". *North Wind* 21 (2002), 26-37 plus discussion 38-70.

Phillips, Michael. *The Curate's Awakening.* Minneapolis: Bethany, 1985.

Prickett. Stephen. "Death in *Lilith*." *Inklings* 13 (1995): 159-68.
---. "The Two Worlds of George MacDonald". *North Wind* 2 (1983): 14-23.
---. *Victorian Fantasy*. 2nd ed. Waco: Baylor UP, 2005.
Reis, Richard. "The Ignorant/Stupid Narrator in *Lilith*". *North Wind* 13 (1994): 24-28.
Robb, David. *George MacDonald*. Edinburgh: Scottish Academic Press, 1987.
Roberts, Leonard and Stephen Wildman. *Arthur Hughes: His Life and Work*. Woodbridge, Suffolk: Antique Collectors Club, 1997.
Ruskin, John. *The King of the Golden River*. London: 1855.
---. *The Queen of the Air*. London: 1869.
---. *Sesame and Lilies*, London: 1865.
Sadler, Glenn. A*n Expression of Character: The Letters of George MacDonald*. Grand Rapids: Eerdmans, 1994.
Trexler, Robert. "The Season for the Hawthorn to Blossom." *Inklings Forever 4* Upland, IN: Taylor UP, (2004). 34-40.

"Ha! art thou here?" he said.

And to the eyes of all a creature like a bat was plainly visible, perched upon his forefinger, and waving up and down its filmy wings. He looked at it for a moment, bent his head to whisper, and then addressed it out loud.

"Go," he said, "alight upon the head of him or of her who hath wrought the evil thou knowest in this house."

from Chapter 37 of St. George and St. Michael

Chapter 8

"Phantastic" Parallels in George MacDonald's *St. George and St. Michael* and *Phantastes*

Ginger Stelle

It has been well established in the field of MacDonald scholarship that MacDonald, a minister by education, felt an urgent need to communicate his message to a spiritually needy world through whatever means afforded him the best opportunity. Equally well established is that the lukewarm reception received by the 1858 publication of *Phantastes* did much to push MacDonald in the direction of the realistic Victorian novel as his best means of reaching out. The majority of the book-buying-and-reading public was simply not ready for the type of visionary work *Phantastes* represented. Furthermore, critical consensus has it that, overall, MacDonald's realistic novels are far below the quality of his fantasies and have, as a result, been largely ignored. What is not universally acknowledged is the fact that MacDonald's realistic novels, inferior though they may be to the fantasies, are nonetheless the work of an artist and a craftsman who, as Richard Reis puts it, "generally had a fairly clear idea of what he was doing and why" (46).

By virtue of their sheer number, the novels are important if one is to come to any true understanding of MacDonald. The transition to the realistic genre did not, as David Robb points out, leave MacDonald unable to "[express] much of what was important to him or . . . [doom him] to artistic failure" (12). Rolland Hein argues that, upon close examination, the difference between the realistic novels and fantasies "is less than one might at first suppose. His writings in both forms abundantly attest to his strong conviction that a transcendent reality is so closely related to the world of immediate human experience that it is also immanent in it" (113). Furthermore, to quote Reis once again, "[s]ince MacDonald had the same general didactic purposes in mind whatever he wrote, he offers an opportunity to study the different ways in which the same 'message' may be conveyed" (30).

MacDonald himself, though at the time of writing he could not have known the direction his life would take, posed the question at the end of *Phantastes*; as Anodos muses: "Could I translate the experience of my travels [through Fairy Land] into common life? This was the question. Or must I live it all over again, and learn it all over again, in the other forms that belong to the world of men, whose experience yet runs parallel to that of Fairy Land?" (184). After his fantasy met with mixed response, MacDonald spent the greater part of his writing career answering this question, exploring in concrete and realistic forms the same issues he sought to illuminate in the fantastic. Though the form was different, Rolland Hein explains that MacDonald's "purposes nowise changed; they simply became more directly and explicitly revealed. In the novels, MacDonald considers moral imperatives and theological insights less symbolically, more directly; symbolic embodiment tends to give way to illustration in the lives of characters that appear as real people" (114). One prominent example of this occurs in *St. George and St. Michael*, published in 1876.

St. George and St. Michael is MacDonald's only genuine historical novel. Set during the English Civil War in the 1640s, this novel tells a fairly typical story. Dorothy Vaughn and Richard Heywood are childhood friends and would-be sweethearts until the Civil War interrupts their romance. As is so often the case in such situations, her allegiance lies on one side while his is on the other. Following his father, Richard joins forces with Cromwell. Dorothy seeks refuge in Raglan Castle, a Royalist stronghold, as a waiting gentlewoman to Lady Margaret, daughter-in-law of the Marquis of Worcester. As the war progresses, they each encounter a variety of challenges, and each, at some point, holds the fate of the other in hand. Through it all, they realize that love outlasts all other considerations, and, in the true spirit of Victorian fiction, live happily ever after. Along the way, in typical MacDonald fashion, the reader is instructed in a variety of subjects.

In this book, however, MacDonald takes his usual transplantation of themes a bit further. With a setting at least somewhat alien to his readers, separated by a distance of two hundred years, MacDonald took the liberty of indulging, however slightly, his love of fantasy. MacDonald infuses *St. George and St. Michael* with a quasi-fantastic quality that is absent from most of his realistic fiction (with some exceptions). Among his chapter titles are "The Witch," "The Magician's Vault," "The Enchanted Chair," "The Apparition," and "The Horoscope." A powerful magician (19), foul beasts (29), familiar spirits (274), and a spectral appearance (212) grace the pages of MacDonald's novel. Ultimately, MacDonald grounds everything in the realistic world, explaining the seemingly supernatural elements of his story with a more modern understanding of science and nature than his characters would have possessed. The "witch" simply knows the local plants and their uses better than others (31). The "magician" is simply decades ahead of his compatriots in his understanding of science and technology (133). The beasts are big cats (176); the familiar is a mechanical bat (276), and the spectre is Richard, alive and well (213). Nonetheless, in the actual telling of the story, MacDonald calls upon the language of fantasy more than a contemporary setting would have allowed him.

Furthermore, he takes full advantage of this freedom to directly address the question he poised at the end of *Phantastes*. Into the midst of this conventional wartime love story, he introduces a secondary character by the name of Rowland Scudamore. Rowland's story is interwoven with those of Dorothy and Richard; he plays an important role in the development of their relationship. But Rowland's story is interesting in its own right. Nearly twenty years after sending Anodos to Fairy Land, while remaining firmly entrenched in a realistic environment, MacDonald sends Rowland on a journey which parallels that of Anodos, living the same questions in the world of men and learning the same lessons.

Anodos is introduced in *Phantastes* encountering a "tiny woman-form" emerging from a chamber in his father's desk. Despite the testimony of his own senses, Anodos cannot believe what he sees. Furthermore, when the lady promises to grant him a wish, he questions her ability to do so because of her size. On both counts, he is chastised for his foolish arrogance (7). A few moments later, after she has become a full-sized lady, he reaches to embrace her, and is again called "foolish boy" and warned against touching her (8). Anodos' gesture is an implicit sexual overture, and it demonstrates both an impulse for self-gratification and a general lack of respect towards womankind. Basically, Anodos is introduced being cocky and unjustifiably sure of himself while making unwanted advances towards a lady of recent acquaintance for whom he lacks respect.

In *St. George and St. Michael*, Rowland's first appearance comes as Dorothy is asking him to leave. MacDonald writes, "Taken with his new cousin, the youth had lingered and lingered; and in fact Dorothy had been unable to get rid of him before an hour strange for leave-taking" (51-52). He is further described by MacDonald as having "an easy tone of superiority" (52) and by Richard as "The ape! The coxcomb!" (58). His attitude of superiority is further demonstrated when he chastises Richard for shouting, then proceeds to shout himself twice on the same page (59). Furthermore, he has a strong sense of entitlement based on his position in a Royalist household, threatening to abscond with Richard's mare on the grounds of Richard's Parliamentarianism (59). He also demonstrates a profound lack of respect for women when he says to Richard, "[L]ook after your mare, for I vow I have fallen in love with her. She's worth three, at least, of your Mistress Dorothies" (59). So, like Anodos, Rowland is introduced as cocky and unjustifiably sure of himself while making unwanted advances towards a lady of recent acquaintance for whom he lacks respect.

Having established this foundational similarity between Rowland and his predecessor, I note how MacDonald proceeds with Rowland's story. There is no point-for-point comparison between Rowland's journey and that of Anodos, but his next significant appearance is in a situation unmistakably echoing Anodos' encounter with the Alder-maiden. In this incident, Anodos is seeking his ideal woman, the White Lady he freed from her enchanted alabaster bed. In song, he calls for his lady in what Rolland Hein terms, "animal sensuality" (62). Seemingly, his wish is granted. A lady appears. Although, as Anodos notices, "there was something . . . in the sound of the voice . . . that did not vibrate harmoniously with the beat of my inward music," he goes with her, and what follows can only be described as a sexual encounter (44-46). In the morning, however, Anodos awakes to find, not his White Lady, but:

> a strange horrible object. It looked like an open coffin set up on one end; only that the part for the head and neck was defined from the shoulder-part. In fact, it was a rough representation of the human frame, only hollow, as if made of decaying bark torn from a tree . . . . The thing turned round – it had for a face and front those of my enchantress, but now of a pale greenish hue in the light of the morning, and with dead lusterless eyes. (46)

Anodos is powerless to protect himself from the Alder-tree or her associate the Ash, to whom she delivers him. Anodos is narrowly saved from destruction as a result of this encounter through the intervention of Sir Percivale, himself a victim of the Alder.

Anodos next visits the cottage of a woman well educated about the inhabitants of Fairy Land. Guessing where Anodos has been, she offers some explanation of the Alder-maiden's motivations, "[A]lthough she loves no man, she loves the love of any man, and when she finds one in her power, her desire to bewitch him and gain his love . . . makes her very lovely – with a self-destructive beauty, though, for it is that which is constantly wearing her away within, till, at last, the decay will reach her face" (49). Keith Wilson describes the Alder maiden as the "quintessence of self-referential love" (146). Additionally, in an earlier place, Anodos had been warned against the Alder-maiden with the admonition that "the Alder will smother you with her web of hair, if you let her near you at night" (11).

MacDonald uses some similar images and ideas to describe the woman with whom Rowland becomes involved. Mistress Amanda Serafina Fuller "was pretty, except when she began to speak, and then for a moment there was a strange discord in her face" (105). Furthermore, she "was a twig or leaf upon one of many decaying branches, which yet drew what life they had from an ancient genealogical tree" interested in making "the false impression of plentiful ease"

(223). While MacDonald uses a standard image, the family tree, he nonetheless describes Amanda in terms of rotting vegetation. He goes on to say that her "one redeeming element . . . was her love to her mother, but inasmuch as it was isolated and self-reflected, their mutual attachment partook of the nature of a cultivated selfishness" (225). Later, Rowland refers to "the tightening bonds Mistress Amanda had flung around him" (291). These descriptions clearly evoke the image of the Alder-maiden.

Likewise, the relationship between Rowland and Amanda invites comparison to the relationship between Anodos and the Alder. It is strongly implied, circumspectly, so as not to offend Victorian sensibilities, that this is a sexual relationship. Midnight trysts in secluded areas of the castle (148), veiled references to Rowland's previous conquests (108, 292, 305), and pointed remarks as to the escalating nature of this relationship (143) are all indicators. Just as Anodos is nearly destroyed by his encounter with the Alder-maiden, this relationship nearly leads to Rowland's downfall. After straying into a restricted area of the castle during one of their trysts, Rowland and Amanda only narrowly escape a discovery which would have threatened both of their positions in the household (171-3). Finally, Rowland is only freed from the "tightening bonds" of this relationship through the intervention, albeit indirect, of another of her victims, Richard Heywood. Though we have no implication that Richard was seduced by or involved with Amanda in any way, she nonetheless uses him in a selfish plot to destroy Dorothy's reputation (231). The revelation of this plot leads to Amanda's expulsion from the castle and Rowland's release from her clutches (281). This is not to say that MacDonald paints Rowland as guiltless through all of this, any more than Anodos is guiltless in his encounter with the Alder-maiden. Both men are guilty of giving in to their selfish desires.

Shortly after the Alder-Maiden incident, Anodos acquires a visible sign of his selfishness. It is his shadow, and it remains Anodos' nearly constant companion for some time. Much has been written about this shadow. Drawing on Jungian psychology, Joseph Sigman calls it "the personification of the evil side of an individual that goes unrecognized by him" (214). Hein refers to the shadow as Anodos' "cynical self . . . . [which] intervenes and interferes in various incidents, defeating the good that could otherwise issue and often working definite harm (65). Edward Cusick claims it is the "personification of all those negative traits belonging to the ego – cruelty, cowardice, selfishness and so on" (60). It is arguably all these things, and more. Its presence has an unmistakable impact on Anodos' adventures. His Shadow causes Anodos to consider himself superior to the world around him. He begins to judge Fairy Land, not on its own merits, but through his Shadow's superior discernment. He, more than before, sees the things around him as his for the taking, even when the taking causes harm to another. Essentially, it is a tangible symbol of what Hein calls "a spiritual state of complete self-centeredness" (63).

In a realistic setting, MacDonald could not use such a concrete device as a shadow to illustrate this sense of self at the root of Rowland's troubles. Nonetheless, Rowland suffers from just such a "spiritual state of complete self-centeredness." As already discussed, he is quite self-assured and cocky. MacDonald says that "in the opinion of the household, the marquis did his best, or worse rather, to ruin young Scudamore by indulgence" (87). He is used to having things his own way, to doing what he wants. The Marquis "would have been scandalized to know the freedoms his favourite indulged himself in, and regarded as privileged familiarities" (108). His only real complaint is that his master, as Rowland describes him, "makes much of the ancient customs of the country; I would he would follow them. In the good old times I should have been a squire at least by now, if, indeed, I had not earned my spurs; but his lordship will never be content without me to hand him his buttered egg at breakfast, and fill his cup at dinner with his favorite claret. And so I am neither more nor less than a page" (55). Even this presumed indignity, though, feeds into his smug self image, as he feels indispensable and irreplaceable (307).

In addition, like Anodos, Rowland feels justified in taking what he wants, regardless of the consequences to anyone else. Carrying out his threat from earlier, Rowland steals Richard's war horse. As cavalrymen often have a very strong attachment to their animal, especially when, as in Richard's case, they have been together since the horse was a foal, for Richard, this is quite a loss. In fact, for Richard, it is too great a loss, and he cannot let it pass. He stages a midnight raid on the castle, gets captured, and is seriously, almost fatally, wounded. He manages to escape, but without his horse, and in a poor condition (200-35). Rowland's excuse for his action is simply to claim that "I gave him fair warning two years ago, my lord; and the king wants horses." Whatever justification this might provide, however, is undone by MacDonald's dialogue tag "said Scudamore cunningly" (219). Rowland is a quick thinker, and he does not want to get in trouble, so comes up with something that sounds reasonable and gets away with theft. Clearly, both Anodos and Rowland have much to learn.

Anodos' education accelerates when his wanderings lead him to the Fairy Palace. While there he encounters the story of Cosmo and the mirror. This story tells of a student who purchases a mirror, only to discover that a woman inhabits the reflection. He falls passionately in love with the woman in the mirror. He has to make a choice, however, between keeping the mirror and keeping the lady close, or breaking the mirror and setting her free in the uncertain hopes of gaining a genuine relationship, a choice ultimately between a selfish love and a selfless love. Before he can decide, the mirror is stolen, and only through the sacrifice of his own life can Cosmo break the mirror and free the woman he loves (85-104). Shortly after reading this story, Anodos is put to a similar test. His White Lady is once again under an enchantment. Anodos can free her. He has to follow only one rule, "Touch not!" (107) and, presumably, she will stay around. Unlike Cosmo, Anodos is unable to subdue his baser instincts. Carried away by his sensual desires, he touches her, and the lady is gone from him again (117). The message of Cosmo's story seems to have been completely lost on Anodos.

This time, his actions have consequences for him. He loses the Lady he loves and must pass through a dark and difficult time, full of torment and anguish. Among other things, he is accosted by goblins informing him of his Lady's being loved by a "better man." Realizing, somewhat, that his own unworthiness has led him to this place, he is able to relinquish his claim to the Lady, giving her up to the "better man" for her own happiness (120). Shortly thereafter, at the home of a Wise Woman, he is confronted with a vision of his White Lady with her "better man." This is an agonizing, painful experience for Anodos, but he emerges with the understanding that true love is, as Hein explains, "like a well that gives and is always fresh, rather than like a cistern that is full to stagnation" (56). According to Wilson, with this first act of self-renunciation, Anodos takes a giant step forward "on the path to understanding, and performing, his 'duty'" (149). On that note, he is sent from the Wise Woman's home with the instructions, "Go, my son, and do something worth doing" (144).

Rowland's education, likewise, involves hearing a story. However, in Rowland's case, it is of a very different nature. The events surrounding Richard's attempt to retrieve his horse were never fully explained to the satisfaction of the residents of Raglan. What was known was that, through some unknown means, he gained access to the castle grounds, found his horse, and would have ridden out the main gate. Dorothy, looking out her window, recognized him and, alerting the guard, prevented his escape, Richard being severely wounded in the scuffle. The following morning, when the door to the chamber he was taken to was unlocked, Richard was gone and Dorothy was there. She claimed that in a fit of guilt and worry, she went to check on him, only to find him already gone. To the reader, MacDonald makes it perfectly clear that Dorothy is telling the truth, but to the residents of the castle, she is obviously covering up her own complicity in both his entrance and his escape (212-47).

This story, related to him by Amanda, has a remarkable effect on Rowland. MacDonald describes:

> But as Amanda spoke, Dorothy became to Rowland twice as interesting as ever Amanda had been. There was a real romance about the girl, he thought. And then she looked so quiet! He never thought of defending her . . . . How far Dorothy had been right or wrong in visiting Heywood, he did not even conjecture, not to say consider. It was enough that she who had been to him like the blank in the centre of the African map, was now a region of marvels and possibilities, vague but not the less interesting, or the less worthy of beholding the interest she had awaked (245-46).

Unlike the story of Cosmo, designed to show the importance of selfless love, this story acts very much upon the baser aspects of Rowland's personality. He begins an active pursuit, a pursuit not unlike that of Anodos for his White Lady. Echoing the experience of Anodos with his White Lady, MacDonald describes Rowland's feelings that "Dorothy had become to him like an enchanted castle, the spell of which he flattered himself he was the knight born to break" (291). Clearly, Rowland is not motivated by any degree of selfless love.

The outcome, however, is one that Rowland did not expect. Nothing happens. MacDonald says, "All his endeavours . . . to attract from her a single look such as indicated intelligence, not to say response, were disappointed. She seemed absolutely unsuspicious of what he sought" (291). Unusual occurrence that this is for Rowland, it begins to have an effect on him:

> Strange to say, however, poorly grounded as was the original interest he had taken in her, and little as he was capable of understanding her, he soon began, even while yet confident in his proved advantages of person and mind and power persuasive, to be vaguely wrought upon by the superiority of her nature . . . . unconsciously to himself, the dim element of truth that flitted vaporous about in him had begun to respond to the great pervading and enrounding orb of her verity. He began to respect her, began to feel drawn as if by another spiritual sense than that of which Amanda had laid hold. He found in her an element of authority. The conscious influences to whose triumphs he had been so perniciously accustomed, had proved powerless upon her, while those that in her resided unconscious were subduing him. Her star was dominant over his.

> At length he began to be aware that this was no light preference, no passing fancy, but something more serious than he had hitherto known — that in fact he was really, though uncomfortably and unsatisfactorily, in love with her. He felt she was not like any other girl he had made his shabby love to, and would have tried to make better to her, but she kept him at a distance, and that he began to find tormenting. (292)

Though clearly not literally analogous to Anodos' trek through the darkness in search of his lady, Rowland's experience nonetheless leads him into emotional darkness and torment caused by Dorothy's lack of favor. And as Anodos grows into a fuller understanding of selfless love through his journey, Rowland begins to understand how shallow his previous perception of love had been.

Eventually, driven to speak more plainly, Rowland confronts Dorothy about her indifference:

> "Wilt thou never love me, Dorothy? — not even a little?"
> "Wherefore should I love thee, Rowland?"
> "We are commanded to love even our enemies"
> "Art thou then mine enemy, cousin?" . . . .
> "Must I then be thine enemy indeed before thou wilt love me?"
> "No, cousin: cease to be thine own enemy and I will call thee my friend . . . . I know thee better than thou thinkest, cousin. I have read thy title-page, if not thy whole book."
> "Tell me then how runneth my title-page, cousin."
> "The art of being willfully blind, or, The way to see no further than one would" . . . .
> "If thou can'st not love me, wilt thou not then pity me a little?"
> "That I may pity thee, answer me what good thing is there in thee wherefore I should love thee."
> "Wouldst thou have a man trumpet his own praises?"
> "I fear not that of thee who hast but the trumpet — I will tell thee this much: I have never seen in thee that thou didst love save for the pastime thereof." (294-5)

She goes on to confront him with his own dishonorable actions in his relationship with Amanda, and, for probably the first time in his life, Rowland finds himself denied something he desires on the basis of his own unworth (296). Dorothy is undeniably harsh in her words, but this is something Rowland needs to hear if he is ever to change. As MacDonald explains, "while one's good opinion of himself remains untroubled . . . hostile criticism will not go very deep, will not reach to the quick. The thing that hurts is that which sets trembling the ground of self-worship, lays bare the shrunk cracks and worm-holes under the golden plates of the idol, shows the ants running about in it, and renders the foolish smile of the thing hateful' (295-96). Chastised and humbled, Rowland begs forgiveness, and like the Wise Woman's farewell to Anodos, Dorothy's answer sends Rowland on the next phase of his journey. She says, "[H]ow should I forgive thee for being unworthy? For such thing there is no forgiveness. Cease thou to be unworthy, and then is there nothing to forgive" (305-06).

Having both been sent on a quest to do something worthy, both Anodos and Rowland take the route of combat. Anodos is enlisted to aid two brothers preparing to fight three giants (150). They are victorious, but both brothers are killed, leaving Anodos the "sole survivor" (156). He suffers a brief attack of survivor's guilt (157), but upon entering an enchanted forest, he begins to feel an unwarranted pride in his accomplishments. He even has to "remind [himself] that [he] had only killed one [of the giants]" (159). Furthermore, he likens himself to Sir Galahad (160). Additionally, his shadow, which had reappeared after the battle with the giants, seems to have disappeared. Suddenly, he is confronted by another knight, his own double, only "larger and fiercer." Cowering before him, Anodos is led into the forest and imprisoned in an empty tower. With a flash of insight, Anodos realizes that the knight was actually his Shadow. So he sits, a prisoner of himself, of his own selfishness and pride. His one consolation is the moonlight coming through the lone window in the tower which, for the duration of the moon gives him the sense that he is free, only to be imprisoned once again with the rising of the sun (161-62).

Rowland enters the service of the king and is present for the Battle of Naseby. Severely wounded in a scuffle with Richard, he is brought back to Raglan. In describing his condition upon his return, MacDonald, as he did with Amanda and the Alder-maiden, uses imagery that evokes a definite parallel to Anodos and his tower:

> The poor fellow was but a shadow of his former self, and looked more likely to vanish than to die in the ordinary way . . . . [H]e lay lapped in ignorance and ministration, hidden from the world and deaf to the gnarring of its wheels, prisoned in a twilight dungeon, to which Richard's sword had been the key. The world went grinding on and on, much the same, without him whom it had forgotten;

but the over-world remembered him, and now and then looked in at a window: all dungeons have one window which no jailer and no tyrant can build up. (336-38)

MacDonald clearly invokes the prison motif in examining Rowland's illness.

Furthermore, as Anodos sits in his tower, so Rowland sits in his sick room, wallowing in self-pity. A visitor comes to the castle, another cousin of Dorothy, the poet, Henry Vaughn. In the hopes that Henry might be able to help Rowland, Dorothy takes him to the sick chamber. Rowland is in a rather pitiful state, caring about nothing and wishing for death. With great insight, Henry asks him:

> Have you not the notion that if you were hence you would leave behind you a certain troublesome attendant who is scarce worth his wages? . . . . Shall I tell thee who hath possessed thee? — for the demon hath a name that is known amongst men, though it frighteneth few and draweth many, alas! His name is Self, and he is the shadow of thy own self . . . . But if he be cast out and never more enter into thy heart, but remain as a servant in thy hall, then wilt thou recover from this sickness, and be whole and sound (345).

Although one is imprisoned in Fairy Land and the other in England of the 1640s, both men are prisoners of the same jailer.

Likewise, for both men, the remedy is the same, a conscious decision to slay their jailer and leave their prison. Anodos hears singing and opens the door of his prison (164). He could have left at any time, but he had to decide to use the door. Finally convinced of his own unworthiness, he divests himself of his armor and, in his own words, "knew the delight of being lowly" (166). Before long, he realizes that his shadow is no longer with him. Unfortunately, this brings with it another danger. Anodos explains,

> Now, however, I took, at first, what perhaps was a mistaken pleasure, in despising and degrading myself. Another self seemed to arise, like a white spirit from a dead man, from the dumb and trampled self of the past. Doubtless, this self must again die and be buried, and again, from its tomb, spring a winged child . . . . Self will come to life even in the slaying of self, but there is ever something deeper and stronger than it, which will emerge at last from the unknown abysses of the soul (166).

He has lost his shadow, but must ever remain vigilant, lest it try to return.

Rowland's recovery is not so simple, perhaps due to the nature of reality as opposed to fantasy. He has reached the point of despising himself, but as Anodos points out, this is a "mistaken pleasure." Not until he begins to "think more and brood less" does he actually begin to recover. MacDonald describes his progress:

> By and by he began to start questions of right and wrong, suppose cases, and ask Dorothy what she would do in such and such circumstances . . . . Slowly his health began to return, and slowly the deeper life that was at length to become his began to inform him. Heartless and poverty-stricken as he had hitherto shown himself, the good in him was not so deeply buried under refuse as in many a better-seeming man. Sickness had awakened in him a sense of requirement – of need also, and loneliness, and dissatisfaction. He grew ashamed of himself and conscious of defilement. Something new began to rise above and condemn the old (347-48)

Slowly, but undeniably, Rowland achieves a measure of victory over his own shadow. And, with the promise of "the deeper life that was at length to become his," MacDonald indicates that he will continue to grow and mature.

MacDonald ends Rowland's story with one final incident which parallels an earlier adventure of Anodos. While traveling through the dark, tormented by the goblins, and again after seeing the vision of her with Sir Percivale, Anodos relinquished his claims on the White Lady in favor of the "better man." After yet another encounter with Richard results in an aggravation of his earlier wound, Rowland receives treatment from an acquaintance of Richard's. Richard visits daily, and as the two spend time together, they come to a better understanding of one another. Like Anodos, Rowland must do something which is painful. In the course of conversation, he says to Richard, referring to Dorothy:

> "By heaven, but it were a pity you should not come together! Surely the same spirit dwelleth in you both! For me, I should show but as a shadow cast from her brightness. But I tell thee, Roundhead, I love her better than ever Roundhead could."
>
> "I know not, Scudamore. Nor do I mean to judge thee when I say that no man who loves not the truth can love a woman in the grand way a woman ought to be loved."
>
> "Tell me not I do not love her, or I will rise and kill thee. I love her even to doing what my soul hateth for her sake . . . She loves thee." (378)

This is something very difficult for Rowland to do, and it hurts him deeply, but like Anodos, Rowland is finally able to relinquish his White Lady to the better man. He has learned the painful lesson of self-sacrifice, of loving another enough to desire her happiness even at the expense of his own.

Could the lessons of Fairy Land be translated into common life? While public tastes may have dictated that MacDonald confine his writing to the realistic form, he was nonetheless able to explore the ideas and themes he held important. Despite taking place in completely different universes, the adventures of Rowland Scudamore in England of the 1640s provide an interesting parallel for those of Anodos in Fairly Land. Both have similar personalities and character flaws. They are both vain, selfish, and controlled by base desire, and both must learn to overcome those elements in their nature. Each loves a woman they cannot have and must come to a place of self-renunciation for the good of their beloved. For both Anodos and Rowland, their journey is ultimately about learning to subjugate the Self and escape the lonely captivity of selfishness. With these similarities, *St. George and St. Michael* represents one example of MacDonald's attempt to answer the question he poised at the end of *Phantastes*.

Works Cited

Cusick, Edward. "MacDonald and Jung." Raeper 56-86.
Hein, Rolland. *The Harmony Within: The Spiritual Vision of George MacDonald.* Grand Rapids, MI: Wm. B. Eerdmans, 1982.
MacDonald, George. *Phantastes.* 1858. Grand Rapids, MI: Wm. B. Eerdmans, 2000.
---. *St. George and St. Michael.* 1876. Whitethorn, CA: Johannesen, 1996.
Raeper, William, ed. *The Gold Thread: Essays on George MacDonald.* Edinburgh: Edinburgh UP., 1990.
Reis, Richard H. *George MacDonald.* New York: Twayne, 1972.
Robb, David S. "George MacDonald's Scottish Novels." Raeper. 12-30.
Sigman, Joseph. "Death's Ecstasies: Transformation and Rebirth in George MacDonald's *Phantastes*." *English Studies in Canada*.11.2 (1976): 203-226.
Wilson, Keith. "The Quest for 'The Truth': A Reading of George MacDonald's *Phantastes*." *Etudes Anglaises* 34 (1981): 140-152.

He lifted his eyes, and saw a great globe of light — like silver at the hottest heat: he had once seen silver run from a furnace. It shown from somewhere above the roofs of the castle: It must be the old princess's moon! How could she be there? Of course she was not there! He had asked the whole household, and nobody knew anything about her or her globe either. It couldn't be! And yet, what did that signify, when there was the white globe shining, and here was the dead white bird in his hand? That moment the pigeon gave a little flutter. "It's not dead!" cried Curdie, almost with a shriek. The same instant he was running full speed toward the castle, never letting his heels down, lest he should shake the poor, wounded bird.

Chapter 2, The Princess and Curdie

Chapter 9

Curdie's Intertextual Dialogue:
Engaging Maurice, Arnold, and Isaiah

Kirstin Jeffrey Johnson

The Princess and Curdie (1883) has bemused and frustrated critics of George MacDonald. Most agree that there is something inherently different between this book and its predecessor, *The Princess and the Goblin* (1873) — something more than merely a ten-year lapse between publishing dates. The book's conclusion is the most discussed and the most disagreed upon aspect. Beginning as a happy fairy tale that brings the reader once again into the realm of the miner-boy Curdie, the young princess Irene, and the royal great-great grandmother Irene, The *Princess and Curdie* has the expected "fairy-tale-ending," only to be followed abruptly by devastation and annihilation in four short sentences. Although these sentences seem to cause little concern to child-readers, adult critics have often been confounded. They have proposed that MacDonald is going through a crisis in faith; that he has he lost his faith altogether; that he is in an "apocalyptic mood" "convinced that evil triumphs in the end" (Wolff 176); that this "startlingly bleak" ending is meant to signify "the passing of Christendom"(Prickett, *Victorian Fantasy* 187, 188).

Such propositions seem to me inconsistent with MacDonald's corpus as a whole. Roderick McGillis' introduction to the Oxford University Press double-edition of the two *Princess* books is a notable exception of considering the text within the body of MacDonald's work. He concludes that the end portrayed here is "a sign of renewal, of new beginnings" (xviii).[1] Perhaps one of the greatest weaknesses of much MacDonald scholarship is the infrequency of such consideration of his body of work as a collaborative source of insight and, indeed, of considering of his work contextually.[2] Revelations abound for the scholar willing to traverse this territory because MacDonald frequently points the observant reader directly to a source — often with explicit quotations. As regards the contentious ending of *The Princess and Curdie*, as well as its other perplexities, a close look at part of the particular 'book' which MacDonald claims to have read and valued more than any other, provides helpful insight. Combining this with a consideration of one of the men he claimed most influenced him, F. D. Maurice, and an awareness of the contemporary dialogue with which Maurice engaged — particularly as embodied in the arguments of Matthew Arnold — can provide revelatory illumination to the *Curdie* dilemma.

The Bible is the text MacDonald claims to have read more than any other (156 qtd in Sadler).[3] Unfashionable a text as it may be in the 21st century, it is nonetheless crucial for unraveling much of previous Western Literature, and the work of MacDonald is no exception — as he makes evident in his explicit ruminations upon its influence.[4] The role of the Bible — its place in both culture and literature — was an issue of much debate in MacDonald's day, and one text in particular received specific attention from academics: the book of *Isaiah*. It is thus of particular interest to note that MacDonald gives significant attention to this book throughout his work. Frederick Denison Maurice and Matthew Arnold also give extensive attention to the book of *Isaiah*, and a close look at how they do so reveals that *The Princess and Curdie* does not stand independent of their commentary. Indeed, a reading of Maurice's and Arnold's work reveals that *The Princess and Curdie* may be a text of greater critical import than it has hitherto been given credit for. And its ending, when read in light of these *Isaiah* dialogues, perhaps not so disastrous after all.

A brief look at the repeated use of the book of *Isaiah* within MacDonald's work, and at its context in the Victorian era, will assist us in understanding why MacDonald might have granted it such dominance in the shaping of *The Princess and Curdie*. Much more time could be given to explore the role of *Isaiah*, and looking at its extensive influence upon MacDonald, yet the purpose of this chapter is to look at why MacDonald chose *Isaiah* to be such an overarching framework for this fantasy. It must be noted that while many critical questions about *The Princess & Curdie* can be answered through the recognition of an intentional relationship with the Old Testament text of *Isaiah*, it is by no means the only book, story, or poem with which *The Princess and Curdie* has a relationship — MacDonald enjoyed the interplay of texts and ideas far too much to limit himself in such a fashion; it would probably not even be possible for him. In this case, however, *Isaiah* has a critically unique role.

From MacDonald's first realistic novel, *Isaiah* stands forth as a text of particular note. In *David Elginbrod* (1863), Chapter 40 of *Isaiah* is read in its entirety — three times. Not only is it clear on each occasion that this is the saintly Elginbrod's favorite chapter, but each time there is a small exposition on some aspect of the chapter (4, 208, 367).[5] "The Wow O' Riven" (1864) ends with a significant quotation from *Isaiah* 60, which calls for the reader to reflect upon the story anew (189). In *Annals of a Quiet Neighbourhood* (1867), the book of *Isaiah* is mentioned several times, and in Chapter 40 it receives an extended exegesis, beginning with the words: "And the sermon I preached to myself and through myself to my people, was that which the stars had preached to me" (512). This

Isaiah sermon is a turning point in the novel, and is undergirded by several performances of pieces from Handel's *Isaiah*-inspired *Messiah*. In *Thomas Wingfold, Curate* (1876) reflection upon words of the prophet Isaiah is part of an awakening for the curate (330), and paraphrases from *Isaiah* are scattered throughout the book.[6] In the midst of the great storm in *Sir Gibbie* (1879), Gibbie remembers the words of the prophet "Esaias" (as MacDonald sometimes spells it), and thus we see how this story too is significantly shaped by the Old Testament text (202; indeed Gibbie is so frequently named a 'prophet' that it is hard to overlook the parallels). In *What's Mine's Mine* (1886), the mother's memory of her husband preaching from *Isaiah* 28 is a pivotal moment in righting her relationship with her son and their land (306); obedience to God and relationship with the land are key themes, just as in *Isaiah*. In *There and Back* (1890) Isaiah's vision is brought to mind so that we can better understand protagonist Richard's change. In *Hope of the Gospel* (1892), the book of *Isaiah* and the prophet himself are referred to frequently. At one point MacDonald gives particular emphasis to the fact that the text from which Christ read aloud when returning to his home synagogue was *Isaiah* – thus identifying himself as fulfillment of its prophecy (63).

Isaiah is, of course, the scriptural source for the character of Lilith, who figures in MacDonald's novel of the same name (1895), and whose name is also given to a character in the short story "The Cruel Painter." Such explicit references continue. The implicit references are almost innumerable. Of course *Isaiah* is also frequently referred to in the *Unspoken Sermons* (I-1866; II-1885; III-1889). And Greville MacDonald shows that the recitation of *Isaiah* is a habit which spanned his father's lifetime: as a schoolboy the young George regaled his friends with "a free metrical version of the 14th chapter of *Isaiah*" (a fairly lengthy chapter!); late in MacDonald's life, according to a friend, "it was worth a journey from London [to Italy] to hear [him] read the 43rd chapter of *Isaiah*: 'The Divine Voice itself seemed to come to us as he finished by saying, "Take it to yourself personally: what He said to Jacob, He says to you"' (Greville 61,507).[7]

MacDonald is not unique among Victorian writers in giving particular attention to the book of *Isaiah*, though his emphasis is extensive. Indeed, *Isaiah* was receiving significant attention culturally. Handel's *Messiah* (largely based on excerpts from *Isaiah*, and emphasizing the fulfillment of this prophetic text in the person of Christ) was experiencing a revival.[8] *Isaiah* was dominant in many of the era's best-known hymns, including "The Battle Hymn Republic" and "O Come, O Come Emmanuel" (Sawyer 8). *Isaiah* 32:8 was used as a public epitaph by Queen Victoria, for herself and Albert. The celebrity Victorian preacher Charles Spurgeon, claiming that a verse from *Isaiah* had converted him, preached frequently from that book (Sawyer 148). F. D. Maurice's *Prophets and Kings of the Old Testament*, published in 1852/3, gave an unperturbed response to heated discussions of *Isaiah in the field of Biblical Criticism and Historical Critical Method*. Matthew Arnold published four different works commenting on *Isaiah*[9], making his own significant contribution to the new biblical study methods, and moving the influence of those methods promptly into the classroom. He points out in his classroom text: "Isaiah is styled the greatest of the prophets, the evangelical prophet, and St. Jerome calls him not so much a prophet as an evangelist, and Ambrose told Augustine to read his prophecies the first thing after his conversion, and this prophet is of all Old Testament writers the one far most quoted in the New" (*Prophecy* 4).

That the book of *Isaiah* was receiving such attention is not as unusual as it might at first seem. Long known as the "fifth gospel," it has always held a unique place as a text combining the prophet, poet and evangelist. Even intratextually Isaiah has a unique place because, as Arnold points out, "this prophet is of all Old Testament writers the one far most quoted in the New" (*Prophecy* 4).[10] Amongst early Church Fathers, *Isaiah* had particular influence on the writings of Augustine, and Jerome claimed that it contains "all the mysteries of Christ" (Sawyer 43, 48). In its role as Messianic prophecy and a call to Gentiles, *Isaiah* has worked its way significantly into Chaucer, Dante, Dunbar, Milton, Bunyan, Herbert, Shakespeare, Mendelssohn, Brahms, Byrd, Bach, Pope, Byron, Shelley – to name but a few. In the late eighteenth century Robert Lowth's *Isaiah: a New Translation*, ensured that *Isaiah* remained a text of principal literary interest. As widely read for Lowth's introductory comments on the relation of prophetic and poetic language as for the translation itself, this and Lowth's other writings on *Isaiah* were especially notable in their influence on Coleridge, Wordsworth and Blake. That Isaiah the prophet was also a poet was a significant attraction to both preRomantics and Romantics. He was a model for them to imitate.[12]

Being a text of such historical and literary significance – the "fifth gospel"[13] – and yet, safely, not a gospel, *Isaiah* became the perfect test case for the Historical Critical Method. Its aptness was furthered by the discussion over 'Deutero-Isaiah.' As scholars considered the possibility of the book actually having two authors (the possibility of a Tertio-Isaiah was yet to be raised), many questions arose in regards to who had actually written the book, when it was written, what the actual identity was of those referred to in the text, what explanations there were for apparent inconsistencies, and what were the probable text sources. Many Victorians held the King James Version of the Bible in such high esteem that some were even unaware that it was a translation; resistance to a new translation was high amongst the general population (McGrath 301, 302). That such questions were challenging the accuracy of a long-accepted translation was disturbing for many people, and the suggestion that the ink in their 'Authorized Versions' might also have possible errors in regards to authorship, that there might be further inconsistencies, was for some plain heresy. Prominent public figures, such as George Eliot, John Ruskin, and Leslie Stephen, lost their faith over some of these issues. Wrote Arnold: "This is what everyone sees to constitute the special moral feature of our times: *the masses* are losing the Bible and its religion" (*Dogma* 175). In large part it seemed like the church was in a divide, either liberally welcoming this new and revolutionary trend in biblical scholarship or closing conservative doors soundly. And in the midst of this weighted, vested discussion sat the nonconforming George MacDonald, with his love of the book of *Isaiah*, and his insistence upon the import of the poesis within it.

Any reader of MacDonald familiar also with *Isaiah* will quickly recognize particular themes from *Isaiah* informing MacDonald's writing, as the above review of *Isaiah*'s appearances within his work indicates. Such themes include: the call to obedience, responsibility to social justice, the primacy of Light over darkness, the theme of servanthood, the interconnectedness of the people and the land, the realization that "nobleness of thought" is impotent without nobleness "of deed" (*Phantastes* 138). Perhaps the most obvious image correlation between Isaiah and *The Princess and Curdie* is Curdie's preparation for a mission he has offered to go on even though he does not know what it will entail. Just like Isaiah in *Isaiah* 6, with his renowned "Here am I, send me," Curdie is commissioned before a royal throne, prepared with coals. Both Isaiah and Curdie confess to deeds ill done. Both are given the means to assess people's hearts, and the weight of a message the people will not want to hear. And both accept the mission.

But this is far from all: the fine details of correlations abound throughout the story – even down to the specific actions of the caterpillar creature (*Isaiah* 33:4; *Curdie* 181) and the maggoty scullery (*Isaiah* 14:11; *Curdie* 181). Wider strokes include such parallels as when Peter and Curdie walk in the mines and "see a great light" – the great-great grandmother (*Curdie* ch.6; *Is*.9:2).[14] In the mine Curdie and Peter are told, rather startlingly: "And now I am going to tell you what no one knows but myself: you, Peter, and your wife both have the blood of the royal family in your veins. I have been trying to cultivate your family tree, every branch of which is known to me, and I expect Curdie to turn out a blossom on it. Therefore I have been training him for a work that must soon be done" (53). Similar words are said again and again by the prophet: "The Lord formed me from the womb to be his servant, to bring Jacob to him again"(Is.49:5); "Thou shalt inherit the land forever, the branch of my planting, the work of my hand" (*Is*.60:21); "And there shall come forth a rod out of the stem of Jesse, and a Branch shall grow out of his roots: And the spirit of the Lord shall rest upon him, the spirit of wisdom and understanding, the spirit of counsel and might [...] and he shall not judge after the sight of his eyes, neither reprove after the hearing of his ears" (*Isaiah* 11:1-3). Israel shall: " take root...blossom and bud" (*Isaiah* 27:6). Thus is Curdie of royal seed as Isaiah is of royal seed, and soon he is, as bold and wise counselor, to judge men with his hands rather than eyes or ears.[15] Lina matches all too well the description of "a little child shall lead them" (*Isaiah* 11:6), the creature with the hand of a child leading her group of Uglies, together numbering fifty, and making Curdie not unlike the Isaiahan description of the prophet being a "captain of fifty" (*Isaiah* 3:3). In both texts the palace of corrupt courtiers, who poison wine, is cleansed by wild beasts (*Curdie* 173-183; *Isaiah* 28:7,8; *Isaiah* 57:9)[16] In battle, the five face thousands, and victory is enabled by their ensign on a hill, with a cloud as doves also coming to the rescue. *Isaiah* 30:17 tells the same story.[17] Well over a hundred direct textual correlations exist between the two texts, including exact quotations.

But a look at *Isaiah* within the writings of MacDonald's mentor, Frederick Denison Maurice, quickly reveals that MacDonald has more than just the biblical text of *Isaiah* in mind. Maurice's *Prophets and Kings* proves to be a surprisingly useful tool with which to explore the interplay between *Curdie* and *Isaiah*; when MacDonald wrote of Curdie's adventure he seems to have been particularly influenced by *Isaiah* as seen through Maurice's eyes. Maurice's sermons deeply enter the *story* of *Isaiah*, and they draw his listeners into the story, to help them understand the book's complexities. They also guide the unfolding of Curdie's tale. Those sermons, in the same manner as the novel, detail the ermine-covered mountains and a degenerate hero who requires a rejuvenation before he is able to rescue a further degenerate people; they sketch the progression to the designed royal heritage of a protagonist who continuously needs to see the truth beneath the surface of appearances. And it is not just the generalities of Maurice that correlate, but again a multiplicity of specifics.[18] In "Sermon XIII, 'The Vision of the King,'" a sermon beginning with the text of *Isaiah* 6:1, Maurice's description of Isaiah's vision parallels closely Curdie's 'commissioning' visits to the great-great grandmother, Queen Irene. In parts Maurice's descriptions appear the direct blueprint for MacDonald's book. It is, therefore, useful to notice how definitely Maurice's theological reading and commentary guide MacDonald – himself a seasoned writer and thinker at this point.[19] For example, Maurice tells us that in Isaiah's vision, "Each object was the counterpart of one that was then or had been at some time before his bodily eyes yet it did not borrow its shape or color from those visible things" (222). Just as for Curdie in his visits to the room of the great-great grandmother, a "bare garret, a heap of musty straw, a sunbeam, and a withered apple", or later, a moonbeam, a rickety spinning wheel, and an old withered woman, become completely transformed into glorious counterparts. Maurice tells us, "For it is true of earthly symbols, still more of heavenly visions, that they are meant to carry us out of words and above words; not so that we despise them or think lightly of them, but that we seeing the reality of the invisible may not be greatly disturbed by the processes and conceits of our minds" (222), and this invocation of centuries of discussion about the limitation of words to convey meaning is paralleled in the great-great grandmother's request of Curdie: "Listen to the wheel." For then we learn that to Curdie has been communicated something beyond even what the great-great grandmother can capture within words...yet Curdie is somehow able, again in a mysterious manner beyond words, to convey back some of his reception of this revelation to her, and she 'words' what she can of it, and the reader is able to read "something like the words of its song" (*Curdie* 64, 65).[20] Maurice tells us that it is the holiness of God that is being expressed ineffably in the seraphims' hymn, that which is beyond word and even beyond image. He writes of how the prophet says, "Woe is me! For I am undone! Because I am a man of unclean lips, and I dwell among a people of unclean lips. For mine eyes have seen the King, the Lord of Hosts"(223).

Curdie too first stands before the great-great grandmother "as a culprit, and worst of all, as one who had his confession yet to make." And as he makes his confession he comes to realize that it is not his most recent deed which he is in most need to confess, but rather that his whole way of living has become 'unclean', or, as Curdie himself phrases it, "the wrong had soaked all through me": although he had "done right for sometime," he had "forgotten how" and was now "doing the wrong of never wanting or trying to be better ... didn't want to hear the truth" (*Curdie* 30). He is like the prophet of whom Maurice says: "All his uncleanness had come from this. He and his people were impure because they had lost that common life and love which belonged to them while they were living as the people of God."[21] Maurice makes clear that,

> In such a revelation the discovery of personal evil comes first. The man does not look about him to compare his offences with those of other men and try which are the heavier. It is not this or that particular offence, no, nor a multitude of particular offences, that overwhelms him; it is the feeling of a root of bitterness; not 'I have

done this or that wrong,' but 'I am wrong.' Not however that this thought could long be separated from the one of which it must take precedence. "I dwell among a people of unclean lips." There is the same pollution in them which there is in me. Each of us is living to himself. Each is living apart from that God who has called us to be holy as He is. He is attended by obedient Spirits, Spirits united in obedience, working together as His servants, for the fulfillment of His purposes. We are separate and broken; every man following a way of his own; not a people, because we do not believe that a King is with us (224-5).

It is not long before the reader learns that the sin Curdie needs to repent of is the same sin from which the people of his country suffer. Yet he must first deal with his own faults before he his able to serve the great-great grandmother in his mission — a mission to the city where the people have ceased to believe that their King is one with them (let alone that the likes of the great-great grandmother may exist and thus is 'with them'), and where each has explicitly begun "living to himself" (Maurice 225), their "first fundamental principle (being) that every One should take of that One," their proclaimed responsibility the "well-being of the original self" (*Curdie* 189).

A thorough exploration of both Maurice's sermons and the book of *Isaiah* answers many of the perplexities that critics have with *The Princess and Curdie* — including the book's conclusion. For Maurice reiterates throughout his sermon series that the central message of *Isaiah* is this: that though the whole land be shaken and seem to die, the Prince of Peace shall never pass, that his word endures forever (Maurice 231) — a message which is also one of *Isaiah*'s most familiar and redundant refrains. Veiled as it is, I would argue that Maurice's interpretation of what he calls a key passage for understanding *Isaiah* is also a key for understanding what happens, what is being conveyed, at the end of *The Princess and Curdie*. All that MacDonald leaves of the mighty gold-filled rock, and the city which crowned it, is "a stone-obstructed river" (*Curdie* 221). Barely even a remnant. The very name of the town passes from the lips of men. However, the reader may remember that the city forms only part of this tale's setting...that the land of the miners, of even the mostly unkind villagers, yet remains. And perhaps even more important is the forest where the "Uglies" dwell — the Uglies for which we have even more hope now that we know that the woman-turned-Lina-with-the-hand-of-a-little-child has gone through her refining by rose-fire. Yet most importantly of all — and the Maurice-reading makes very clear that this is the crucial point — no child fears for the eternal great-great grandmother. She had been untouched by the former flood which had filled the countryside-castle for days and days – indeed when Curdie expressed fear for her, especially in knowing that the castle might fall, Irene had assured him that, "My grandmother is in no danger.....you see my grandmother knows all about it, and isn't frightened. I believe she could walk through that water and it wouldn't wet her a bit" (*Goblin* 303). The people of Gwyntystorm who were "worse even than in the old time"(*Curdie* 219) are now gone, but the great-great grandmother – the apparently eternal Princess Irene – is in no danger. She will carry on in being a lasting guiding light, a wise counselor, and as her name indicates, a Princess of Peace to her people.[22] This, in light of Maurice's reading, is the crux: that the reader does not see the continuation of any particular human person or family as the most important goodness – rather it is assurance in the eternal great-great grandmother that is essential. MacDonald does not explicitly state this, and although one may wonder why, it appears inherently true.

Maurice tells us that he has belabored so carefully this part of *Isaiah*,

> because I believe that it leads us into the very heart of *Isaiah*'s teaching, and that all the portions of it which we shall have to consider hereafter, are but expansions of the hints in this opening vision.... And if there should come a convulsion in that land, such as neither thou nor thy fathers have known, be sure that it signifies the removal of such things as can be shaken, that those things which cannot be shaken may remain (235).[23]

The city ends in destruction: is this MacDonald's intimation that it has all been for naught, that his faith is in ruins? Aside from all else, such an interpretation does not follow coherently on the tail of such a story (were the tale written centuries earlier one might hear calls for a 'deutero-MacDonald'). But reading Maurice gives clarity to a reader still convinced this is a representation of calamity in MacDonald's faith. Gwyntystorm had been redeemed by the royal prophet who was sent by the great-great grandmother.[24] But when he is gone, and the people forget yet again all that they have been taught, including their own redemption, this time their descent is complete. Nothing is left of the city once its foundational pillars "left standing to bear the city" are overmined in greed, and collapse (219). "And from the girth of an oak of a thousand years, they chipped them down to that of a fir tree of fifty...one day...the whole city fell with a roaring crash...then there was a great silence. Where the mighty rock once towered, crowded with homes and crowned with a palace, now rushes and raves a stone obstructed rapid of a river. All around spreads a wilderness of wild deer, and the very name of Gwyntystorm had ceased from the lips of men" (219-221). In light of Maurice, the reader understands that it is not the continuation of any particular human person or family that is the most important goodness, but rather, the eternal nature of the great-great grandmother. Instead of making this explicit, MacDonald makes it implicit – and yet inherent to the cohesiveness of the tale as a whole. She has always been greater than just this one tale – even allusions by the king and Curdie's mother keep us minded of that (*Curdie* 23,167).

The closer one reads Maurice, the more light is shed on plot decisions and designs within *Curdie*. It is worth reminding ourselves, however, that not all perplexities are cleared by reading Maurice. Reading him is but the beginning, because for MacDonald, as indicated earlier, there is always a multiplicity of engagement with other sources. While *Isaiah* provides, arguably, the dominant framework, it is still only one of the many sources shaping *The Princess & Curdie* – for other texts include biblical tales, ancient pagan myths, Scottish folklore; MacDonald also draws upon Dante, Coleridge, Shakespeare, Shelley – a vast treasure trove; deceptively simple in appearance, this tale actually is very intentional in its complex array of interweaving and re-presenting.[25] And a close read reveals quotations and explicit allusions in abundance. This is a MacDonald trademark.[26] Consistent with that trademark is the intimation that something more than mere imitation is occurring here. George MacDonald uses the commentary of his mentor Maurice as a veritable guide. However, alert to the significant nineteenth century dialogue about reception and evaluation of biblical text, and aware that *Isaiah* is frequently used as the test case text for this Historical Critical dialogue, MacDonald predictably embeds his own studied answer to that conversation. He actually engages with a particular hermeneutic method, used by Maurice, yet pushes it even further in a direction being given little thought by those involved in the exegetical debate. He situates it in a direction diametrically opposed to the one being successfully touted by a man not shy about his actual abhorrence of Maurice's methods: Matthew Arnold.[27]

Stephen Prickett's *Romanticism & Religion* established that a study of the differences between contemporaries Maurice, Arnold, and MacDonald has much to divulge to the student of nineteenth century criticism.[28] Bringing into dialogue their mutual interest in the text of *Isaiah* both intensifies and clarifies some of the pertinent issues, and the result is perhaps surprising in its significance. Arnold himself gave considerable time and attention to the concerns of criticism in the context of the book of *Isaiah*; he actually wrote four complete works on *Isaiah*. The ethos of these works stands in direct conflict with Maurice's writings – and with the writings of MacDonald. Did MacDonald have Arnold in mind when he wrote *The Princess & Curdie*? A close look at this seemingly simple fairy tale certainly indicates MacDonald believed an important element had been overlooked in the ongoing critical dialogue – or, more precisely with Arnold, had been deliberately devalued – and MacDonald consciously draws his readers right into this element: the essential story-ness of the text.

Maurice and MacDonald read *Isaiah*

In the midst of the culturally significant discussion about how to read and assess scripture – a key issue in the Victorian academy – Arnold's voice was that of educated reason, calling out for the historicity of the Bible as an influential text, as a time-proven guide to morality and ethics and a beautiful literary resource, not to be lost merely because some of the historical facts seemed not to hold true, and some of the traditional translations seem inadequate (Arnold *Bible Reading* 3-4). Maurice's voice, though far too liberal for many "evangelicals" of the day, was yet a considerable distance from Arnold: even if traditional understandings of the text – both in content and history – were being challenged, he did not see this as a threat to faith and the greater Truth of the text. Maurice saw a place for the questions and was not threatened by the answers – neither those he agreed with nor those he disagreed with. He was convinced, however, that scripture was more than a well-crafted morality guide. Although he did not wholly endorse the Historical Critical Method, recent scholarship has shown that he engaged with it, and more positively, than he has previously been given credit for (Rogerson 33; Prickett).[29] His major point of contention appeared to be when the Bible was objectified, when it was made "an object that was in an inferior position to the critic" (Rogerson 53). He saw the Historical Method critics as "not sufficiently literary in their approach"; ultimately, "they remain[ed] systematisers" (Prickett 133). He wanted readers to see that the God engaging with humans in Old Testament times was the same one with which they of the nineteenth century could relate. To endorse a historical reading in this manner is to say that in and of itself, before the text even folds out into the Messianic readings relevant to Christians, that text has important things to say about its own world, and thus to the reader about their world. This is a claim Maurice scholar J.W. Rogerson calls a "brave thing to do in Britain in the Church of England in 1852" (35) – and it was a theological claim which Arnold certainly could not accept.

Prickett's *Romanticism and Religion* is helpful in calling to mind something often overlooked in the contemporary specialization of disciplines: "Anyone who has read both literary criticism and theology in the Victorian period soon comes to realize how deeply the two are intertwined. The nature of literary criticism (and the kinds of sensibility it implies) cannot be understood in the nineteenth century without reference to contemporary theology, just as the contemporary theology cannot be understood without reference to the literary criticism of the period" (4). The explorations of both Maurice and his mentor Coleridge into the multiple levels in which Scripture works, how it is stereoscopic in its function of revelation, how language points beyond itself, and how it is both the vehicle and symbol used as history shapes and conditions the way we interpret the present, all contributed to MacDonald's understanding of Story – biblical and otherwise. Coleridge's concept of biblical narrative as "living educts of the Imagination" (*The Statesman's Manual* as qtd in Prickett 17), drawing out and eliciting something deep within us, fortified MacDonald's belief that stories could indeed "wake up" something within the reader or listener ("Imagination" 319).

In *Curdie*, MacDonald has represented elements of the book of *Isaiah*, educing them from the "living educt" of one story into the living educt of another...rather than etherizing them upon the table of exegesis. Curdie's new story, conceived in part through the old story of *Isaiah* – a text seen by the Church to be both independently complete and simultaneously a forerunner of the Gospel – reflects back upon that old story of *Isaiah* while giving light as well to all of its later representations. For MacDonald, this intertextual interweaving of universal truths that enhances the reality – each of the other – is revelation functioning on multiple levels of time, space, and experience. He obviously delights in this as much as did all his literary mentors before him, those who not only loved the interplay of Scripture within itself, but also with the Ancient Myths and great classics – think of Dante, Milton, Shakespeare!

As poet, MacDonald is acutely aware of the challenge of ambiguity that language brings to scripture. Each word can carry with it a myriad of overtones, allusions, insinuations; language is polysemous. Particular phrases are embedded with histories. Yet despite these accompanying challenges, MacDonald delights in the multiplicity of meanings and ever deepening intertextual dialogue.[31] He discovered in his own struggles with translation that it is virtually impossible to carry all of a context over into a world of another language which functions within its own context. And yet he does believe it is worth the effort to convey as much as is possible if the text is important (*Rampolli* v)[32]– he spent over twenty years struggling to make his own translation of Novalis more adequately representative of the text (Sadler 295).[33] He was keenly aware of the challenges of translating his own work.[34] And he had a growing awareness of the inadequacies of some existing translations of the Bible.[35] "After all," he says "translation is but a continuous effort after the impossible. There is in it a general difficulty whose root has a thousand ramifications, the whole affair being but an accommodation of difficulties, and a perfect translation from one language into another is a thing that cannot be effected. One is tempted even to say there is no such thing as a synonym."[36] MacDonald knew, and found to be true, Coleridge's proposition that as "living educts" of the imagination, language grows from within a community, developing as it grows, imbued with the story and belief of that people. The language and text of the King James Bible played this role in Britain as no other text ever had (or has since). And yet that shaping is not something exclusively unique to the King James Bible; it is a role that other texts (sometimes themselves shaped specifically by the King James Version) also fill. Coleridge believed that the symbolic language of the Bible "changed the way a reader thinks and feels," yet he also believed that all great literature functioned in this fashion, expressing more than any one reader could know in any one time or place (Prickett 26). And this brings us back to MacDonald's words on why he writes what he writes: "The best thing you can do for your fellow, next to rousing his conscience, is – not to give him things to think about, but to wake things up that are in him; or say, to make him think things for himself" (*Imagination 319*). And thus he contributes what he can to 'knowing God' by writing stories like *The Princess and Curdie*, stories that might just act so that the reader, or listener, is "woken up."

Rogerson claims that Maurice allows that "a writer who was concerned to understand the principles of God's government could meditate upon an old story, and re-present it. In re-presenting it, this writer would be less concerned with what had originally happened than with bringing out the truths about God's Government that he saw in the story" (52).[37]

This is an accurate description of what MacDonald does with *Isaiah* and *Curdie*. He weaves aspects of great literature – taking the language and symbols he believes to convey Truth – to present it again. Perhaps for some readers this re-presentation will help what MacDonald sees as the 'truth of the story' to go yet deeper. Whether the reader makes a direct connection to the story – is not important; what is important is that he is, in Maurice's words, "bringing out the truths about God's Government that he saw in the story" of *Isaiah*. The resulting work offers an exegetical hermeneutic of *Isaiah* that stands in significant contrast to that of Arnold's contemporary works on *Isaiah*.

MacDonald both cared for and respected Arnold, but he disagreed with him in regards to biblical and literary criticism. His disagreement is evident in the manner in which *The Princess and Curdie* stands in significant contrast to Arnold's work on *Isaiah*. Indeed, particularly as Docherty and Manlove have suggested,

MacDonald has a propensity for conversing with contemporaries in his fictional texts; it is conceivable that the Maurice-influenced *The Princess and Curdie* was, in part, a response to Arnold.

Both MacDonald and Arnold agreed that there was a need for a more accurate translation of the Bible, but as to what such efforts might achieve, they did not agree. MacDonald pointed out that words could be translated in different ways, could hold more than one meaning – but more importantly, that the text as a whole was infinitely full of multiple-dimensioned truths which could never be successfully explained or contained by academic analysis. Indeed a fairy tale served to show just how full and complex even part of that text could be. Arnold, however, was convinced that academic advances, scientific advances, meant that all ambiguity would be – and should be – eradicated. Arnold fears people will say: "The Bible takes for granted [stories] and depends on the truth of [them]; what, then, can rational people have to do with the Bible?" (*Dogma* 175).

Arnold's Discord

While Maurice may have felt that if forced to choose, the truths were more important than the facts, Arnold believed that the facts were everything. "Myth" being a manner of conveying something "wider and deeper than the rational and propositional" (Prickett 240) was, for Arnold, dangerous and deceiving. Maurice had welcomed Coleridge showing how deeply theology and literature are inextricably entwined. Arnold saw the Bible as a beautiful piece of literature and argued vociferously for the cultural import of not just the Bible, but of the King James Version specifically. However, he feared that legend, superstition and fairy tale[38] had "grown up around the basic moral truths of Christianity" and were, "in danger of strangling it" (*Literature and Dogma* as qtd in Prickett 213). Arnold goes on to write:

> That men should, by help of their imagination, take short cuts to what they ardently desire, whether the triumph of Israel or the triumph of Christianity, should tell themselves fairy-tales about it, should make these fairy-tales the basis for what is far more sure and solid than the fairy-tales, the desire itself- all this has in it, we repeat, nothing which is not natural, nothing blamable…In religion, above all, *extra-belief* is in itself no matter, assuredly, for blame. *The object of religion is conduct*; and if a man helps himself in his conduct by taking an object of hope and presentiment as if it were an object of certainty, he may even be said to gain thereby an advantage.

And yet there is always a drawback to man's advantage in thus treating, when he deals with religion and conduct, what is extra-belief and not certain [,] as if it were a matter of certainty, and in making it his ground of action. *He pays for it.* The time comes when he discovers that it is not certain; and then the whole certainty of religion seems discredited, and the basis of conduct gone. (*Dogma* 80,81)

Literature and Dogma shows how Arnold was persistent in attempting to demythologize religious belief, showing that modern man needed to move beyond "fairy tale" belief in scripture (58), and, as Prickett phrases it, "separate the kernel of abstract truth from its poetic husk" (214). Rather than embracing an existing paradox, as had Coleridge, Arnold could only believe in "one world." As Prickett explains: "For him, values must ultimately be deduced from the same material world as science and technology, because there was and could be no other" (216). For Arnold, this one world was decidedly not multidimensional as it was for MacDonald. The importance of this emphasis becomes evident in Arnold's various studies of *Isaiah*.[39] Arnold indicates that it is possible for a translator to aim to be "purely scientific" when translating, "to render his original with perfect accuracy" (Arnold *Prophecy* 11).[40] Indeed he lauds T.K. Cheney's objective with *Isaiah*, in 1870, which is "simply scientific, to render the original with exactness" (*Prophecy* 11). Arnold calls Cheney "one of that new band of Oxford scholars who so well deserve to attract our interest, because they have the idea, which the older Oxford has had so far too little, of separated and systematized studies" (13).[41] Arnold believes that, "To have one version universally received is of the greatest advantage" (2). This articulation may not sound surprising until one stops to consider that Arnold, like MacDonald, Coleridge (and even Maurice) is a poet. The desire for a single sufficient translation of this Hebrew poetry is not as disconcerting as the implication that Arnold believes that such a feat is possible.

Arnold is careful to make clear that such a feat is not possible for him, for his own grasp of the language required is not sufficient. And so with his commentaries, while awaiting the forthcoming "officially revised version," he offers something different. He differentiates between "correcting the English Bible" – the task he sets out to do with *Isaiah* – and "retranslation in an aim of scientific exactness" (*Prophecy* 15). He claims that any alterations he is making to the text are merely to remove comprehension difficulties. He is intent on making clear that he leaves "the physiognomy and movement of the authorized version quite unchanged"(1). Arnold is obviously conscious that any change whatsoever to the King James Version raises a delicate issue. Again and again, almost to a point of paranoia, he stresses that the old text of the English Bible is "a literary work of the highest order"; indeed, "the Book of Isaiah, as it stands in our Bibles, is this in a double way. By virtue of the original it is a monument of the Hebrew genius at its best, and by virtue of the translation it is a monument of the English language at its best...the power of the English version must not be sacrificed" (12).

Yet what Arnold *does* change is curious. His mandate is clarity: "A clear sense is the indispensable thing" (8). For Arnold this means that he *will* make corrections to the text where the King James Version is confusing. However he will not change any text just because he knows the translation to be wrong – not if keeping that wrong translation retains clarity. "Even where the authorized version seems wrong, I have not always, if its words give a clear sense, thought it necessary to change them" ...only if the correct translation gives a higher "poetic propriety and beauty" than the King James Version will he change it (8). And yet he had said he regarded it "quite forbidden" to "alter by guess the original" no matter how "pleasing and ingenious" (10-11). The very man who has called for a "scientific" treatment of the text, is here approaching the text himself in an entirely subjective fashion, taking it upon himself to decide when he can assist a portion of the text to a higher beauty, and, when to allow the translation of the text to stand incorrect. While disagreeing with Maurice that "truth" is more important than facts, here Arnold is acting in a manner that claims that beauty is more important than either truth or fact. Hardly a scientific approach. Arnold seems truly a man of Victorian disillusionment. He is torn between wanting indisputable and provable theological clarity, and yet remaining intrinsically a poet by nature. He has been persuaded of the power of science to prove all things with concrete fact, and yet he is still in love with the abstract poesis of language (12-14). What Arnold tries to argue is quite opposite to Maurice, who had claimed: "the mere sentimental feeling which attaches a particular passage to a particular name will be readily sacrificed by a lover of truth. The more firmly we believe the Bible to be from God, the less serious will that sacrifice seem to us" (qtd in Rogerson 34).

Arnold in his quandary is an interesting contrast to MacDonald, whose university training was in physics and chemistry. MacDonald continued to love and be fascinated by science, but he saw Science as another dimension to the same truth of which Poetry was a part. Indeed he says: "Poetry is as true as Science, and Science is holy as Poetry" ("Development" 51).[42] In the essay, "A Sketch of Individual Development," which makes utterly clear MacDonald's stance on this issue, he writes of a young poet who, in "a new phase of experience...has wandered over the border of what is commonly called science," and is now unable to grasp that true science and true poetry cannot be at odds. MacDonald shows the youth struggling between "quantitative analysis" and the poetry of Coleridge. It seems fairly clear that this "young poet" is a Type of young Matthew Arnold (*Development* 51).[43]

MacDonald is comfortable with the interplay of science and poetry. For this man who writes of multiple dimensions and the refraction of light, and for whom inexactitude implies a possibility of even more truths rather than a proof of none, the very sense of fairy tale is an inextricable aspect of the essence of scripture. That very thing that Arnold believes obscures the essence of scripture, MacDonald insists is crucially inextricable from it. Arnold insists that the essence of scripture is moral conduct, and MacDonald believes that the import of moral conduct is something that the mythic element of scripture will convey; being woven into the very fabric of that element, moral conduct itself is *not* the purpose of scripture or religion. That purpose, MacDonald claims, is the very poetic – and non-systematic – revelation of the love of God. MacDonald seems to have Arnold's ideas in mind when he describes Gwyntystorm's celebration on "Religion Day," when the priests "talked ever about improvement": "The book which had, of late years, come to be considered the most sacred, was called *The Book of Nations*, and consisted of proverbs, and history traced through custom: from it the first priest chose his text; and his text was, 'Honesty Is the Best Policy'" (*Curdie* 188-90).[44] When the head priest is removed by one of Curdie's beasts, he is dropped "into the dust hole among the remnants of a library whose age had destroyed its value in the eyes of the chapter." And then the new priests rename themselves "The Party of Decency" (188-190). MacDonald makes clear with these images that a religion or movement *based* on good moral conduct is vacuous, and such a venture, which believes itself above the wisdom of the ages, will remain ineffectual.

MacDonald's "extra-belief" frees him in a way Arnold's lack does not.[45] Arnold believes that "the object of religion is conduct," and that any "extra-belief" runs the risk of setting one up for disillusionment and thus a loss of even the "basis of conduct" (*Dogma* 80). He also believes that scripture can be translated with exactitude and that one ultimate version can result. And yet Arnold spends pages and pages dancing around the revered reputation of the English Bible with which he is about to tamper...in the name of clarity. MacDonald, who is tied to an old-fashioned "fairy tale" belief, full of things difficult to prove, is infinitely more comfortable with re-presenting the "word of God." In part it seems that for Arnold, the King James Version has become more "holy" than what he calls "the original." For MacDonald, the "original" is undoubtedly more holy than the King James Version, and still yet the *essence* of the "original" more holy than the words upon the page.

But MacDonald the poet goes further than making clear that no single English translation could ever adequately represent the "original" Hebrew or Greek scriptures. He is so bold as to retell aspects of the stories himself, within his own tales...his own answer to Arnold's attempt to "clarify" scripture. Rather than anguishing over "scientific exactitude" versus clarity of phrase versus higher beauty, he re-presents that which is mythic within the same medium: the ancient tradition (used even in scripture) of story telling story, of story conveying the meaning of that which words alone cannot capture. It is arrestingly ironic that it is Arnold who writes:

> Whoever began with laying hold on this series of chapters [*Isaiah*] as a whole, would have a starting-point and lights of unsurpassed value for getting a conception of the course of man's history and development as a whole. If *but for a certain number* of readers this could happen, what access would they thus gain to a new life, unknown to them hitherto! What an extending of their horizons, what a lifting them out of the present, what a suggestion of hope and courage! (*Prophecy* 32-33. Italics added)

It is indeed ironic that these words come from Arnold because one realizes, when comparing the work of these two authors, that for "a certain number of readers" who have followed their imaginations into the fairy story of *The Princess and Curdie*, it is *MacDonald* who has accomplished exactly the extending and uplifting that Arnold describes.

Arnold had argued that the age of fairy stories – of extra-belief – was past. MacDonald's response, guided and shaped by Maurice and Coleridge, was that the age of fairy stories – the age of Bible Stories – is the age of humanity. One could be so bold as to say that for MacDonald, Maurice, and Coleridge an age of poesis is an age of Truth – and thus they do not believe that the age shall ever pass, although at times it may suffer from the lack of apprehension of that Truth. Coleridge had stood as a reminder that there was an ancient tradition of religious thought that was not "systematic," an aeons-old tradition in which the theological and the literary were inseparable, a tradition in which poesis was an essential means of conveying Truth. Maurice and MacDonald included themselves in that tradition, and saw in it an answer to a vacuous sterility that they felt was being created by the polarized approaches to scripture in their day.[46] Maurice, Coleridgean in his understanding of Scripture and Story, did not simply deconstruct the text in his sermons. While exploring the Truths he found within the text, instead of doing so by sifting away the story, he attempted rather to make the story more accessible, flushing out its sight and sound, attempting to draw those attending further in. He is much freer with the text than the agnostic Arnold, because he values it so highly – *because* he believes that it is "from God."

MacDonald, aware of the contemporary theological dialogue which intimately involved Isaiah – so valued, so influential, and yet so difficult to understand – seems to respond to Arnold's anti-Coleridgean, anti-Maurician approach by showing, by doing, what his mentors had talked about. Rather than attempting to clarify each and every aspect of the text in a supposedly ultimate "clear sense," he shifts the angle. Almost subversively. It is obvious that he has 'meditated deeply upon an old story' (in the words of Maurice) and is now "re-presenting it...[seeking to bring] out the truths about God's Government that he saw in the story," in true Maurician fashion. He has spent time with the Hebrew text, as well as the King James Version and Maurice's explorations. And the story itself is simultaneously shaped in a tribute to both Maurice and Coleridge, and contains many allusions to both. Also, MacDonald takes care to reveal that the text remains as contemporary and relevant as Maurice has argued the book of *Isaiah* to be – whether regarding such 'Isaiahan' issues as trust and obedience, political deceit, materialism, or social welfare. Should MacDonald's readers return to the *Isaiah* text they might be doing so with renewed interest or understanding. If they do not, they have nonetheless journeyed through a story that seeks to re-present some of the same truths.

MacDonald goes further than not divorcing 'Literature and Dogma;' he says that such a thing is simply impossible. He will not even allow that Science and Poetry can be divided. He delights in bringing the tools of Science to the text – not only to better understand the meaning or context of a word, but to better understand the poetry! He explores theories of evolution and of geology, and he uses these explorations to enrich metaphors and deepen understanding of what he believes to be Truth. *The Princess and Curdie* begins with a lengthy poetic lesson in one of the trendiest Victorian sciences: geology.[47] And MacDonald revels in being able to wrestle with the technicalities of linguistics as he mines the Greek and Hebrew languages. His approach is neither Scientific nor Poetic – in his desire to stay true to the text he shows that he does not believe that 'either/or' is actually possible.[48] And Arnold's inconsistency is, for MacDonald, proof of this.

In *The Princess and Curdie*, MacDonald enters a tradition and a dialogue poetically exploring a famous, oft quoted, notoriously-difficult-to-read text. He unveils its ability to function on multiple levels of time, space, and experience. The result is a gift to both those who value *Isaiah* merely for its literary and historic import, as well as those who consider it one of yet deeper worth. An engagement with this intent of MacDonald's puts the ending of *The Princess and Curdie* – and indeed its role in the context of the story as a whole – into an entirely new perspective than one of conclusive doom and despair. As Arnold laboured over his commentaries on *Isaiah*, seeking to attain a single "clear sense," he mused that, "To make a great work of soul pass into the general mind is not easy [.....] the more these chapters sink into the mind and are apprehended, the more manifest is their connexion with universal history, the key they offer to it, the truth of the ideal they propose for it" (*Prophecy* 31, 32). Instead of telling *his* readers what to think, MacDonald invites them into the Story – a living Story. It is Story that passes a "great work of soul" not only into the mind, but into the soul.

> When His Majesty was awake, the princess read to him - one storybook after another; and whatever she read, the king listened as if he had never heard anything so good before, making out in it the wisest meanings. Every now and then he asked for a piece of bread and a little wine, and every time he ate and drank he slept (*Curdie* 150).

Endnotes

1. Joseph Sigman also suggests that the nihilistic readings do not ring true – his Jungian reading suggests rather that it points to "deeper levels of existence" (193). Sigman does take other MacDonald texts, and even some biblical texts, into account, yet interpretation is determinedly focused through a Jungian lens.
2. Although Prickett has pointed out the need to consider MacDonald contextually as a Victorian, David Robb the need to consider him contextually as a Scot, and Colin Manlove the need to consider him as part of a Scottish *and* Christian tradition of fantasy, few have actually done so over the last couple of decades, and fewer have integrated these aspects. Manlove and John Docherty have pointed out how willing MacDonald is to engage in intertextual dialogue with his contemporaries, and one suspects that their discoveries are but the first of many yet to come. (The papers from the centennial conference have revealed renewed interest in contextual methodology.)
3. "Indeed, I have studied [Shakespeare] more than any book except the Gospels." Throughout the letters MacDonald refers to reading his Bible daily – with occasional 'seasons of fallow' (qtd in Sadler 275), indicating that such breaks are

the exception, rather than the norm. He is particularly delighted when he can read the Greek New Testament daily (275, 278, 283, etc).

4. "For he has come, The Word of God, that we may know God: every word of his then, as needful to the knowing of himself, is needful to the knowing of God, and we must understand, as far as we may, every one of his words and every one of his actions, which, with him, were only another form of word. I believe this the immediate end of our creation. And I believe that this will at length result in the unraveling for us of what must now, more or less, appear to every man the knotted and twisted coil of the universe" (Imagination 2). "But I do say that all my hope, all my joy, all my strength are in [God]; that all my theories of life and growth are rooted in him"; "I will try to show what we might be, may be, must be, shall be – and something of the struggle to gain it" (qtd in Sadler 153; 288).

5. The title character of this book is based on MacDonald's revered father, who for him was also a spiritual mentor (Greville MacDonald 323). Henceforth the biography by MacDonald's son will be referred to as *Greville*.

6. Indeed the word "comfort", which begins Isaiah 40:1 in the familiar phrase "Comfort, comfort my people," appears in various forms 123 times throughout the novel – surely a few too many to be unintentional!

7. 'Jacob' refers to the nation of Israel, as addressed through the words of *Isaiah*.

8. Furthering this revived interest was *The Works of John Newton* (author of "Amazing Grace"), published in 1820, which contained a series of 38 sermons featuring the Handel libretto (Sawyer 8). The MacDonald family was amongst the fervent admirers of Handel's *The Messiah,* and Louisa and some of the girls were in the Handel Choir of the Crystal Palace (ref: archived letters). MacDonald referred to *The Messiah* in his sermons and novels, and his son Greville talks of "Handel's Largo from the far Jerusalem" being one of the modes of drawing to conclusion their evening services (Greville 508). Louisa famously pounded away at the Hallelujah chorus on a church organ during an earthquake in Borghiderra (Greville 515). In *The Elect Lady*, a performing Handel is described: "I saw him with his white rapt face, looking like a prophet of the living God sent to speak out the heart of the mystery of truth!" (113).

9. *A Bible-Reading for Schools: The Great Prophecy of Israel's Restoration (Isaiah, Chapters 40-66), Arranged and Edited for Young Learners (with commentary).* London: Macmillan, 1872; "Isaiah of Jerusalem, " an article in *Nineteenth Century* 13 (April, May 1883): 587-603, 779-94; *Isaiah XLLXVI; with the Shorter Prophecies Allied to It* (1875), arranged and edited with notes, Macmillan and Co., London; *Isaiah of Jerusalem, in the Authorized English Version with An Introduction, Corrections and Notes*, London, Macmillan, 1883.

10. And Sawyer points out that it is indeed the most directly quoted or alluded Old Testament text, with possible exception of the Psalms, within the Gospels, *The Book of Acts*, Paul's epistles and *The Book of Revelation* -- the last being notably shaped by *Isaiah*'s imagery (21).

11. Augustine translates Isaiah 7: 9 into the Greek as: "If you do not believe, you will not understand" – words that mind us of Irene and Curdie both, in both *"Princess"* books.

12. William Blake is the most explicit of these (Sawyer 163); Coleridge makes use of Lowth's translation in his 1795 lectures, and through Hugh Blair, Lowth's thought on *Isaiah* also influences Wordsworth's *Prelude*. Blake also, in his writings on *Isaiah*, reveals his familiarity with Lowth (Jeffrey 381). This distinction is not surprising when one discovers that in his introduction Lowth reconsiders what is understood to be the basic elements of poetry – and pointing out that for the Hebrews, poetry was not necessarily defined by meter or rhyme (Lowth introduction).

13. The "fifth gospel" is a term that has come to be applied to *Isaiah* precisely because of its perceived integral relation with the four Gospel texts.

14. Isaiah passage in full: "The people who walked in darkness saw a great light" – a passage traditionally understood to mean the light of God.

15. Curdie's proper name, Conrad, is Old German for "bold counselor" or "wise counselor" – another phrase from *Isaiah* made particularly familiar through Handel's *Messiah* (Isaiah 9:6). Curdie's parents being Peter, "the rock", and Joan (feminine form of John), "God is gracious," Curdie has a rich lineage indeed. The Celtic church (through Lindisfarne and Iona) deferred to the authority of St John, 'the contemplative'. The Roman church traced its lineage from the authority of Peter, the man of faithful action, the rock on whom Christ had promised to build his Church. In 644 this diversity was addressed in a significant and divisive synod. The Great-great-grandmother has indeed been intentional in her reunifying 'genetic engineering' of Curdie's lineage.

16. As the once imprisoned now "take them captives, whose captives they were" (Isaiah 14:1): "woe to those that spoilest…thou shalt spoil" (Isaiah 33:1). The worst is reserved for the treacherous courtiers who "wentest to the king with ointment, and didst increase thy perfumes, and didst send thy messengers far off, and didst debase thyself" (Isaiah 57:9) – MacDonald shows them doing these precise things, as they falsely flatter the king, lead his messages astray, and poison him. Not only do they poison the king's wine, but they also deny "thy bread to the hungry" king (Isaiah 58:7, *Curdie*, p.140).

17. "There were thousands to one against them, and the King and his three

companions were in the greatest possible danger. A dense cloud came over the sun, and sank rapidly toward the earth,"(*Curdie* 210). The four companions on the field plus the one above on the hill will be the victors, and *Isaiah* 30:17 reads: "One Thousand shall flee at the rebuke of one; at the rebuke of five shall ye flee: till ye be left as a beacon upon the top of the mountain, and as an ensign on a hill." "Who are these that fly as a cloud, and as doves to their window?" (*Isaiah* 60:8): the cloud is indeed an army of the Great-great-grandmother's white doves. Down they swoop on the invaders, and "it was a storm in which the wind was birds, and the sea men" (*Curdie* 210): "But the wicked [were] like the troubled sea, when it cannot rest, whose waters cast up mire and dirt. [There is] no peace, saith my God, to the wicked"(*Isaiah* 57:20-21). Up on that hill, around that ensign – she who is 'maid/Queen Irene/Peace' – rush the birds as a wind, returning to her raised arm for renewal, and with "trebled velocity" rushing out to wreak justice (*Curdie* 210). *Isaiah* repeatedly refers to the intervening arm of the Lord, which he raises before the eyes of the nations, bringing salvation where there is no justice (e.g., *Isaiah* 59:16). "So shall the Lord of hosts come down to fight for Mount Zion, and for the hill thereof. As birds flying, so will the Lord of hosts defend" (*Isaiah* 31:4,5).

18. A more extensive account of these and further *Isaiah* correlations may be found on the Internet, under the title: "Curdie's Isaiah: A detailed account of some of the *Isaiah* correlations within MacDonald's *The Princess and Curdie*."

19. The close relationship between Maurice and MacDonald is well established. Maurice was godfather to one of MacDonald's sons (and, incidentally, one of Tennyson's), and MacDonald dedicated *Robert Falconer* to Maurice. MacDonald also gives not only a description, but a defense of Maurice in *David Elginbrod* -- that book which focuses so closely on *Isaiah* 40. Maurice suggested in 1869 that he and MacDonald collaborate on a book of prayers, meditations and hymns, though that did not transpire due to Maurice's ill health. He died in 1872 (*Greville* 399ff).

20. *Curdie*, p.64, 65. "The music of the wheel was like the music of an Aeolian harp blown upon by the wind that bloweth where it listeth" (*Curdie*, p.65), "The wind bloweth where it listeth, and thou hearest the sound thereof, but canst not tell whence it cometh, and whither it goeth: so is every one that is born of the Spirit," John 3:8. The words of the song which Curdie hears, laden with familiar biblical imagery, has a strong semblance to the poem "Prayer", by one of MacDonald's favorite poets, George Herbert; it also serves homage to Coleridge's poem "The Aeolian Harp."

21. *Prophets and Kings*, p.226

22. Accompanied, undoubtedly, by her "white winged army of heaven" (211). Irene means, of course, Peace. And the eternal nature of this Princess of Peace is underscored by the king's remembrance of overhearing *his* grandfather speak of her (*Cudie* 167). Her supernatural nature receives further unveiling in her multiple forms: old woman by the wayside, majestic queen, vision in the mines, the castle maid, the titan overseeing living sacrifice – her deeds aside. Yet, as she told Curdie at the beginning: she is still and ever "the same all the time" (56).

23. Italicizing mine. One is reminded again of Louisa MacDonald pounding away Handel's *Hallelujah* chorus on the organ during the earthquake! The "stone-obstructed river" also stands as a reminder that the rock on which this city was founded, filled with stone which caused men like the baker to "stumble," mined by the petrous Peter and ruled by Curdie Peterson, yet remains, though the city is shaken out of existence. It is not unlikely that Victorian readers familiar with Isaiahan refrains referring to the Messiah as the "stone that makes men stumble" (Isaiah 8:14), and "Trust in the Lord forever, for the Lord is the Rock eternal…he lays the lofty city low; punished them and brought them to ruin, wiped out all memory of them" (Isaiah 26:5, 14) would notice the resonances.

24. For remember, miner as he is, Curdie is of royal blood – like his predecessor, Isaiah.

25. Occasionally MacDonald scholars have postulated that the obvious presence of such influences as mythology or Romanticism makes evident that MacDonald's message cannot be of Christian intent, but I would argue that this is to misunderstand, and gravely underrate, the depth and complexity of dialogue within MacDonald's texts – as well as his understanding of Christianity.

26. Numerous quotations and explicit allusions were not unusual within the body of a fictional text in MacDonald's time – indeed, it was almost an expected acknowledgement that one was rooted within the tradition of literature. But MacDonald is particularly intentional, if not excessive. In *David Elginbrod* alone, for example, over 90 works of literature are *explicitly* mentioned – this is not including unreferenced quotations and allusions. And it is not only in MacDonald's 'realistic' novels that this occurs – in his fantasies he also has many direct quotations (not all marked out by quotation marks – *Curdie* has both methods), and often direct mentions of other titles of literature.

27. Arnold called Maurice "that pure and devout spirit, – of whom, however, the truth must at last be told, that in theology he passed his life beating the bush with deep emotion and never starting the hare…" and claimed his declarations both mischievous and vain (*Dogma* 200). Prickett shows how even after Maurice's death Arnold still holds him in *intellectual* contempt, and indeed attacked him bitterly

(215, 225).
28. Indeed, inspired by Prickett's study, I turned to Arnold to see if he had engaged at all in his writings with *Isaiah* – and discovered a literary jackpot.
29. In conversation, Rogerson has called Maurice "quite ambivalent, really" about German Historical Criticism (Gladstone Library, April 27, 2004).
30. As the reader of Prickett will already be aware. Regarding Coleridge, I use the word 'mentor' guardedly – Maurice, like MacDonald after him, was well-able to sort what he considered dross from gold in the writings of those he considered worth attending. This is a point of crucial note in understanding MacDonald.
31. For example, 'Derba,' the name of the woman who takes Curdie in when no one else will, is also the name of a town that does the same for reformers Peter and Barnabas (*The Book of Acts*, chapter 14). MacDonald's Derba also takes in the wicked servants when they are expelled from the castle and denied help by their fellow citizens. In Gaelic Derba's name means "free man" – and indeed she is free of the envy and suspicion that rule her fellow citizens. In Middle English her name means, "place where the deer graze" – a foreshadowing the place where the deer will graze (as the reader is told) once Gwyntystorm is no more. It was unlikely to have passed the notice of a man who turned an anagram of his own name into the family motto – "*corage, God mend al*" – that Derba is also an anagram for the potent symbol, Bread.
32. MacDonald, *Rampolli* (California: Johannesen Publishing, 1995) p. v
33. Letter dated 1879.
34. "It is possible that you may be aware that I have paid a great deal of attention to translation, though I have not done a large amount of work in it. I remind you of this merely to establish a sort of right to an opinion. Of very little translation that I have read could I say it was well done; of most I think abominable, but I know some translations that are as translations works of art. Among these is one of *David Elginbrod* into German by the lady [Miss Julie Sutton] I now use the right of friendship to present to you. I think she spent more earnest labour turning it into German than I did in making English (or Scotch) of it. So much pleased was I with it that I gave a copy to Prince Louis of Hesse Darmstadt." 13 May, 1881 (Sadler 304); for another example, see p. 20 in *The Elect Lady*, a discussion that ends: "I will reconsider the passage. We must not lightly change even the translated word!"
35. MacDonald is exuberant when given a Greek New Testament of his own by Mrs. Cowper-Temple in 1878, and he becomes even more aware of questionable – or errant – translations than he had been before: "Still I have the old story to tell you – more and more delight in my New Testament. I had no idea how

inadequate was the English of the Epistles, nor how much I should learn from the Greek." (July 20, 1878)

36. MacDonald, *Rampolli* (1897), p.vi. MacDonald discusses this issue in this collection of translated poems; He also writes, in his 1870 text *The Miracles of Our Lord*, "For he has come, The Word of God, that we may know God: every word of his then, as needful to the knowing of himself, is needful to the knowing of God, and we must understand, as far as we may, every one of his words and every one of his actions, which, with him, were only another form of word. I believe this the immediate end of our creation. And I believe that this will at length result in the unraveling for us of what must now, more or less, appear to every man the knotted and twisted coil of the universe." (*Miracles* 1)

37. Italicizing mine. It is amazing that Rogerson wrote this before having any awareness of the MacDonald-Maurice connection (discovered in conversation, April 27, 2004).

38. Prickett suggests that Arnold's use of the word "fairy story" is a colloquialism for what Coleridge meant by 'myth' (p.214)

39. Of Arnold's four different pieces specifically on *Isaiah*, three were commentaries, with introductions that are quite detailed in outlining not only the importance of the text of *Isaiah*, but also the importance of the King James Version translation of that book. One of these commentaries was a text for school children – a more formative and influential venue for Arnold's voice than perhaps has been given consideration. This "Religious Education" textbook highly lauded by *The Times*, and written by the man who was also prominent 'Inspector of State Schools,' undoubtedly shaped an entire generation of young thinkers.

40. Cheyne's influential volume *The Prophecies of Isaiah* was first published in 1880. In 1870 he had published an earlier work on *Isaiah*, which "aimed at reconciling in some degree English style and Hebrew scholarship." (T.K. Cheney, *The Prophecies of Isaiah*, 5th Edition, (London: Paul, Trench and Trubner Publishing, 1889) p.ix

41. It is worth recalling at this point that Maurice studied at that 'older Oxford', under the Colridegean, Hare.

42. This is a consistent theme throughout MacDonald, even to be found in his fairy tales.

43. The line of Coleridge's verse which he quotes, "moving moon...nowhere did abide," and which is highly reminiscent of the Great-great-grandmother's evasive moon, is from *Rime of the Ancient Mariner* (51).

44. An interesting juxtaposition to Arnold's discussion of the same phrase, "Honesty is the best Policy," in *Literature and Dogma* (211).

45. Arnold abstracts his term "extra-belief" from the German word *Aberglaube* (*Dogma* 58).
46. After them, stepping likewise into this tradition, will come two writers significantly shaped by George MacDonald: C.S. Lewis and J.R.R. Tolkien. Both are notably strong proponents for an understanding of the gospel as True Myth, *the* True Fairy Tale – Tolkien's argument for which actually played a significant role in Lewis' conversion to Christianity.
47. The highly acclaimed 'Geological Society of London' was founded in 1807. It is worth noting that not only was MacDonald's friend John Ruskin one of the best known enthusiasts of this science, but also that two of MacDonald's mentors, Goethe and Novalis, were involved in the mining industry. For them too Art and Science were inextricable.
48. Indeed most of MacDonald's writings take time, either explicitly or implicitly, to establish this point.

Works Cited

Arnold, Matthew. *A Bible-Reading for Schools: The Great Prophecy of Israel's Restoration* (Isaiah, Chapters 40-66), Arranged and Edited for Young Learners (with Commentary). London: Macmillan, 1872.

---. *Isaiah Xl-Lxvi: Great Prophecy of Israel's Restoration with the Shorter Prophecies Allied to It.* London: Macmillan, 1875.

---. "Isaiah of Jerusalem." *Nineteenth Century* 13 (1883): 587-603, 779-94.

---. *Isaiah of Jerusalem, in the Authorized English Version with an Introduction, Corrections and Notes.* London: Macmillan, 1883.

---. *Literature and Dogma: An Essay Towards a Better Apprehension of the Bible.* Popular Edition ed. London: Smith, Elder, 1904.

Cheney, T.K., *The Prophecies of Isaiah* 5th Edition. London: Paul, Trench and Trubner, 1889.

Coleridge, Samuel Taylor. *Rime of the Ancient Mariner.* London: Palgrave Macmillan, 1999.

Docherty, John. *The Literary Products of the Lewis Carroll - George MacDonald Friendship.* Lewiston, NY: Edward Mellen, 1995.

Jeffrey, David L., ed. *The Dictionary of Biblical Tradition in Literature.* Grand Rapids, MI: Eerdmans, 1992.

Johnson, Kirstin Jeffrey. *Curdie's Isaiah: A Detailed Account of Some of the Isaiah Correlations within MacDonald's the Princess and Curdie.* <http://www.quod-est-dicendum.org>.2005.

Lowth, Robert. *Isaiah: A New Translation; with a Preliminary Dissertation and Notes,* 13th Edition. London: Balne Brothers, 1842.

MacDonald, George. "The Imagination: Its Function and Its Culture." *A Dish of Orts.* Whitethorn, CA: Johannesen, 1996. 1-42.

---. "A Sketch of Individual Development." *A Dish of Orts.* Whitethorn, CA: Johannesen, 1996. 43-76.

---. "St George's Day." *A Dish of Orts.* Whitethorn, CA: Johannesen, 1996. 77-140.

---. "The Cruel Painter." *Adela Cathcart.* London: Sampon Low, Marston, Searle, & Rivington, 1890.

---. *Annals of a Quiet Neighbourhood.* London: Kegan Paul, Trench, Trübner, n.d.

---. *David Elginbrod.* London: Hurst & Blackett, n.d.

---.*The Elect Lady.* Whitethorn, CA: Johannesen, 1992.

---. "The Wow O' Riven". *Gifts of the Child Christ.* Ed. Glenn Sadler. Grand Rapids, MI: Eerdmans, 1973.

---. *Hope of the Gospel*. Whitethorn, CA: Johannesen, 1995.
---. *The Miracles of Our Lord*. Whitethorn, CA: Johannesen, 1995.
---. *Phantastes*. Grand Rapids, MI: Wm. B. Eerdmans, 1981.
---. *The Princess and Curdie*. Middlesex: Puffin, 1979.
---. *The Princess and the Goblin*. London: Blackie & Son, n.d..
---. *Rampolli*. London: Longmans, Green, 1897.
---. *Sir Gibbie*. Eureka, CA: Sunrise Books, 1988.
---. *There and Back*. Whitethorn, CA: Johannesen, 1998.
---. *Thomas Wingfold*, Curate. Eureka, CA: Sunrise Books, 1988.
---. *Unspoken Sermons* (Series One) Eureka, CA: Joseph Flynn Rare Book Publishers, 1989.
---. *Unspoken Sermons* (Series Two). Eureka, CA: Joseph Flynn Rare Book Publishers, 1989.
---. *Unspoken Sermons* (Series Three). Eureka, CA: Joseph Flynn Rare Book Publishers, 1989.
---. *What's Mine's Mine*. Eureka, CA: Sunrise Books Publishers, 1994.
MacDonald, Greville. *George MacDonald and His Wife*. London: Allen & Unwin, 1924.
Manlove, Colin N. *Modern Fantasy: Five Studies*. Cambridge, N.Y.: Cambridge UP, 1975.
---."George MacDonald's Early Scottish Novels." *Nineteenth-Century Scottish Fiction: Critical Essays*. Ed. Ian Campbell. Totowa, NJ: Barnes and Noble, 1979. 68-88.
Maurice, Frederick Denison. *The Prophets and Kings of the Old Testament: A Series of Sermons Preached in the Chapel of Lincoln's Inn*. London: Macmillan, 1852.
McGillis, Roderick. "George MacDonald's Princess Books: High Seriousness." *Touchstones: Reflections on the Best in Children's Literature*. Ed. Perry Nodelman. Vol. One. West Lafayette: Children's Literature Association, 1985. 146-62.
---. "Introduction." *The Princess and the Goblin and The Princess and Curdie*. George MacDonald. Ed. Roderick McGillis. Oxford: Oxford UP,1990. vii-xxiii.
---, ed. *For the Childlike: George MacDonald's Fantasies for Children*. Metuchen, NJ: Scarecrow, 1992.
McGrath, Alister. *In the Beginning; the Story of the King James Bible*. London: Hodder & Stoughton, 2001.
Prickett, Stephen. *Romanticism and Religion: The Tradition of Coleridge and Wordsworth in the Victorian Church*. Cambridge: Cambridge UP, 1976.
---. *Victorian Fantasy*. Sussex: Harvester Press, 1979.

Robb, David S. *God's Fiction: Symbolism and Allegory in the Works of George MacDonald*. Eureka, CA: Sunrise Books, 1987.

Rogerson, J.W. *The Bible and Criticism in Victorian Britain*. Sheffield: Sheffield Academic Press, 1995.

Sadler, Glenn, ed. *An Expression of Character: The Letters of George MacDonald*. Grand Rapids, MI: Eerdmans, 1994.

Sawyer, John F. A. *The Fifth Gospel: Isaiah in the History of Christianity*. Cambridge: Cambridge UP, 1996.

Wolff, Robert Lee. *The Golden Key*. New Haven: Yale UP, 1961.

"Isaiah." *The Holy Bible, Authorized King James Version*. Chicago: John A. Dickson Publishing. 1973.

Chapter 10

George MacDonald and 'Ethicized' Gothic

Susan Ang

George MacDonald's fantasy has received much commentary; as it is a denizen of the house of gothic; however, it has received considerably less attention. I consider this second 'affiliation' here. Yoked strangely – and perhaps uneasily – to an otherwise benevolent and protective ethos, MacDonald's work contains a noticeable strain of the terrible and fearful – certainly, at any rate, the unsettling. These affects emerge out of tropes that are now accepted as part of the standard gothic matrix or vocabulary. A quick list of these might include metamorphosis, transgression, imprisonment, mirrors, doubling, labyrinthine tunnels, imprisonment, the distressed damsel, the tyrannical parent figure, vampires, werewolves and other creatures of the dark and liminal. To this list we might add epistemological uncertainty and structural discontinuity, etc., which have come to be seen as formal properties frequently associated with the gothic (see Napier, Haggerty and Anne Williams) and also Freud's notion of the uncanny, or *das unheimliche*, which finds a special resonance in MacDonald's writing.

What I suggest is that in MacDonald's hands, the gothic is often "ethicized," that is, "invested with an ethical element" (*OED*), and as such it becomes a mode both recuperative and recuperated. To render something ethical is nicely Victorian, and it is an incidental, but perhaps not unsurprising, fact that the only listings given by the *OED* of the verb "to ethicize" are late Victorian – the *OED* cites James Martineau in 1885 and Boyd Carpenter in 1889; in addition, the earliest given use of "ethicality" – the property of being ethical – is that by J. H. Stirling in 1890.

(I use "ethicize" rather than "Christianise" because while a fair number of MacDonald's gothically-troped works are capable of being read as Christian allegory, not all lend themselves readily to this; and the ones which are capable of being so read are also capable of sustaining more general meanings than the specifically Christian. It seems to me correct, therefore, to refrain from arrogating to Christianity what MacDonald was happy to leave unspecific. It is, however, an interesting fact that his theological writing and his gothic fiction draw at times on a common vocabulary, as I will point out later in this chapter.)

"Recuperation" may be understood as "restoring," as the *OED* phrases it, "a person or thing to a proper state," and this definition, in fact finds a correspondence in MacDonald's observation in *Hope of the Gospel* (1892) that "[t]he return of the organism to its true self, is its only possible ease" (qtd in *Life Essential* 14). That which is to be recuperated may either be a character in a work or perhaps also the reader. But it is also true that the gothic, in being so invested with ethicality, is itself rehabilitated and rescued from its perceived depravity, and so made an honest genre/mode. (In speaking of "perceived depravity," I am not speaking of how the gothic is nowadays understood within the academy; I am here referring to the popular perception of the genre as one pandering to a taste for the vicious, the cheap thrill and the deliciously illicit. This view – give or take a few degrees of disapproval – would have been held by a good many at the time of MacDonald's writing. To treat gothic fiction as the skeleton in the literary closet was in fact fairly common until not all that long ago. The last couple of decades or so have seen a significant critical rehabilitation of gothic literature; however, as Coral Ann Howells comments in her Preface to the reissued *Love, Mystery and Misery: Feeling in Gothic Fiction*, when her book first came out in the late '70s, the status of gothic novels was such that one had to "argue for the legitimacy of Gothic as a proper subject of literary study" (vii).

I argue that "ethicization" and "recuperation" are achieved through the deployment of the tropes, properties and affects of the gothic, the principal of which is, arguably, terror. Ann Radcliffe and her contemporaries had conceived of terror in terms of the Burkean sublime, i.e., as a thing to "expand the soul" as she says in her posthumously published essay on terror in 1826 (Radcliffe 315); this "expansion of the soul," however, was an experience more essentially aesthetical than ethical or even religious in nature. In MacDonald's works, however, terror acquires a nobler, more elevated, role as a chastening force which works to reorient and return one to a true self or proper state; in a "discourse delivered" on the 13th April, 1873, MacDonald suggested that even torture would not be avoided by God in his efforts to rouse those sleeping the sleep of spiritual death (*George MacDonald in the Pulpit*, 22). For the word "torture" one might here read "terrorize," for terror, in MacDonald's work frequently acts as a means to awaken the moral or spiritual somnambulist to the dangerous truth of the reality which he inhabits, but which he has hitherto walked ignorant of. There are, as the premise of Neil Gaiman's book of that title goes, "wolves in the walls"; or, in MacDonald's formulation, goblins underground, undermining the foundations of the home. They were always there; we only failed to know it.

(Incidentally, in *The Portent*, we have an instance of actual somnambulism. Lady Alice, a sleepwalker in both the literal and metaphorical sense, wakes reluctantly, phasing through bewilderment, alarm and anger. To wake is to become aware of a world of distress and terror where to dream was comfort; the comfort was, however, false, and Lady Alice's waking marks the start of a process of increasing awareness on several levels. And apropos of nothing in particular, while one might not go so far as to say that it is a near-double of *The Woman in White*, *The Portent*, which was published in the *Cornhill* in 1860, bears certain uncanny similarities to Wilkie Collins's novel, which appeared in serial format in *All the Year Round* over the period 1859-1860.)

Returning to my claim that MacDonald enlists gothic as a mode whereby to articulate an ethical state, as well as to recuperate it, I briefly discuss, before proceeding, certain of the more significant elements in play within MacDonald's gothic works. In addition to the use of terror, quite a few of the standard gothic tropes are active in MacDonald's work, whose meaning is in many cases capable of being understood within a relatively straightforward economy of symbols, for instance the mirror, the labyrinth, the prisoner, etc. A few, however, are particularly freighted, for instance the werewolf and beast-human (e.g. Lina in *The Princess and Curdie*) and appear to stand for a compromised humanity, one precariously balanced between the possibilities of loss and gain, salvation and damnation. The home, which will be looked at later in more detail, is another prominent trope, which in MacDonald's hands becomes a complex thing – both the (static) expression of a condition as well as a sign for a dynamic process which addresses and works towards the redressing of that condition.

The short story, "The Cruel Painter," which first appeared in *Adela Cathcart* (1864), and which later formed part of the collection *The Portent and Other Stories* (1909) may be read as an emblem for MacDonald's ethicized and ethicizing gothic. In "The Cruel Painter," a story with obvious debts to the work of the German Romantics, we have a work haunted by gothic elements. The story is set in Prague in 1590, a town in which rumors of vampiric activity are rife. In this town live a painter, Teufelsbürst, or Devilsbrush, whose wife has died under mysterious circumstances, and his daughter, Lilith, who appears strangely heartless, a near-double of the "Light Princess" in another of MacDonald's stories, or is, perhaps, if one wants to put this differently, another instance of the sleepwalker or sleeper waiting to be awakened.

Teufelsbürst is an artist who depicts human suffering and who does so for no apparent reason other than the enjoyment of it and that it tickles his evil fancy, and in this sense, he is the true vampire of the story, a feeder off the suffering of others. His art, which concentrates on the representation of people in pain and enduring torture, their agony heightened by attendant demons, might perhaps be seen as a symbol for Gothic art or literature itself, which has not infrequently indulged in the contemplation of various mishaps and terrors – people languishing in the dungeons, or on the torture racks of the Inquisition, languishing in the caves of bandits, languishing in the castles of would-be ravishers, suffering the (presumably unwanted) attentions of bleeding nuns and vampires, being under threat of death, rape, imprisonment, taking the veil either in the sense of being forced to marry or forced into a cloister, etc.

However, there is a second emblem for the Gothic text in the story (emblems of the Gothic proliferate in this tale), and this second emblem is Lilith, who has a doubled existence, both as herself and as a reiterated figure in her father's canvases – in a sense, she could be said to be a prisoner of his paintings. Both the paintings and Lilith are productions of Teufelsbürst and both are incomplete, lacking in something, this "something" being an ethical awareness.

The paintings depict suffering for its own sake; there is neither meaning given to that suffering, nor any edification in it; nothing is taken away from the viewing of suffering except a certain questionable pleasure. We could say that the paintings represent the lack of an ethical dimension in art. Lilith, similarly, is lacking – she is an incomplete figure, one of many in MacDonald's fiction. Both the paintings, and Lilith – the most celebrated beauty in Prague – are examples of art without a heart. Karl Wolkenlicht, the student who is in love with her, notices Lilith's incompleteness, and the fact that in the paintings, as in life, she is represented as lacking a proper capacity for feeling:

> She did not hate, she did not love the sufferers: the painter would not have her hate, for that would be to the injury of her loveliness: would not have her love, for he hated. ... Sometimes she would stand in the crowd as if she had been copied there from another picture, and had nothing to do with this one, nor any right to be in it at all. Or when the red blood was trickling drop by drop from the crushed limb, she might be seen standing nearest, smiling over a primrose or the bloom on a peach. ("The Cruel Painter" 17)

Something in this description almost anticipates Wildean notions of art, for here, we have the suggestion of an art that exists narcissistically, for its own sake, without reference or connection to, without care for, a wider world, and which appears to appropriate everything to itself, even suffering which it aestheticizes.

The last sentence of the quotation juxtaposes the "red blood trickling drop by drop" and the "bloom on a peach" – these are presented as artistic images to be savored. However, the sentence also presents its components, i.e., these two experiences, as equal in value. Further, through their juxtaposition, they are presented as parts, seemingly, of the same aesthetic experience, and the sentence thus subtly suggests a failure to distinguish between them in any way, to register that there is, in fact, a difference between a crushed limb trickling blood and the bloom on a peach.

To fail to register that such a difference exists presupposes an ethical lack, and this ethical vacuum is located primarily in the painter, the painting's grammarian, as it were, whose compositional syntax has caused to be juxtaposed the elements under discussion. However, the lack of moral/ethical sense is not only the painter's. It is also the represented Lilith's, whose attention to the bloom of the peach constitutes a neglect of suffering in need of alleviation. The represented Lilith, however, is a double of the real girl, and any ethical lack in the one may also, I think, be understood to exist in the other.

Teufelsbürst experiments on the unwitting Wolkenlicht, who has enrolled as his apprentice; Wolkenlicht collapses, appearing to be dead. The painter then attempts to take a cast of what he assumes is an emaciated corpse for future use in his art, and in this, we may see Teufelsbürst producing Wolkenlicht as yet another gothic text. The cast – or perhaps overcast apprentice – (Wolkenlicht, after all, translates as "Cloudylight") – is not dead, but returns to haunt his former master, serving up to him the terror and pain that Teufelsbürst has been in the habit of dispensing to others. Teufelsbürst thinks that the dead, or rather, un-dead, Wolkenlicht has returned as a vampire. Wolkenlicht, though not a vampire, is now a secret sharer of the house, a gothic haunter, and as such, has returned, as Freud argued that the repressed always does. As the gothic haunter of the house, Wolkenlicht renders it *unheimlich* – or "unhomely" to its inhabitants Teufelsbürst and Lilith, thus initiating the ethicizing process.

Earlier, we have seen Teufelsbürst as a figuration of the Gothic artist, and Wolkenlicht as a forced reader of his gothic texts. Now, Wolkenlicht becomes in turn the writer of a new gothic, as well as an editor of the old while Teufelsbürst becomes the conscripted reader of the rescripted gothic. The editorial-cum-authorial role is evident in MacDonald's description of Wolkenlicht's activities. Wolkenlicht, for example, "edits" Teufelsbürst's paintings, one of which is "rewritten" or repainted with Teufelsbürst as the figure of the torturer, the figure of Lilith having been replaced by a "dim vampire reiteration of [Karl's] body that lay extended on the table" (45). The two young men also drip red wine in "blots" meant to simulate blood over the plaster cast made by Teufelsbürst. These blots suggest at one level a re-writing of the (gothic) text – as they elaborate and add to it in an attempt to revamp it, so as to make it more effective and terrifying.

The wine that, in this new gothic narrative, becomes blood, is an image drawing specifically on Christian imagery, within which framework it has a tremendous power and significance. Blood carries a redemptive charge, and it might be noted that the metaphorically transubstantiated blot, configured as a contested site which is simultaneously inhabited by gothic and Christian, becomes a sign for the recuperative and recuperated gothic, the one eventually dispossessing the other and driving it out. Wolkenlicht, like this transubstantiated blot, might also be seen as such a site – he is, in Teufelsbürst's narrative, a vampire. But in a Christian narrative, as a figure risen from the dead, he could also be said to have a Christ-like function, the more so as he is the agent by which the recuperation in "The Cruel Painter" is carried out. Here again we find, simultaneously residing in one image, the gothic and the Christian. The gothic image is a mirror or inverted image of the Christian – both are 'staked' – but one takes blood and life, the other gives them. Again, we could argue that one image exorcises, chases out, or replaces the other.

I have been using transubstantiation as metaphor, and using it with the mildest of irony. An interesting question, however, emerges from this metaphor, for the wine-turned-blood invites us to think about the nature of the image, from which certain 'theo-logics' would follow. What is at issue is the nature of the Eucharist itself, as it is interpreted within the separate remits of Catholic and Protestant doctrine. In the one, it is a mystery, in the other a mimesis. Blood is either real or it is a representation. In "The Cruel Painter," the blood is, patently, representation (that is, the blood here is not blood, but only a simulacrum; and furthermore, the blood is harnessed in the service of representation) – a point congruent with MacDonald's own Protestantism, and this reading is backed up by its context: as I was reminded,[1] – the story is set in Prague in 1590 – and Prague was a point from which Reformational energies had spiraled in the fifteenth century, directed by Huss, and, in the 1590s, was still a site fiercely contested by both Catholics and Protestants; the second Defenestration of Prague occurred in 1618. "The Cruel Painter" shows the blood as a representation; it also shows Teufelsbürst believing in the blood's reality; it is difficult not to read the story as MacDonald pushing a Protestant point, i.e., suggesting a recuperation (of a Catholic imagination?) formulated in Protestant terms.

In toying with (and it is really no more than a toying with) the notion of "The Cruel Painter" as Protestant Gothic, I also suggest that the story is a work that, in the taxonomy of the fantastic evolved by Tzvetan Todorov, falls into the realm of the uncanny. That is to say, it does not employ truly supernatural phenomena which our notion of reality cannot accommodate, and is, hence, not "marvelous"; it has none of the sustained hesitation between the rationalized uncanny and the unrationalizable marvelous which, Todorov says, defines the mode of the fantastic;

it is thus uncanny – the supernatural in this tale is ultimately explained to have a basis in reality. My reason for bringing this up here is that – as with the Protestant interpretation of the Eucharist which could be said to 'demystify' it by reducing it to symbol rather than presenting it as miracle, the text "The Cruel Painter," in its alignment with the uncanny rather than with the marvelous, could, arguably, be a similarly demystified, and hence Protestant, form of gothic. Gothic he has had the marvelous drained from it.

Earlier, I suggested that the dripping of the wine, or the "blotting" of the cast, the wine also representing ink, might be seen as a rewriting or editing of the gothic text. The word "blots," however, has other resonances: it suggests smudging or spoiling, transgression (blotting one's copybook), eradication or deletion (to blot out) – the wine is not just blood but also the ink of the irritable editor – and finally, to 'blot' something, for example, using blotting paper to remove some kind of excess, for the purposes of preventing smudging or staining; blotting paper replicates the image being blotted, but in reverse.

MacDonald, in his essay "The Fantastic Imagination" (1893) avers that a "genuine work of art must mean many things" and "the truer its art, the more things it will mean" (*Complete Fairy Tales* 7), and I take this as my license for reading a multiplicity of meanings into the figure of the blot. The blot, as I suggest above, is polysemous; and if we conflate its various possible meanings, then what perhaps emerges is a sense of how the "blotting" out (removing, deleting, eradicating) of a blot (smudge, transgression) may, paradoxically, first involve the duplication of the blot, whose produced image, is, however, an inverted version of the original blot.

"Blotting" (the eradication of a smudge by a mirroring process) is what Teufelsbürst is subjected to as he is terrorized by Wolkenlicht's duplication and reversal of the gothic (he was "writer"; he is now "reader"). Wolkenlicht's terror works to cure him of his sadistic tendencies: "[a]lready Teufelsbürst had begun to experience a kind of shrinking from the horrid faces in his own pictures, and to feel disgusted at the abortions of his own mind" (43). The terror that he is made to feel is, in fact, not terror for sensationalism's sake, but terror with a purpose. MacDonald writes, in "The Fear of God" from the *Unspoken Sermons, Second Series*, that "fear is natural, and has a part to perform [which] nothing but itself could perform in the birth of the true humanity" (qtd in *Creation in Christ* 84). And while here he is speaking, specifically, within a theological context, and the fear he speaks of is the fear of God rather than the generalized fear or terror which is generated by the *unheimlich* experience, the point is, nonetheless, one that may be legitimately exported; terror, as I earlier argued, in MacDonald's gothic acquires a didactic, ethicizing, function.

Not all of MacDonald's gothic tales, of course, use gothic as a form of recuperation. Certain of these, notably "The Gray Wolf" (1871), are pointedly recalcitrant in this regard. The werewolf girl in "The Gray Wolf" is neither restored to a proper state at the level of the physical nor at the level of the moral/ethical. The story ends ambivalently, with the werewolf in girl form weeping briefly upon the bosom of the student, presumably in grief and/or remorse, before it – having phased into wolf form – dashes up to the cave from which the "sound of bones crunched in rage and disappointment" emerges along with sounds of a "mingled moaning and growling" (*The Gray Wolf* 8), in a kind of moral schizophrenia. Earlier I suggested that the werewolf might, for MacDonald, stand for a precarious balance between bestiality and humanity. This balance is not seen to shift positively within the limits of the "The Gray Wolf." But the balance is capable of so shifting. That the man-beast is seen as capable of redemption is suggested in *The Princess and Curdie* (1872), in which Lina ultimately earns, through faithfulness and good works, the right to enter the rose-fire and have her beast-self consumed.

I now move on consider the usefulness of a particular insight that has had a modest but stable career in gothic studies, i.e., Freud's notion of das *unheimliche*, to which he gave shape in his essay, "The Uncanny." Published in 1919, a decade and a half after MacDonald's death, the essay offers, despite its post-dating MacDonald's work, a set of ideas that help to illuminate his writing. Freud's discussion of *das unheimliche*, which muses upon the relations between the home, secrecy, the familiar and unfamiliar, and the way in which the known and the unknown change places to produce in the reader a sense of unease, finds an obvious application in a work like *Lilith*.

The German word *unheimlich* formally translates as "uncanny"; however, as Freud notes, it "corresponds etymologically to the word 'unhomely'" (Freud 124). "Unhomely" might appear a trifle awkward and ungainly, but is in fact surprisingly apt. It is clumsy, *gauche* – (French for "left," which if Latinized, interestingly, becomes "sinister"). It is a dissonance; it is not comfortable, not 'at home' in the language; as a translation, it is a sign for, and reminder of, a foreign-ness which resists being, and can never totally be, assimilated and naturalized. In this, it represents that which is strange and "other," that which is neither domestic nor familiar.

And thus even as uncanny, the officially-approved rendering of *das unheimliche*, designates the untamed, undomesticated space of strangeness, the smoother, more polished translation "uncanny" at the same time represents the force of civilization that would overwrite or colonize the more barbaric, or gothic, "other." "Uncanny," then, ironically, suppresses the resistant strangeness of the word "unhomely," the irony residing in the fact that the choice of word ends by blurring the point that Freud's archaeological excavation through the linguistic layers of '*das unheimliche*' had striven to make. It re-covers what had been recovered. And the irony is compounded by the way that what we might call the "politics of translation" is twinned with the politics of gothic itself, in which the impulse to bring to light that which is hidden is always struggling with the impulse to repress and bury.

Freud's sense of the '*das unheimliche*' turns upon the transformation and inversion, or metamorphosis, of the meaning of the word itself. Rather in the same way that the word "individual" has undergone an about-face from signifying that which was non-dividual or non-dividable from a larger whole to become that which is in fact distinct and separate from the mass, the sea change suffered by *unheimlich* has seen it evolve to take on the meanings formerly associated with its opposite: *heimlich* or *heimisch*. A quick recapitulation of the main points of Freud's basic argument:

Starting from the homely and domestic [and hence associated with the familiar, comfortable, friendly], there is the further development towards the notion of something removed from the eyes of strangers, hidden, secret [because within the home]. This notion is extended in a number of ways (see "The Uncanny" 133).

This alignment of *heimlich* with the concealed and the secret plays out in the realm of knowledge, where, according to Freud, *heimlich* denotes the mystic and allegorical, the occult, and also, "in a different sense, as withdrawn from knowledge, unconscious" (133), and the word also suggests that which is "locked away, inscrutable" (133). These associations with *heimlich* thus come to take on the coloration of the "hidden and dangerous," and *heimlich* thus becomes increasingly ambivalent, until it finally merges with its antonym, *unheimlich*. The uncanny (*das unheimliche*, "the unhomely" is in some way a species of the familiar (*das heimliche*), "the homely" (134).

A few things are worth thinking about here: the first and most obvious is the ambivalence of the home, which can be both a safe, familiar and protecting space as well as that which is the repository of the secret, and for that reason a source of unease. Another thing worth noting is the play of paradox: that a thing can be itself and its opposite; that apparent antitheticals may in fact be identical. Interestingly, the notion of "unhomeliness" is one that MacDonald specifically names, although he does not use it as Freud would do in 1919, but invokes it within the context of his Christian writings to make a theological point. In "Self-denial," from *Unspoken Sermons III*, he speaks of "Christ [being] the way out, and the way in; the way from slavery, conscious or unconscious, into liberty; the way from the unhomeliness of things to the home we desire but do not know" (qtd in *Creation in Christ* 279). And in *Hope of the Gospel*, he again speaks of man's essential alienation in the world – what we might call his "unhomed-ness":

Here we find one main thing wherein the Lord differs from us: we are not at home in this great universe, our father's house. We ought to be, and one day we shall be, but we are not yet. This reveals Jesus more than man, by revealing him more man than we. We are not complete men, we are not anything near it, and are therefore out of harmony, more or less, with everything in the house of our birth and habitation. Always struggling to make our home in the world, we have not yet succeeded (qtd in *Life Essential* 29).

All this is worth attending to because it shapes for us a sense of the meanings assigned by MacDonald to the notions of home and homeliness – and, by extension, to the inverted forms of these terms. Home in his writing invokes all of Freud's complex meanings: it is ambivalent, alternating between the safe and familiar and the strange and fantastic; it is full of secrets. However, in addition to this, the home or house turned *unheimlich*, turned strange proceeds to alienate its inhabitant, or rather, make him aware of his own essential alienation in the world for which the house/home is only a metonymy. The house inverts itself, and in turning itself inside out, dispossesses him, turning him out of itself and forcing him to embark on a quest to find the "real" home.

We see this pattern played out repeatedly in MacDonald's fiction. A couple of examples are easily located in *The Princess and the Goblin* (1872) and *At the Back of the North Wind* (1871) which, though works for children, have aspects which can be frightening, and which could be argued to make use of gothic elements in a form slightly modified for use in juvenile fiction, but without losing the ethical content with which MacDonald invests the mode.

In *At the Back of the North Wind* Diamond's home is suddenly turned inside out, and so made strange, as Diamond discovers that his home and the North Wind's are, in a sense, inversions of each other: a hole in his bed is one of the North Wind's windows; and, as the North Wind says huffily, Diamond's mother has three windows into her dancing room, and Diamond three into her garret. As one moves further away from a point which is known and familiar in order to journey towards a point which is neither, *heimlich* and *unheimlich* switch places, becoming each other – as the point departed from recedes into the distance it gradually becomes strange and unhomely, while the region ahead, formerly strange and unfamiliar, beckons, the journey there thus taking on the shape of a homecoming.

This is the pattern at work in *At the Back of the North Wind*. Traveling with the North Wind, Diamond leaves his home for a series of spaces increasingly further afield: the lawn, the summer house, the cathedral, Sandwich, etc. These are points along a metaphysical journey representing the increasing estrangement of the individual from the world-as-home, and these points culminate in the place which represents the ultimate *unheimlich*. This place is the country at the back of the North Wind, which, while a country, is also a house, or home, as the image of the North Wind sitting on the "doorstep," herself the "door" through which Diamond must pass, suggests. And when Diamond returns from this first visit to the North Wind's country, he finds that "home" as a signifier has become detached from its original signified, and now refers to a new place; his father has lost his job due to his master's financial collapse, and both families have had to move. As we are told, "[b]efore Diamond was well enough to be taken home, there was no home for him to go to" (111). We see here a process whereby "home" becomes a gradually estranged and reformulated term, this process only ending when Diamond returns, this time for good, to the place at the back of the North Wind.

The North Wind, like the old Princess Irene in the *Curdie* books, may perhaps be seen as the figure of the gothic within the text. Both are metamorphs, both have a double aspect to the self, and both have a didactic function. As at one point the North Wind takes on the form of the wolf in order to chastise a drunken nurse, so she later sinks Mr. Coleman's ship in order to "try to make an honest man of him" (110), for, in his financial speculations, he has been led into a certain dishonesty. As the North Wind tells Diamond – her "ugly" face, the face of terror, exists in order to "make ugly things beautiful" (17), and once again the "ethicization" and recuperation are at work.

The North Wind, in conversation with Diamond, who is puzzling over her 'doubleness' – that she has a kind and a cruel self, says:

> "Ah! But which is me? I can't be two mes, you know . . . You know the one me, you say, and that is good."
>
> "Yes."
>
> "Do you know the other me as well?"
>
> "No. I can't. I shouldn't like to."
>
> "There it is. You don't know the other me. You are sure there is only one of them?"
>
> "Yes."
>
> "And you're sure there can't be two mes?"

"Yes."

"Then the me you don't know must be the same as the me you do know – else there would be two mes?" (62)

Perhaps like the word *unheimlich* itself, the meaning of the North Wind, to borrow Freud's words, "thus becomes increasingly ambivalent, until it finally merges with its antonym" or opposite (134). The North Wind, as pointed in the extract above, is double and singular, known and unknown, familiar and unfamiliar, thus constituting in herself an antithesis to herself; she is both God and Death.

In *The Princess and the Goblin*, we find a recurrence of the pattern indicated above. The Princess Irene loses herself in her home, running up stairs and through corridors unexplored and unsuspected, becoming terrified until she discovers her mysterious great-great grandmother. The house, like the old Princess Irene herself, metamorphoses, appearing not to stay in a stable state, becoming *unheimlich*, – the paths one traces through it fail to map it, and do not necessarily lead where they had led before. The house is also a repository of secrets. One of these is the great-great grandmother herself who can only be found under certain circumstances, but is hidden at others, and in addition, as we subsequently discover, under the supposedly safe home lie secret and subterranean tunnels populated by those gothic creatures of the dark, the goblins. The image of Irene's home finds its dark reverse in the palace of the goblins that lies beneath it, and to which they want to bring her.

The home, however, turns unhomely for a purpose that is half-divined by Irene when she says to her nurse Lootie: "I went upstairs and I lost myself, and if I hadn't found the beautiful lady, I should never have found myself" (22). This metamorphosing of the house from homely to unhomely is echoed later, when Irene, encountering a creature of the goblins in her own home, is "dispossessed" by the now *unheimlich* house, out of which she runs in terror. Only while she is outside of it – in that sense alienated from it – does she see the glowing globe of her great-great grandmother and return home. The ambivalent figure of the estranged/estranging house, then, exists in order that people may lose and then find themselves – the implication is that the self that is found is a deeper, enriched one, just as the home that one finds at the end of one's journey is the real home.

Finally, we come to *Lilith*, that most gothic of MacDonald's tales in which all its standard elements: the house, the mirror, ghostly figures, the vampire, the raven, the ravening parent, and metamorphosis come together. *Lilith* begins with the house, the narrator's home, which is swiftly established as uncanny in both senses of Freud's term. The narrator declares that "no description of it [his home] is necessary to the understanding of [his] narrative" (5), and thus, curiously, the reader first registers the home, which would normally serve to define and contextualize, as a largely blank site, a space undefined, unknowable. Excepted from the general absence of detail is the library, a place creepily presented as a thing almost alive and in the process of consuming the rest of the house: "an encroaching state [which had] absorbed one room after another until it occupied the greater part of the ground floor" (6). From the library, strangeness, like a contagion, spreads out. Vane, the narrator, sees a figure of a tall thin man in his library, and follows him up stairs and along passages to places which Vane has not explored, coming at last to a mirror in the garret. Vane looks for a reflection but in vain: the mirror, which shows altogether another place than the garret, is also a door into that other place. Walking through it, the narrator finds himself "on a houseless heath" (11). The house expels Vane from itself into a place where it is not.

This place might be seen as a heterotopia, which Foucault says,

> constitute[s] a sort of counter-arrangement, of effectively realized utopia, in which all the real arrangements, all the other real arrangements that can be found within society, are at one and the same time represented, challenged, and overturned: a sort of place that lies outside all places and yet is actually localizable. In contrast to the utopias, these places which are absolutely other with respect to all the arrangements that they reflect and of which they speak might be described as heterotopias. Between these two, I would set that mixed experience which partakes of the qualities of both types of location, the mirror. It is, after all, a utopia, in that it is a place without a place. In it, I see myself where I am not, in an unreal space that opens up potentially beyond the surface; I am down there, there where I am not, a sort of shadow that makes my appearance visible to myself, allowing me to look at myself where I do not exist: utopia of the mirror. At the same time we are dealing with a heterotopia. The mirror really exists and has a kind of come-back effect on the place that I occupy: starting from it, in fact. I find myself absent from the place where I am, in that I see myself in there.
> Starting from that gaze which to some extent is brought to bear on me, from the depths of that virtual space which is on the other side of the mirror, I turn back on myself, beginning to turn my eyes on

myself and reconstitute myself where I am in reality. Hence the mirror functions as a heterotopia, since it makes the place that I occupy, whenever I look at myself in the glass, both absolutely real – it is in fact linked to all the surrounding space – and absolutely unreal, for in order to be perceived it has of necessity to pass that virtual point that is situated down there (Foucault 352).

This long quotation effectively sums up the function of the mirror and the place-beyond-the-mirror. The mirror-space is simultaneously real and not-real, like Freud's *unheimlich*, both itself and its opposite. It is a not-space which contests the space of the real by inverting and counteracting it, in which the invisible self is rendered visible and substantial to itself by means of its shadow, and which one traverses in order to return to a "reconstituted self." It enables reflection – in both literal and metaphorical senses.

Vane enters mirror-space, in which, the Raven tells him, he must learn to be at home – the *heimlich* - *unheimlich* pattern repeating again – and then he wanders through this space in search of himself; the work is a *Bildungsroman*. Vane's name is suggestive of the vanity or emptiness of the world-as-home that he must learn to detach himself from.

A defamiliarization is at work here. I am not only using the term as it is commonly used, in the Shklovskyian sense, to describe a process of cognitive estrangement by which a familiar thing is presented strangely, so as to de-link the observer from his standard responses to that object and also in order that the haeccitas, or essence, of the object, the "stoniness of the stone" being re-presented can be recovered (Shklovsky 12). This sense of "defamiliarisation" is certainly important, because of its recuperative function if nothing else, and certainly, we may see this sense being brought into play in *Lilith*, firstly through the metamorphic quality of the world and also through the technique employed by MacDonald, in which a thing is not only represented but constantly re-presented in such a way that perception is not allowed to stabilize, and that one is always having to re-negotiate an understanding of that which one is being shown. We see an early example of "defamiliarisation" in this, first, sense in Vane's interaction with Raven:

"Look at me," he said, "and tell me who I am."

As he spoke, he turned his back, and instantly I knew him. He was no longer a raven, but a man above the middle height with a stoop, very thin, and wearing a long black tail-coat. Again he turned, and I saw him a raven. (14)

Here, Raven is a constantly changing being that requires the watcher to keep "cognising," rather than merely "re-cognising" it/him. This is one kind of "defamiliarisation." But the "defamiliarisation" I meant when I spoke of the way in which Vane's journey through mirror-space is a journey of detachment from home refers to a slightly different process, one in which, as with Diamond earlier, a familiar thing – in this case home – is distanced from the self and so rendered unfamiliar. A reluctant sojourner in mirror-space, wanting to return to his own familiar domain – what would nowadays probably be referred to as his "comfort zone" – Vane nonetheless recognizes that returning would accomplish nothing, as home is something already irretrievably lost:

> All about me was a pine-forest, in which my eyes were already searching deep, in the hope of discovering an unaccountable glimmer, and so finding my way home. But, alas! How could I any longer call that house home, where every door, every window opened into – Out, and even the garden I could not keep inside. (21)

What use *At the Back of the North Wind* implicitly makes of the home-turned-unhomely as metaphor, *Lilith* makes explicit.

The gothic elements in the work are invoked to aid in the process of what Keats would have called "soul-making" (the phrase comes from a letter to George and Georgiana Keats dated 14 Feb to 3 May 1819). The house and the mirror, the macabre skeleton dancers without faces, the sleeping dead in Raven's house who are ripening into life, and Lilith herself – the vampire-princess of Bulika – all exist in Vane's mirror-space as elements of the language that will speak his invisible self into being and point it towards its proper goal.

While the realm on the other side of the mirror may have an 'objective' existence, as suggested by the fact that other members of Vane's family, we are told, have traversed it before him, it might nonetheless be suggested that the mirror-space exists in a particular relation to the individual who confronts it and walks through the door of the mirror. What you seek when you look in the mirror is yourself. And what I am suggesting is the possibility that what one encounters in mirror-space are symbols of that self, or of its tendencies.

The gothic images – Raven, the skeletons, and the dead who wait to wake, and even perhaps the vampire Lilith, neither fully dead nor alive when Vane first finds her – might be seen as emblems of Vane or of his state of being. These emblems are complex. "Vane" is a partial acronym of "Raven" (and perhaps thus an incomplete version of which 'Raven' is the perfected type), and at some level, arguably, Raven is a mirror version of Vane. The library of the one is an inverse image of the other. At one level, Raven, Lilith, the skeletons, the dead, etc. are Vane's mirrors, reflecting back to him his "deadness," and also his lack of a face – the symbol of being and identity. Emblems of death derive their ability to terrify from the fact that they inspire the viewer to a recollection or remembrance of the inescapability of his own coming death; here, they are reminders that one is already in some sense dead. Raven is a bird of ill-omen, generally associated with coming death – as Lady Macbeth says, "the raven himself is hoarse that croaks the entrance of Duncan under my battlements" (*Macbeth*, I, v, 38-9). At one level, Raven and the other images work precisely by virtue of their ability to terrify, or at any rate to discomfort.

Gothic has often been viewed as sensationalist; it is not within my present purpose to challenge that in any sustained way. But I might be a little provocative and put the case that if a genre is sensationalist, and also wildly popular, it might be because that sensationalism feeds a need in the readership for the experience of sensation itself. In saying this, I am also saying that to require something strongly sensational in order to know that one is feeling something might suggest the existence of a callused or dulled consciousness that can only respond to jolts of a greater voltage. Burke had held that "the ideas of pain are much more powerful than those which enter on the part of pleasure" (36), and perhaps MacDonald's use of the gothic as a means to inspire terror derives from the parallel notion that the dulled or desensitised soul requires a sharp stimulus rather than a mild one.

However, interestingly, MacDonald in *Lilith*, after invoking the spectre of terror, dismisses it: the images of the dead and of the skeletal dancers without faces are not there to work solely at the level of a terror meant to prod one in the right direction. Having accomplished this recuperation, this reorientation, the gothic trope then dismantles itself as such; as befits an image in mirror-space, its meanings become inverted, reversed, and the gothic trope is reconstituted as something else. Raven, that bird of death, is also, by virtue of its being a scavenger, a carrion fowl, that which consumes decaying flesh, leaving clean skeleton behind – the dry bones which God shows Ezekiel in the *Book of Ezekiel* (*Ezekiel*, 37: 3), asking if they "shall live?" The Raven, who is sexton is also librarian – the sexton buries the dead; the librarian keeps the book of life.

Those animated *memento mori*, the skeletal dancers, dissolve; and while they primarily function as reflectors or mirrors of Vane's own 'unfaced' state, they also signify that faces might yet be acquired – these dry bones shall indeed live – (Lewis must have read the skeletons this way, given his title *Till We Have Faces*). If the skull acquires a face, it is no longer a skull, and hence no longer has the ability to terrify; the gothic image is thus potentially capable of being exorcised through its being recuperated. A better example of how the gothic image in *Lilith* is dismantled and reconstituted differently, however, are the figures of the dead in the woods and in Raven's cemetery, which terrify Vane when he first encounters them. The bed of death, in the heterotopic mirror space, comes to be understood as the cradle of real life; life, as Vane has known it, is a state of mere-un-deadness. The formerly terrifying image (i.e., the dead) has now been rehabilitated and reconstituted.

Endnotes

1. I owe the initial observation, regarding the Eucharistic imagery, to Alistair Chew, Esq. who teaches Chemistry at Anglo-Chinese School, Singapore, and the refinements regarding the implications of the conflicted image in Protestant/ Catholic terms with regard to the story, to Richard Nolan, Esq., Fellow of St. John's College, Cambridge (Faculty of Law), who also reminded me of the connection between Prague and the Counter-Reformation. I am very grateful to both.

Works Cited

Burke, Edmund. *A Philosophical Enquiry into the Origins of our Ideas of the Sublime and the Beautiful*. [1757] Ed. Adam Phillips. Oxford: Oxford UP, 1990.
Foucault, Michel. "Of Other Spaces: Utopias and Heterotopias." [1967] Trans. Jane Newman and John Smith. *Rethinking Architecture: A Reader in Cultural Theory*, ed. Neil Leach. London and New York: Routledge, 1997. 350-355.
Freud, Sigmund. "The Uncanny" [1919] Trans. David McLintock. *The Uncanny*, London: Penguin, 2003. 123-162.
Gaiman, Neil. *Wolves in the Walls*. London: Bloomsbury, 2003.
Haggerty, George. *Gothic Fiction/ Gothic Form*. University Park: Pennsylvania State UP, 1989.
Howells, Coral Ann. *Love, Mystery and Misery: Feeling in Gothic Fiction*. London and Atlantic Highlands, NJ: Athlone Press, 1978, 1995.
Keats, John. *Selected Letters of John Keats*. Edited by Grant F. Scott. Cambridge, MA: Harvard UP, 2002.
Lewis, C.S. *Till We Have Faces*, [1956]. Glasgow: Fontana, 1978.
MacDonald, George. *At the Back of the North Wind*. [1871] Harmondsworth, Middlesex: Puffin, 1984.

---. "Awakening," in *George MacDonald in the Pulpit: The Spoken Sermons of George
    MacDonald*. Compiled by J. Joseph Flynn and David Edwards. Whitethorn,
        CA: Johannesen, 1996. 9-26.
---. "The Cruel Painter." [1864] *The Gray Wolf and other stories*. Grand Rapids,
    MI and Cambridge: Wm. B. Eerdmans, 1980. 11-53.
---. "The Gray Wolf." [1871] *The Gray Wolf and other stories*, 1-10.
---. *Life Essential: the Hope of the Gospel*. [1974] Ed. Rolland Hein. Wheaton, Il:
    Shaw Books, 1978.
---. *Lilith: A Romance*. [1895] Grand Rapids, MI and Cambridge: Wm. B.
    Eerdmans, 2000.
---. *The Princess and the Goblin*. [1872] Harmondsworth, Middlesex: Puffin,
    1964.
---. "Self-Denial." [1891] *Creation in Christ: Unspoken Sermons*, ed. and abridged
    by Rolland Hein. Vancouver: Regent College, 1976.
Napier, Elizabeth. *The Failure of Gothic : Problems of disjunction in an
    eighteenth-century literary form*. Oxford: The Clarendon Press, 1987.
Radcliffe, Ann. "On the Supernatural in Poetry." [1826] *Gothic Readings: The First
    Wave*, 1764-1840, ed. Rictor Norton. London: Leicester University Press,
    2000. 311-315. (The essay was originally published in the *New Monthly
    Magazine*, 16, in 1826.)
Shklovsky, V. "Art as Technique," *Russian Formalist Criticism: Four Essays*.
    Trans. and ed. Lee T. Lemon and Marion J. Reis. Lincoln and London:
    University of Nebraska Press, 1965. 3-24.
Todorov, Tzvetan. *The Fantastic: A Structural Approach to a Literary Genre*. Trans.
    Richard Howard. Ithaca and New York: Cornell UP, 1975.
Williams, Anne. *Art of Darkness: A Poetics of Gothic*. Chicago: U of Chicago P.
    1995.

Chapter 11

Fantasy as Miracle
George MacDonald's *The Miracles of Our Lord*

Roderick McGillis

I think a true man should be able to rule winds and waters and loaves and fishes, for he comes of the Father who made the house for him. Had Jesus not been capable of these things, he might have been the best of men, but either he could not have been a perfect man, or the perfect God, if such there were, was not in harmony with the perfect man. Man is not master in his own house because he is not master in himself, because he is not a law unto himself-is not himself obedient to the law by which he exists. Harmony, that is law, alone is power. Discord is weakness. God alone is perfect, living, self-existent law.

(*The Miracles of Our Lord*)

... a fantasy constitutes our desire, provides its coordinates; that is, it literally "teaches us how to desire." (Slavoj Žižek 7)

George MacDonald is a great theorist, as well as a great practitioner, of fantasy. Indeed, he informs much of our contemporary understanding of the literary genre we label, fantasy. We can catch a glimpse of MacDonald's ideas in Tolkien's well-known essay, "On Fairy stories," and we know how indebted C. S. Lewis was to MacDonald. In practice, MacDonald's fantasy work incorporates such aspects of the fantastic as the uncanny, the secondary world, faerie, the horror story (especially the vampire story), the quest romance, and the parodic fairy tale. MacDonald's attempt to articulate his sense of what we now call "fantasy," in his essay "The Fantastic Imagination," turns up in many accounts of the genre. The comparisons of fantasy stories, or what MacDonald terms fairy tales, to "a butterfly or a bee" and to a "sonata" (*A Dish of Orts* 318) allow him to typify the genre without defining it. The first of these comparisons, the fairy tale is like a butterfly or a bee, reminds us of the naturalness of the genre. Fairy stories are beautiful and delicate, like the butterfly; they are busy and productive, like the bee. They result from much psychic business on the part of their authors, and they produce much that is nourishing for the reader. What they create is possibly allegoric, but definitely not an allegory because they are too busy (like the bee) and too beautiful (like the butterfly), MacDonald implies. These stories are like nature in that they evoke meanings, but do not force them. Like the butterfly and bee, such stories are only beautiful and productive while alive – not pinned to a corkboard or held under a microscope, not murdered in dissection. And since these stories are "live things," they remain elusive, changing, and even growing. Like the butterfly, fantasies are the result of transformation; they bring imaginative potential to fulfillment. And like the bee, fantasies are productive and what they produce is sweet and restorative.

The second comparison, the fairy tale is like a sonata, attunes us to the harmony the tales create. "Harmony" is a word MacDonald likes. He uses it in sermons and in essays on the imagination. For example, in his essay "The Imagination: Its Function and Its Culture," he asserts: "For all is God's; and the man who is growing into harmony with His will, is growing into harmony with himself" (*A Dish of Orts* 36). In the essay on the fantastic imagination, MacDonald speaks of the "harmony between the laws by which the new [fantasy] world has begun to exist" (314). In other words, he suggests that whatever kind of world an author creates, that world must have consistent and harmonious laws. The notion of harmony sounds throughout this essay in MacDonald's insistence that fairy tales are like music, like a gathering storm or like a limitless night (319). The latter two comparisons intensify the sense of a form that elicits an emotional response, and the storm reference might loosen our sense of harmony. Harmony is a feature of both the beautiful and the sublime. We can find passages in *At the Back of the North Wind* that accurately illustrate the harmony manifest in storms (see for example, Chapter 6: "Out in the Storm").

Without offering his reader anything specific in the way of formal features for fairy tales, MacDonald insists that this form of literature works not on the ratiocinative parts of the mind, but on the imagination. And the imagination, he argues, reacts most vigorously when it confronts "the region of the uncomprehended" (318). His sense of fantasy has something of the sublime attached to it. Fantasy keeps us in touch with the vast, and although terror and pain may not be necessary as a response to the sublime, awe and astonishment are. He does not define the region of the uncomprehended, but we might surmise that this region comprises miracles in the sense of things – objects, creatures, happenings – that are unaccountable in our mundane philosophy. Certainly, young Diamond finds some of North Wind's actions both strange and unaccountable.

Another metaphor at work in MacDonald's discussion of fairy tales is sleep. He speaks of fairy tales waking things in the reader, things "that are in him" (319). He expresses here what Blake termed "rousing the faculties to act." Or, as

MacDonald says, he is interested in having his reader "think things for himself" (*A Dish of Orts* 319). The metaphor of waking suggests that we spend much of our time asleep, in a dream world or perhaps a shadow world, a world of unreflection. Plato is never too far from MacDonald's thinking, or at least Plato filtered through Plotinus and then the later neo-Platonists and closer to home, the Cambridge Platonists of the seventeenth century. MacDonald was a close reader of another neo-Platonist, Shelley, and in *Prometheus Unbound* (Act 3, Scene 3), he would have read:

> Death is the veil which those who live call life;
> They sleep, and it is lifted.

What MacDonald does is reverse this idea: rather than envisaging life as death-in-life and the end of death as a sleep, MacDonald often sees life as sleep, and death as that which awakens us to life. MacDonald's sleep/death/wake metaphor is nowhere more forcefully apparent than in *Lilith* where Adam and Eve's great cemetery is the culmination of life, and a prelude to the ultimate waking. People such as Mr. Vane, and he is fairly representative of the rest of us, pass through life in a waking dream, and only when they leave their self-made dreams behind and wake up are they truly alive. In short, for MacDonald death is not only "good death," it is also not death at all, in the conventional sense. It is more life. The relevance of this metaphor of waking to MacDonald's conception of fantasy is that for MacDonald, fairy tale or fantasy, being a human creation fashioned from God's creation, is, as it is for Shelley, a lifting of a veil, a mysterious revelation of that which waits beyond this sleeping condition. While we sleep, we are in a state of stupefaction; when we wake, we see through to the heart of things. The magnificent apocalyptic waking near the end of *Lilith* is MacDonald's attempt to express the true state of waking: "The world and my being, its life and mine, were one," says Vane (412). The world Vane experiences in the journey home is a miraculous world in which the "microcosm and macrocosm were . . . at length in harmony" (412).

The passage from *The Miracles of Our Lord* that I quote for my first epigraph contains a couple of words that remain active in postmodern discourse: law and power. We might construct a Foucauldian fiction that sees miracles as the working out of power, as the transforming of a free-floating current of power into an unexpected law, a law that appears to counter our expectations of the way things are supposed to work in the material world we, in our somnambulant state, think we inhabit. When such an unexpected law is manifest, then we have an occurrence we take as abnormal, as not within the bounds of common experience, as unheard of in our philosophy – in short, we have something fantastic. A fantasy. But the Foucauldian fantasy derives from a power that comes under the direction of a particular force, often an aggregate force we might call a government or some other institutional entity, a university or a corporation. From a psychoanalytic perspective, such a fantasy replaces an institution with a singular figure – a parent who holds the subject from experiencing everything the fantasy related to power might offer. All fantasies of power, indeed all fantasies, stop short of accomplishing the fulfillment of desire (see for example, the ending of Philip Pullman's "*His Dark Materials*" trilogy). Fantasy works out the way in which desire comes under law. In short, fantasies, wherever we locate them, have something to do with power and that which attempts to direct and control power, law. When power passes from self-aggrandizement to love, from the Shadow to the great Father, we have fantasy that illustrates desire at its most constructive.

My epigraph from *The Miracles of Our Lord* also signals another aspect of fantasy, although it does so implicitly rather than explicitly. When MacDonald speaks of perfection, of a man being able to rule winds and water and loaves and fishes, he speaks of that most powerful of fantasies – the fantasy of the individuated self, the self fully in harmony with inside and outside, the self capable of exerting a creative power because of a beautiful integration with the things of this world. In his meditation on the New Testament miracles, MacDonald is at pains to account in a sensible way for what appears unaccountable. In other words, for MacDonald miracles are the product of the everyday; they reveal heaven around us, "God in all things, truth in every instinct, evil withering and hope springing even in the path of the destroyer" (*Miracles*). Speaking of Jesus' "miracles in bread and wine," MacDonald says these "were far less grand and less beautiful than the works of the Father they represented, in making the corn to grow in the valleys, and the grapes to drink the sunlight on the hill-sides of the world, with all their infinitudes of tender gradation and delicate mystery of birth" (*Miracles*). No absolute difference exists between the common and the uncommon, he says. "Uncommonness is not excellence, even as commonness is not inferiority. The sign, the wonder is, in fact, the lower thing, granted only because of men's hardness of heart and slowness to believe" (*Miracles*). The ultimate miracle is the working of creative power, something MacDonald links with love. Love is, he says, "the power of power, which alone can create" (*Miracles*). In *Phantastes*, Anodos learns "that it is by loving, and not by being loved, that one can come nearest the soul of another" (179).

MacDonald's argument for the believability of miracles has something in common with what we now hear termed "intelligent design." He argues that natural laws do not "go wheeling on of themselves in a symmetry of mathematical shapes," but rather that these laws are "the expression of a perfect intellect informed by a perfect heart" (*Miracles*). His fantasy work delivers many examples of the world about us informed by intellect and feeling: perhaps the best examples are the many female figures who represent a harmonious nature – North Wind, Irene's grandmother, the grandmother dressed in green with a tinge of green in her hair ("The Golden Key"), the Wise Woman in white ("The Lost Princess"). These women are miracles of grace and action. They are reminders of an intelligence watching over the human community, and working to encourage goodness and justice. In both *Phantastes* and *Lilith*, we can sense the workings of a benign force. For example, as Anodos lies beneath an "ancient beech-tree" at the end of *Phantastes*, he seems to hear words in the "sound of the leaves overhead." What he discerns are words of reassurance: "A great good is coming – is coming – is coming to thee, Anodos" (182). And in *Lilith*, Eve informs Vane that, "all must sleep" in the great cemetery; and not long after she tells him this, Adam informs Lilith that the Shadow too will "lie down and sleep" (384, 388). Everything moves toward the great awakening.

As we well know, MacDonald complicates his sleep metaphor near the end of *Lilith* when he has Vane's waking prove to be yet another dream. As long as we remain this side of the bar, as it were, we drift in a somnambulist's dream. And then MacDonald closes his narrative with a sentence from Novalis that he has invoked before: "Our life is no dream, but it should and will perhaps become one" (420). Now, it seems, we are awake, or at least if we are asleep then we are in a dreamless sleep, and we will only come home, find harmony, activate thoroughly the power that is love, when the world we experience will be permanently a dream. And the dream brings us back to desire. Dreams are manifestations of our desire, but more often than not they are incoherent. We remember the epigraph from Novalis MacDonald used for *Phantastes*. Robert Lee Wolff points out that the epigraphs MacDonald used for *Phantastes* contain an apparent contradiction because first Novalis hails narratives without coherence and later he calls for them to be coherent (43). Wolff says the inconsistency is not Novalis', but rather his editors', and then he goes on to say that MacDonald had accepted Novalis' call for incoherence. I am not going to defend the coherence of *Phantastes* here or argue for its productive incoherence, but I am going to suggest that the seeming contradiction between coherent and incoherent fits with MacDonald's sense of the fairy tale or fantasy as a form that gives glimpses of both this life whether we call this life waking or dreaming, and the life after death whether we call this waking or dreaming. In other words, fantasy expresses the collision of this life and this life extended; it insists on seeing things in a dual perspective as when Mr. Raven tells Vane that he smells "Grieg's Wedding March in the quiver of those rose petals" (204). MacDonald's use of synesthesia nicely captures his sense of fantasy's gathering of that which seems disparate into harmony. To put this sense of two opposed worlds conjoining another way, I might say that MacDonald's fantasy is both coherent and incoherent. It moves toward a moment of clarity knowing that clarity is not possible. The word "glimpse," a word Tolkien picks up for similar purposes, adequately articulates what MacDonald's fantasy offers, glimpses of a coming harmony not yet arrived.

My second epigraph derives from Slavoj Žižek's *The Plague of Fantasies* (1997). Žižek may seem an odd choice for a thinker for me to place beside MacDonald, since Žižek's focus is psychoanalytical rather than spiritual. But when Žižek asserts that fantasy "teaches us how to desire," he gives us a clue to MacDonald's conception of fantasy. In *The Miracles of Our Lord*, MacDonald speaks of the human being who suffers experiencing respite from suffering, "for some precious moments at least." For a few moments, the sufferer has "a sense of the blessedness of being, an openness to calm yet rousing influences." This momentary feeling of blessedness is what Žižek, after Lacan, might call *jouissance*. Tolkien would later refer to narratives of faerie providing us with consolation, and this consolation tucked into the eucatastrophe that typifies faerie is a form of *jouissance*. For MacDonald *jouissance* results from integration or unity, an integration or unity that is both spiritual and material, that is of the mind and of the body. The experience of Anodos in the penultimate chapter of *Phantastes* articulates *jouissance* as well as anything I know. Here Anodos tells us of his experience after death. He finds that he had not in any way "ceased to be what I had been" (178). He says his "passions were dead," and yet "the souls of the passions . . . yet lived, yet glowed, with a pure undying fire" (178). He burns with a hard gem-like flame. Passion remains important, but passion in its "real" sense – and I use "real" in both a Lacanian and a Platonic sense here. Anodos' experience combines the physical with the nonphysical. In *Miracles*, MacDonald makes it clear that both body and soul are important. He tells us that Jesus "respected the human body." The "cure of the body and the cure of the soul" are related. And so Anodos finds not only spiritual purity in death, but also a physical satisfaction and an assurance that true love will "behold its own image in the eye of the beloved, and be humbly glad" (179).

But how do MacDonald's fantasies "teach us how to desire"? Desire, we remember, is a function of lack, and lack is inevitable as long as we are, in MacDonald's terms, imperfect. MacDonald's characters are most often imperfect, in need of chastening, suffering, and learning. As he puts it, "the correlative of creation is search; that as God has made us, we must find him" (*Miracles*). I move between spiritual and psychoanalytic discourses because I feel more comfortable with the latter, but know MacDonald more often than not employs the former. At some level, as his essay "A Sketch of Individual Development" will indicate, these two discourses come together, as we might expect with a thinker who strives for harmony and integration. And so, for example, a character such as Mr. Vane in *Lilith* experiences a fantasy world that has clear connections with spiritual growth with its evocation of Adam and Eve, Mara, and other types of biblical metaphor. Vane's experience is also clearly related to his psyche, a word that nicely articulates the bringing together of spirit, mind, and body. We get to know something of the workings of Vane's conscious and unconscious impulses. He uses the word "uncanny" upon his first return to his garret from the region of the seven dimensions, and this word nicely expresses the intersection of conscious and unconscious aspects of the mind (197).

Vane's experience corresponds to Lacan's Mirror Stage (*Ecrits* 1-7). When we meet him, he is not eighteen months old as Lacan suggests the child is when he or she experiences the Mirror Stage, but he is, clearly, at a transitional stage in his life, having recently completed his studies at Oxford. He is, like the infant that Lacan considers, about to discover that he is not alone in the world and not sheltered from the storm. His parents are no longer living, and he will shortly assume "the management of the estate" (1). Commentators on *Lilith* sometimes see the plot as chronicling Vane's search for his father, and to a certain extent, this is the case (see Wolf 331; Hein 404, although Hein's "the Father and the Son" differ from Wolff's father). His reading of his father's manuscript starts him on his journey in earnest. But we can, I think, assume that both parents are important for Vane, the mother representing that Home Vane desires and the father representing duty and labor associated with what Lacan terms the Symbolic and what in *Lilith* is the "managing of the estate." I might as well come clean and state that I am using Lacan's three "stages" (the Real, the Imaginary, and the Symbolic) to structure my thinking about *Lilith* here. The Real I am considering as Home. We might think of the Real in a Platonic sense as an Ideal, and this would not be completely askew; however, Lacan's Real is a psychic phenomenon rather than an ideational or spiritual one. It exists at all times as the "place" and the "time" we yearn to return to, and as in Freud it has connections with the Mother; it can be frightening as well as comforting. Vane's desire for a variety of female figures – Eve, Mara, Lilith, and Lona – expresses his desire for the lost mother. These women have no existence outside of Vane's desire; they are symptoms of his desire. In other words, the entire story constitutes Vane's fantasy. We may remember Lacan's infamous assertion that woman does not exist (*Feminine Sexuality* 145). The non-existence of woman is especially clear in the case of Lilith herself. Vane brings her to life when he cares for her beside the stream in Chapters 18 and 19, and later in Chapter 29 Adam reads a poem in which we learn that in the earlier incident Lilith took shape from Vane's own desire. The poem's speaker is Lilith:

> "For by his side, I lay, a bodiless thing;
>   I breathed not, saw not, felt not, only thought,
> And made him love me – with a hungering
>   After he knew not what – if it was aught
>   Or but a nameless something that was wrought
> By him out of himself . . ."   (150)

The paradox is that Lilith is both independent and a symptom of Vane's desire. She says that she clothes herself, "in the likeness true/Of that idea where his soul did cleave" (151). Before Vane gives Lilith life, she is "bodiless," a negation, virtually a nothingness. Clearly, from one perspective Lilith represents the ontological certainty of evil, but from another perspective, she represents only possibility and desire, nothing more and nothing less. We might remember that when Vane first sees her she has little or no power of agency in herself; she needs Vane to restore her, and we can assume that she also needs the Great Shadow that appears to control her. In other words, Lilith is a creature of male desire. She exists as evidence of the male fantasy of fullness. She is, strangely, Vane's *objet a*, that thing that activates and focuses his desire for the Real. Insofar as she is unattainable, she is the Real. She represents indulgence, hedonism, algolagnia, chaos, darkness drawing down, and ecstasy. She is Vane's self as 'other," both attractive and repulsive. We can assume that she will be waiting for him, along with Lona and the others, when he eventually dies into life.

Lilith's counterpart is Eve, the woman as living reconciliation. Whereas Lilith represents the Real as chaos, Eve reflects the Real as "continuous creation" (209). She is white as snow, and yet warm. She reconciles light and dark, life and death. She opens, at least Mara says she will open to Lilith, "the mirror of the Law of Liberty" (384). Just how one "opens" a mirror is not entirely clear to me; however, this mirror of the Law of Liberty, mentioned in James 1:22-25, reflects God's word, law as harmony, the state of perfection we can only imagine and desire. For MacDonald, a miracle occurs when one law stops working because of the intervention of another one we do not understand. What matters, he says, is whether we have a willing suspension of disbelief. Well, MacDonald does not use these words, Coleridge does. What MacDonald does say is that "Our power of belief depends greatly on our power of imagining a region in which the things might be" (*Miracles*). The mirror of the Law of Liberty stands opposite the mirror in which we see ourselves reflected in moments of self-consciousness; it is a counterpart of the mirror through which Vane steps at the outset of *Lilith*. The latter mirror reflects Vane's Imaginary, or in the person of Lilith it reflects Vane's struggle to form or find his Imaginary. He seems to find Imaginary versions of himself, of his 'other self', in the various figures he meets, most intensely with Lilith, but finally resting with Lona as the Imaginary he most desires. As always, however, the Imaginary exists only fleetingly, only as the transition either to the Symbolic beyond the mirror, or to the Real beckoning through the mirror.

Vane comes to Lilith after looking in and passing through a mirror. The mirror stage in Lacan is the moment of separation, the moment in which the subject (in this case Vane) becomes aware of otherness. What the infant sees in the mirror is a reflection of himself; Vane sees not himself when he looks in the mirror, but what he does see is an aspect of himself, his psychic geography, as it were. Manlove comments that "all the figures in *Lilith* are, as it were, parts of one huge imagination" (90). Indeed, everything in *Lilith* is part of Vane's (and by extension, MacDonald's) imagination. Once on the other side of the mirror, Vane discovers that he has an identity problem; as he puts it, he understands that "I did not know myself" (11). Later, when he succors Lilith, he learns for the first time "what solitude meant." He tell us: "I saw now that a man alone is but a being that may become a man—that he is but a need, and therefore a possibility." The perfection of man depends upon otherness. Vane asserts:

> A man to be perfect – complete, that is, in having reached the spiritual condition of persistent and universal growth, which is the mode wherein he inherits the infinitude of his Father – must have the education of a world of fellow-men. (105)

He uses the word "gaze" to indicate his specular relationship to the woman he is nurturing, and this fits with the Lacanian notion of the gaze as the subject's construction of the Imaginary "other" that derives from the reflected self first perceived in the mirror. To put this bluntly, I note that when Vane brings Lilith back to life, he is creating his Imaginary, that ideal self he would like to enjoy. Anodos does something similar when he sings the marble lady into life, and Cosmo von Wehrstahl, in the same book, also finds his Ideal-I in a mirror. The creation or even the awareness of the Imaginary precipitates the subject into the Symbolic, the world most of us inhabit, the world of language and quotidian reality, what Lacan refers to as the "law of the Father." This is the world that

Lilith also inhabits, a world of getting and spending, in which possession and possessiveness are what govern action, and in which the father is envisaged as the great Shadow hovering about in uncanny and sinister fashion. This is the world in which self and other confront each other and communicate with language, in one sense or another. This is the world in which self and other jockey for position, always trying to outmaneuver the other, always trying to control the gaze. In this world, Lilith escapes the creating gaze of Vane until she can be in a position to return the gaze and thereby gain superiority over him. In this world, the vampire lurks trying to lure his or her victim by looking steadily at the prey.

Robert Collins notes that in the world behind the mirror, Vane encounters difficulty with language. He puts it this way: "the most critical incompatibility Vane discovers concerns Language" (2). In Lacan's view, language and the unconscious share a structure. Like aspects of the unconscious, language is arbitrary. Lacan here picks up from Saussurian linguistics the notion that the relationship between a word and that which it signifies is agreed upon uneasily in that word and signification are more often than not elusive, and they are certainly arbitrary. Words are "live things" that scurry from person to person and from meaning to meaning. Vane tells us more than once that he has difficulty matching word and meaning, and the reason for this is simply that words are incompetent to say anything with finality or complete accuracy. At one point, he interrupts the narrative to explain that he is engaged in a "constant struggle to say what cannot be said with even an approach to precision." He notes from his perspective a "single thing would sometimes seem to be and mean many things" (46). MacDonald is here echoing the Romantic idea of what Wordsworth refers to as the "sad incompetence of human speech." But this idea has relevance for the Lacanian notion of language as itself an *objet a*, that which focuses our longing, that which attempts to fill in for the absent home. Language is symbolic precisely because it is always just a cover for that which cannot be said or that which is missing. In other words, language reminds us that we lack the completeness of the Real. Once we re-enter the Real, subject and object, word and meaning will coalesce. Words will be deeds. We have a glimpse of this return to the Real in Chapter 45, "The Journey Home." Vane tell us that the "world and my being, its life and mine, were one" (255). He, Lona, and the Little Ones are on their way "home to the Father!" (255). We know what he means, but perhaps I can take the liberty of inserting a psychoanalytic observation here and point out that the "Father" inevitably represents the world separate from the Mother, and therefore we can know that Vane must find not completion, but incompletion in his journey. The law of the father dictates that the world this side of death is incomplete; this world is as much a vale of longing as it is a vale of tears. Until he is truly dead, Vane can only wait, asleep or awake, wait for the end that we cannot know beyond imaginative projection. He can, in words I draw from *The Miracles of Our Lord*, "honour the laws [he does] know." As for those he does not know, and I draw again on *Miracles*, these laws inhabit "a wide may be around us; and every true speculation widens the probability of changing the may be into the is."

What I am talking about, of course, boils down to something rather simple: fantasy as MacDonald conceives it is a projection of our longing for that perfect place we can read about in various visionary works from the Bible to Dante's *Paradiso*, Spenser's *New Jerusalem*, Milton's *Paradise*, Blake's *Golgonooza*, and MacDonald's "country whence the shadows fall" ("The Golden Key" 240). Fantasies themselves work in the area of the unconscious in that they reflect our desire for that perfect place, and in doing so they use that which is available to us in our quest for fulfillment: language. Language constantly slips close to and away from fullness of expression, signification that matches idea. In other words, the language of fantasy is richly polysemous because it stretches into the unknown "which yet the heart yearns to know" (*Miracles*). It widens our horizons (see *Lilith* 203). MacDonald's fantasies invariably give us characters like Irene or Mossy and Tangle or Diamond who struggle, with greater or lesser degree of ease, to understand apparently impossible things. Even a character like the Princess, in "The Light Princess," encounters miracle; indeed, she herself is a miracle. She may be lightheaded and lighthearted, apparently without a care in the world, but she is also living proof of the existence of an unknown law, a law that overturns the law of gravity. She is a miracle, and as far as the Prince who meets her while she is swimming is concerned, she is a miracle of rare device, a fantasy of the perfect princess. This light story is replete with miraculous happenings: the Prince coming across the Princess in the lake, the Princess Makemnoit using a slithering snake to drain the lake, the sexual play of the Prince and Princess in the water, the effect of water upon the princess, the Eucharistic meal the two lovers share, the tears that come once the Princess begins to think that the Prince has drowned, and finally the miracle of the Princess' final fall, after she learns to shed tears. In this story, the fall into suffering is itself a miracle.

A modern edition of "The Light Princess" sports illustrations by Maurice Sendak, and we know that Sendak is an admirer of MacDonald. In his famous picture book, *Where the Wild Things Are*, Sendak delivers a fantasy that is as miraculous as anything MacDonald produced. In fact, he uses MacDonald as the starting point for this fantasy of a young boy's desire for power and recognition. When Max's mother sends her mischievous son to his room, he stands by his bed and watches his room transform into a forest. In the second chapter of *Phantastes*, we have the source for this transformation when Anodos, lying in bed, suddenly hears the sound of water about him, and "looking out of bed, I saw that a large green marble basin, in which I was wont to wash, and which stood on a low pedestal of the same material in the corner of my room, was overflowing like a spring; and that a stream of clear water was running over the carpet, all the length of the room, finding its outlet I knew not where." He watches the stream flow over his carpet, a carpet designed with daisies and grass, and he sees the flowers and the blades of grass bend and sway with the current. Likewise, he notices his oak dressing table that is decorated with foliage becoming living ivy, We witness, along with Anodos, the transformation of his room into a forest (19-20). We can explain the transformation as the substance of a dream; however, the experiences Anodos has in fairyland have the feel of reality, and certainly while he is experiencing them, he thinks they are actually happening.

The play between dream and reality is familiar in MacDonald's fantasies, perhaps most clearly presented in *The Princess and the Goblin* where Irene's visits to her great-great grandmother have a dreamlike quality. She may go to sleep in her grandmother's tower, but wakes up in her own bed; she may receive a ring from her grandmother, but later the nursemaid tells her she has had the ring for a long time. Then we have Curdie who is wounded by an arrow, and in what he thinks is a dream he receives medication from the grandmother only to wake to find his wound mended. We could multiply examples (e.g., the implication that Diamond, in *At the Back of the North Wind*, sees North Wind while he is in a feverish dream, and yet she has such material effect in the waking world of Victorian London), but the point is that in MacDonald's world dream and reality are blended, ambiguously related so that we find it difficult to tell which is dream and which is not dream. In dreams strange things may happen, things that in waking life will seem impossible – miracles. We either believe these strange happenings or we do not. MacDonald avers: "happy are they who demand a good reason, and yet can believe a wonder" (*Miracles*). He also notes that the "question is whether or not we can believe that the usual laws might be set aside by laws including higher principles and wider operations" (*Miracles*).

When we contemplate the dream/reality ambiguity in MacDonald's work, we might note that dreams are more often than not individual dreams, rather than collective dreams. In other words, the dream mechanism is a manifestation of an individual mind that is working to scroll its fantasies. Dream, like fantasy, has to do with desire. Even when dreams deal with fears, fears are an aspect of desire in that what we fear we desire to avoid. As often as not, that which we fear, we also desire, as Anodos and Vane may indicate. If I move from dream to miracle, I observe that in *Miracles of Our Lord*, MacDonald has a tendency to observe a miracle from the perspective of a particular person. For example, in his treatment of the story in *John*, Chapter 9, of the man born blind, MacDonald asks his reader to imagine "the glory which burst upon [the blind man] when, as the restoring clay left his eyes, the light of the world invaded his astonished soul." He also asks his reader to "Think for a moment" of the delight experienced by the man whose withered hand Jesus restored (*Miracles*). When he discusses the curing of Simon's wife's mother (*Mark* 2:29-31), MacDonald says: "But now let us look at the miracle as received by the woman" (*Miracles*), and he proceeds to describe her torment in some detail. In his discussion of the miracle turning water into wine (*John* 2:1-11), MacDonald speculates as to what Jesus' mother thought when she heard her son speak in a manner she "could ill understand" (*Miracles*). Miracles have their effect upon individuals; they are fantasies come true. MacDonald also suggests that no "two cases" are "treated in the same manner" (*Miracles*). So often in his fantasy work, MacDonald shows us characters who encounter wonders alone: Irene, Curdie, Diamond, Anodos, Vane, Tangle and Mossy, and so on. And yet, as we saw with Vane, a "man to be perfect – complete, that is, in having reached the spiritual condition of persistent and universal growth, which is the mode wherein he inherits the infinitude of his Father – must have the education of a world of fellow-men" (280).

In this passage from *Lilith*, Vane gives us, in spiritual language, a psychoanalytic lesson. He tells us that individuality depends upon otherness. When the infant (and I'll assume a male infant here) in Lacan's narrative looks in the mirror and sees himself, he sees himself as other, as someone immitigably different from himself. In other words, self and other are both the same and separate. Vane puts the situation this way:

> Were all men alike, each would still have an individuality, secured by his personal consciousness, but there would be small reason why there should be more than two or three such; while, for the development of the differences which make a large and lofty unity possible, and which alone can make millions into a church, an endless and measureless influence and reaction are indispensable. (280)

Our fantasies, in other words, begin with our individual consciousness, but they cannot fill out without the presence of another. Were our fantasies ours alone, were we forever trapped in solipsism, then we would remain in that chaotic and fully arbitrary condition of the Real. Facing the mirror, we imagine an other person and then others and our journey through a symbolic landscape begins. And on this journey, as both Vane and Anodos discover (and so too does Curdie), the individual becomes part of a community. Fantasy deals with individuals whose romance is to find community, a home if you will.

This, dare I say, liberal emphasis on the individual as the cornerstone of community allows us to see the political dimension to MacDonald's fantasies. His characters often involve themselves in a group's political struggles: Anodos when he battles the three giants in Chapter 21 of *Phantastes*, Curdie when he saves the King and the city of Gwyntystorm, Vane when he leads an army against the bad queen of Bulika. MacDonald's heroes may contemplate a nostalgic return to innocence – Anodos locked in a tower with his shadow longs "to be a child again, innocent, fearless, without shame or desire" 161) and Vane feels the urge to protect the Little Ones from growing up – but nostalgia is a sickness from which they need to recover. Rather than looking backward, MacDonald looks forward. His vision, his fantasy, is of a nation made up of individuals – the classic liberal state in which individual rights and freedoms take precedence over state control. The individual's interests are the nation's interests. In *The Miracles of Our Lord*, MacDonald puts it this way:

> Even when God deals with a nation as a nation, it is only as by this dealing the individual is aroused to a sense of his own wrong, that he can understand how the nation has sinned, or can turn himself to work a change. The nation cannot change save as its members change; and the few who begin the change are the elect of that nation. Ten righteous individuals would have been just enough to restore life to the festering masses of Sodom – festering masses because individual life had ceased, and the nation or community was nowhere. (*Miracles*)

I am interested in MacDonald's use of the word "elect" in this passage. Here the Scots-born, Calvinist-raised writer secularizes this word, even as he is acutely aware of its spiritual significance. The secular and the spiritual are in harmony. He goes on to assert that a "community is the true development of individual relations."

Fantasy, then, is miraculous because it delivers impossible things, including impossible communities we sometimes refer to as utopias. What has always struck me as nice (in the particular sense of this word) about the ending of MacDonald's *The Princess and Curdie*, is its insistence on fantasy – fantasy as elemental as we could imagine. The book ends with a vision of cleansing so effective that everything is clean, the world begins again, a river "now rushes and raves," and "All around spreads a wilderness of wild deer, and the very name of Gwyntystorm has ceased from the lips of men." Everything is ready for a new beginning, a new development and a new building of the great city. Everything is ready for the next fantasy. The vision is both horrible and uplifting. Fantasy will always give us both that which we desire and that which we fear. This is the miracle of fantasy.

In our fantasies, we cannot escape from our desire to possess what we lack, and we cannot escape from our fear that we will find that what we possess is only a twisted version of ourselves. Tolkien argues that faerie frees us from possessiveness, and this may be true if we take faerie to emanate from what MacDonald calls in *Lilith* "the great Thinker" (206), but if we take faerie or fantasy as a psychic phenomenon, then possessiveness lies at the heart of fantasy because it is that which we both decry and that which we strive for. Fantasy plagues us, but it may also protect us. Without fantasy, we would be truly alone in that fearsome and chaotic and threatening Real that is the true emptiness. Ultimately, what fantasy delivers that touches on MacDonald's constant theme is the miraculous nature of creation itself. Creation keeps us from succumbing completely to the desert of the Real.

Works Cited

Collins, Robert. "Liminality in MacDonald's *Lilith*." March 14, 2004.
    http://www.english.fau.edu/faculty/collins/lilith.htm
Lacan, Jacques. *Feminine Sexuality*. Edited by Juliet Mitchell and Jacqueline Rose. New York: Norton, 1985.
MacDonald, George. *A Dish of Orts*. London: Sampson Low Marston, 1895.
    ---. *The Miracles of Our Lord,* etext: http://johannesen.com/Miraclescomplete.htm
    ---. *Phantastes and Lilith*. Grand Rapids. MI: William B. Eerdmans, 1975).
Manlove, C. N. *The Impulse of Fantasy Literature*. London: Macmillan, 1983.
Wolff, Robert Lee. *The Golden Key*. New Haven: Yale UP, 1961.
Žižek, Slavoj. *The Plague of Fantasies*. London New York: Verso, 1997.

It was plain to Curdie, from the universal hardness among them, that they must all, at one time or another, have been creatures in the mines.

He saw at once what this one was after. The beast had planted his feet upon the floor of the passsage, and stretched his long body up and across the chasm to serve as a bridge for the rest. Curdie mounted instantly upon his neck, threw his arms round him as far as they would go, and slid down in safety, the bridge just bending a little as his weight glided over it.

Chapter 25, The Avengers, The Princess and Curdie

Chapter 12

'Travelling Beastward':
George MacDonald's *Princess* Books
and Late Victorian Supernatural Degeneration Fiction

Geoffrey Reiter

While George MacDonald's realistic books clearly interact with the social, moral, and religious concerns of his day, it can sometimes be tempting to read his fantastic work as more otherworldly, divorced from the pressing issues of Victorian England. Such could certainly be said of his children's novels *The Princess and the Goblin* (1872) and *The Princess and Curdie* (1882), with their mythical settings and supernatural underpinnings. Yet the Princess books are not nearly so disconnected from quotidian reality as one might suppose; indeed, they touch on one of the most prevalent fears of the late nineteenth century: the danger of degeneration. In these books, MacDonald uses the notions of evolution and degeneration to great effect.

MacDonald's regard for Charles Darwin's thought is uncertain; he plays coy about the topic in *The Princess and Curdie*. "Have you heard what some philosophers say – that men were all animals once?" asks the princess' great-great grandmother, shortly before adding, "It is of no consequence" (71). In *The Princess and the Goblin* and its sequel, MacDonald uses degeneration as a literary device, making him a forerunner of many subsequent works that explore this theme by use of supernatural hyperbole. However, unlike many of his successors, MacDonald's Christian worldview prevents his work from falling prey to some of the more problematic aspects of degenerationist thought.

In order to understand where MacDonald fits in this milieu, we must first establish some context. Unfortunately, a working definition of degeneration has proved difficult for critics and historians to articulate. William Greenslade acknowledges the "ambiguity and instability of the term" (16), while Stephen Arata notes that the "protean quality" of the concept resulted in it being so widely held and so little scrutinized in its era that it "was less a coherent system than a form of common sense" (3). However, we can discern some characteristics of the phenomenon within its social context. With over fifty years of historical perspective on his side, Greenslade points out how pervasive degeneration theory was in the discourse – "medical, psychiatric, political" (2) – of the day, being "at the root of what was, in part, an enabling strategy by which the conventional and respectable classes could justify and articulate their hostility to the deviant, the diseased and the subversive" (2). This theory of degeneration became all-encompassing: "Founded on the Darwinian revolution in biology, and harnessed to psychological medicine, the idea of degeneration spread to social science, to literature and art" (16). Kelly Hurley captures the core doctrine, and the core fear, of the idea:

> *Degeneration was evolution reversed and compressed.* Like evolution theory, degenerationism concerned itself with the long-term effects of heredity within the life-span of a species, and with biological variations from type that affected not just the individual, but the generations to follow. But for the idea of evolution towards ever-higher forms of life, degenerationism substituted a terrible regression, a downward spiral into madness, chaos, and extinction.
>
> (66, italics mine)

Such were the fears degeneration invoked. As Gillian Beer observes, "the primordial was comfortless. Instead of a fixed and perfect species, it showed forms in flux . . . Ascent [through evolution] was also flight – a flight from the primitive and the barbaric which could never quite be left behind" (127). Degeneration was terrifying to the average middle class Victorian, because so many fears could be subsumed within the aegis of that one term. On the one hand, it represented a profound socioeconomic fear of the paupers and lower classes. Individually, it could take on physical or mental forms, as perceived degenerates were considered malformed or grotesque in their features and deficient in their intellects. These factors also fed into a fear of moral regression; certain "types" of people were believed to be more inclined to criminal lifestyles.

In *Origin of Species* (1859), Charles Darwin treats the possibility of degeneration only in passing: "It might further be expected that the species of the same genus would occasionally exhibit reversions to long lost characters" (118). For many Victorians, however, it was a necessary corollary of evolutionary theory: if there was the possibility of natural progression, did this not carry with it a concomitant danger of regression? Two years before *Origin of Species* was even published, the French alienist Bénédict Augustin Morel suggested the possibility of degeneration in human beings. In 1869, Francis Galton allowed for the first time the commingling of Darwinian evolution with the concept of human degeneration in his book *Hereditary Genius*. Galton's intensely hierarchical ethnic rubric was of course highly favorable to the English, but also carried with it a dire caveat: "Our race is overweighted, and appears likely to be drudged into degeneracy by demands that exceed its powers" (333). Darwin's book proved to be a pebble in a pond, and its perceived implications created some unexpected ripples. As Greenslade notes,

> In assenting to [Herbert] Spencer's formulation 'the survival of the fittest' in the sixth edition of *The Origin*, Darwin could not have anticipated the transformations which that concept of fitness would undergo, nor the extent to which this process would concentrate such a constellation of fears and foreboding. (36)

In the religious community, meanwhile, responses to evolutionary theory were mixed. Historian Frederick Gregory observes that the English church's initial reaction was, for various reasons, somewhat muted. The more vehemently antiDarwinian elements had to wait fifteen years to find a suitably articulate advocate in American theologian Charles Hodge, but the more conciliatory theologians had already begun addressing the issue by the 1860s. And even if more attention was paid to the former group, a matrix was in place for the more scientifically conversant members of the clergy to adopt principles drawn from *Origin of Species* (Gregory 378-79).

As the church struggled to frame an appropriate response to Darwin, fears of physical degeneration had already begun to haunt Victorian writers throughout the last decades of the nineteenth century. Such apprehensions appeared to find confirmation in the alarming deficiencies of Boer War recruits and the British army's general lack of success; but by this time, the body of literature on the subject was already vast. Fantasists could dramatize the theme more profoundly than their realist counterparts, because they could accelerate the process of regression and show more farreaching consequences. Perhaps no author took this device farther than Arthur Machen. As Adrian Eckersley has noted, Machen produced a series of works in the mid-1890s that dealt directly with physical degeneration. His stories often end with individuals reduced to primordial matter. One becomes "a dark and putrid mass, seething with corruption and hideous rottenness, neither liquid nor solid" (*Impostors* 122). In *The Great God Pan*, he is even more overt: "Here too was all the work by which man had been made repeated before my eyes . . . I saw the body descend to the beasts whence it ascended, and that which was on the heights go down to the depths, even to the abyss of all being" (114).

Most writers did not indulge their imaginations to quite this extent, focusing their attention on the societal implications of such atavism. In *Hereditary Genius*, Galton had "witness[ed] the draggled, drudged, mean look of the mass of individuals" and feared that "[t]he conditions of their life seem too hard for their constitutions, and to be crushing them into degeneracy" (328-29). This attitude was echoed by his contemporaries, yet many also maintained that degeneracy could cut across class lines. Max Nordau, for example, suggested in his book *Degeneration* (1892) that individuals who were "cultivated and well-to-do, or in a commanding position" might be degenerate "ego-maniacs," "commit[ing] misdemeanours peculiar to the upper classes" (260). Such individuals included the Decadents of the *fin-de-siècle*. Galton too was critical of decadence, looking forward to the "steady riddance of the Bohemian spirit of our race" (335).

In *Dracula*, Bram Stoker seizes on this propensity of opposite classes to lapse into degeneracy. As critic Laura Sagolla Croley observes, "Middle- and upper class Victorians took great pains to distinguish the industrious poor from the residuum or, in Marx's terms, the proletariat from the lumpenproletariat" (87).[1] Yet while the character of Dracula, an aristocrat, may be "upper class," he also allies himself with the residuum to achieve his ends: he participates in the socioeconomic degeneration of the society. Dracula acts, in Croley's words, as "the meeting of social extremes . . . he can be land-owner (with its attendant security and power) and vagrant (with its spatial mobility)" (90). And Dracula is not only a social degenerate, he is also clearly a physical and mental degenerate. The physical aspects of Dracula's degeneracy have been widely remarked among Stoker critics.[2] But his intelligence is also suspect, as Van Helsing notes: "The Count is a criminal and of criminal type . . . and qua criminal he is of imperfectly formed mind" (Stoker 296).

H. G. Wells would go even further than Stoker in *The Time Machine*. Here the human race has degenerated into two subspecies: the vapid Eloi (who, "like the Carlovingian kings, had decayed to a mere beautiful futility" [68]) and the monstrous Morlocks ("queer little ape-like figure[s]" [60] who live underground). Wells dramatizes the dangerous divide between social strata by partitioning them into two races, each a regression in its own way. Both races have degenerated mentally, while the Morlocks have also degenerated physically, lapsing into an "ape-like" state.

Superficially, *The Princess and the Goblin* prefigures the socioeconomic and physical degeneration depicted in *Dracula* and *The Time Machine*. The goblin society is composed largely of mine workers but is ruled by a government and royal family "whose chief business, beyond their own simple affairs, was to devise trouble for their neighbours" (5). The goblin miners and royal family work together in their plan to topple the human king. Indeed, despite obvious class distinctions, the goblin miners are laborers with homes, which sets them apart from the parasitic residuum with which Dracula allies himself. Thus, the cooperative relationship between class polarities resembles that in *Dracula*; but the roles played by those classes is more characteristic of the Eloi and the Morlocks, descendants of the bourgeoisie and proletariat. Also like the Morlocks, the goblins are definite physical degenerates, "dwarfed and misshapen" (5). With their "pale, chinless faces and great, lidless, pinkish-grey eyes" (67), the Morlocks are adapted to subterranean life. MacDonald's goblins live underground too, and consequently "had greatly altered in the course of generations"; once human-like, they have become "not ordinarily ugly, but either absolutely hideous, or ludicrously grotesque both in face and form" (4).[3]

Unlike the deterioration evident in Dracula or the Morlocks (or Machen's primordial masses), however, the goblins' physical deterioration is not accompanied by a corresponding mental deterioration. On the contrary, "they had grown in knowledge and cleverness" (4). Though they often behave foolishly, the goblins develop two different strategies to achieve their end of conquering the daylight kingdom, both of which require patience and long-term planning. This strengthening of the organizational or rational mind of the goblins sets *The Princess and the Goblin* apart from virtually all succeeding degeneration fiction, in which physical and mental decline are always inextricably tied together.

Fears about socioeconomic, physical, and mental degeneration were greatly exacerbated in the late Victorian era by a related and even more substantial fear: that of moral degeneration. This anxiety was not so divorced from the aforementioned fears as might be expected. In the late nineteenth and early twentieth centuries, various pseudosciences such as phrenology and physiognomy percolated into the emerging field of psychopathology. Immoral and criminal behavior was looked upon as a physiological problem, and thus it would manifest itself externally. The writings of individuals such as Caesare Lombroso (*Criminal Man*) and Max Nordau (*Degeneration*) helped popularize these views around the turn of the century with works first translated into English in the 1890s.[4]

Not surprisingly, authors of supernatural fiction did not wait long to incorporate these ideas into their books. Whereas some writers, such as Machen and Wells, were content to dwell on hyperbolized physical degeneration, others were quick to assimilate the possibilities inherent in a symbiosis of physical and moral degeneracy.[5] Stoker, for example, mentions Nordau and Lombroso explicitly in describing Dracula (296), who is clearly morally corrupt — and visibly so! Robert Louis Stevenson dramatized the darker side of humanity in the persona of Mr. Hyde. An obvious physical degenerate — "he gave an impression of deformity" and is "troglodytic" (41) — Hyde is a moral failure as well: "Evil besides . . . had left on that body an imprint of deformity and decay . . . because all human beings, as we meet them, are commingled out of good and evil: and Edward Hyde, alone in the ranks of mankind, was pure evil" (79). Oscar Wilde – who ironically warranted inclusion in Nordau's *Degeneration*[6] – creates a similar physiognomic dichotomy in *The Picture of Dorian Gray*. When the eponymous protagonist's corruption at last catches up with him, he is found "withered, wrinkled, and loathsome of visage" (391).

MacDonald's 1872 goblins eerily anticipate Lombroso's "criminal man." The book's physical descriptions and especially Arthur Hughes' illustrations definitely resemble Victorian criminal archetypes: wide faces, disproportionately large ears, and prominent noses. And this is certainly borne out by their scheming and malicious natures. The correlation between their biology and morality is quite evident at the end of the book, when the descendants of the defeated goblins begin to change both in form and conduct: "most of those who remained grew milder in character . . . *Their skulls became softer as well as their hearts*" (241, italics mine).

But MacDonald uses a variant of degeneration to even greater effect in *The Princess and Curdie*. As Richard Reis has noted, MacDonald thought of Darwinism as "another convenient means of symbolizing his ideas about the spiritual education" (132). Stephen Prickett likewise observes that behind MacDonald's "essentially allegorical theory of evolution was the notion that each individual creature, animal or human, is in a constant process of spiritual development or degeneration that could be shown symbolically on the Great Chain of Being" (84). As such, *The Princess and Curdie* employs biological retrogression as a trope for spiritual retrogression, the grandmother stating "that all men, if they do not take care, go down the hill to the animals' country; that many men are actually, all their lives, going to be beasts. People knew it once, but it is long since they forgot it" (72). The young hero Curdie is given the gift of discerning the inner animal nature of other people. This ongoing biological metaphor is taken farther, however, in the character of Lina, a woman who has degenerated into a hideous beast. Lina accompanies Curdie on his task, participating in her own spiritual pilgrimage. Curdie longs to "pull the child out of the beast" (76). But that responsibility lies with Lina herself, and she must complete her own journey. He realizes "that Lina was a woman, and that she was naughty, but is now growing good" (160). Lina must prove herself good rather than naughty in order to be restored. Thus MacDonald allows for a process of spiritual *re-evolution*, a concept which seldom if ever appears in the works of his successors.

Why, ultimately, does MacDonald's treatment of the degeneration motif differ from his successors'? On one level, it may simply be that degeneracy had not yet become a significant societal concern when MacDonald wrote the *Princess* books. Despite Galton's writings, Victorian society did not truly internalize his ideas until the 1880s. *The Princess and the Goblin* predates this surge, whereas *The Princess and Curdie* merely teeters on the cusp of it. By the 1890s, degeneration was looked upon as a genuine danger, but a danger without a solution. As Greenslade has observed, hope did not seem available until the early twentieth century (182-210), and then it was only the false and frightening hope of the eagerly propounded eugenic theory.

More significant than societal matters, however, is MacDonald's underlying Christian worldview. In this, he resembles his friend, clergyman and writer Charles Kingsley, who had assimilated some purposive evolutionary thought as early as 1863, when he published his children's novel *The Water-Babies*. That novel, in the words of Gillian Beer, "fancifully moralise[d] the connections between evolutionary ideas, social theory and Christian teaching" (133). As Kingsley's journal entries on the Irish testify, he also perceived racial degeneration as a serious threat. An undercurrent of degeneration is also present in *The Water-Babies* in the Doasyoulikes, who represent, in Beer's words, "the decay of mankind back into primitivism and thence into animality" (119). Similarly, the grandmother in *The Princess and Curdie* notes that many people may be "travelling beastward," though "[t]here are not nearly so many going that way as at first sight you might think" (72). And within the contexts of MacDonald's theology, influenced as it was by F. D. Maurice and shades of Platonism, all creation is moving toward a greater restoration. Like his compatriot Kingsley, MacDonald held, in the words of Colin Manlove, "the beliefs that evil is not final, that all may finally be saved, and that the state of a being's soul may determine the form of its body" (*Christian* 183). The world of *The Princess and Curdie* is, as Manlove writes elsewhere, a "world poised on the edge of transformation, about to pass away beyond the old husk to a new and more glorious form" (*Scottish* 98). What finally separates MacDonald from his successors, then, is his eschatology. With the hope of a final *apocatastasis*, a final redemption of creation, no transitory earthly degeneration can have any permanence. The child can be pulled out of the beast and be reunited at last with its Father.

Ultimately, where do the *Princess* books fit within the larger context of degeneration literature? As has already been noted, MacDonald's goblins resemble the later degenerates of the *fin-de-siècle*. The affinity he draws between class extremes is a theme which found its way into works like *Dracula* and *The Time Machine*, though it may derive from Galton. Also, there are parallels between Wells' Morlocks and the goblins in their adaptation to a subterranean environment. The interrelation of physical and moral regressive qualities in *The Princess and the Goblin* echoes many times in the succeeding decades in the work of writers such as

Stoker, Stevenson and Wilde.

What might be missed amidst such correspondences is just how innovative MacDonald was. Lest we forget, all the other authors discussed postdate the writing of the *Princess* books. Lombroso, Nordau and others of that ilk had not yet been published in translation. I do not know whether MacDonald took his ideas directly from Galton or another source; he may have extrapolated them directly from Darwin or, as Prickett suggests, he may "owe more to Lamarck than Darwin, but very little directly to either" (82). But whatever their origin, he was clearly one of the first fantasists to recognize the great literary potential for variants of evolutionary theory.

Moreover, there are significant differences between the degeneration in MacDonald's books and those that emerge at the *fin-de-siècle*. For the later Victorians, the degeneracy of the populace represented a significant social concern, and thus their works are more tinged with an underlying terror that such regression might actually occur. With MacDonald, on the other hand, the real threat is almost entirely spiritual. The physical deformities of the goblins do not seem designed to excite the horror of the audience; in many ways, they are more comical. They act as a way for the novel's young audience to apprehend more readily the goblins' evil natures. This is even truer in *The Princess and Curdie*. Lina may be ugly, but she is not terrifying like the Morlocks or repulsive like Machen's oozing monstrosities. Rather, her degeneration into bestial form is a narrative means of depicting her spiritual condition. And unlike any other supernatural literary degenerates such as Mr. Hyde, Dorian Gray, and Dracula, she and the other creatures of MacDonald's *Princess* books are given the opportunity of redemption, of restoration to their original forms.

George MacDonald, then, holds a unique place in the history of this peculiar subgenre. On the one hand, he is one of its progenitors, pioneering the use of Darwinian motifs by hyperbolizing them fantastically. Yet as a Christian apologist, his aims are spiritual more than they are societal, so he does not play on popular fears of reversion as his successors in the 1880s and '90s do. He thus resides *in* the world of degeneration fiction but is not *of* it. In the end, his degenerates are unlike others because their condition is ontological, not physiological: "the change always comes first in their hands – and first of all in the inside hands, to which the outside ones are but as the gloves" (*Curdie* 73).

Endnotes

1. Croley notes that she takes the term "residuum" from Gertrude Himmelfarb's

book *The Idea of Poverty: England in the Early Industrial Age*.
2. Cf. Glover 39-41; Halberstam 337-40.
3. The resemblances between MacDonald's goblins and Wells' Morlocks have been cursorily noted by Gail-Nina Anderson and David Longhorn in their article "Mr. Wells's Goblins."
4. For an analysis of how *fin-de-siècle* writers used Lombroso and Nordau in particular, see Greenslade, especially Chapters 5 and 6 (88-133).
5. Even the cannibalism of Wells' Morlocks is primarily amoral; they are too bestial to be subject to human moral categories. Machen, meanwhile, was simply interested in evoking "a sense of horror with roots more in biology than in spirituality" (Eckersley 285).
6. Further analyses of how Stoker uses Nordau, Lombroso, and other *fin-de-siècle* criminologists can be found in Glover 65-81 and Fontana 25-27.
Wilde is examined in "Book III: Ego-Mania," where he is criticized for his decadent proclivities rather than his homosexuality. According to Nordau, he "apparently admires immorality, sin and crime" (320) – in other words, a literally textbook case of degeneracy.
7. For a further analysis of Kingsley's use of (d)evolution in *The Water-Babies*, see Manlove, *Christian Fantasy* 192-94.

Works Cited

Anderson, Gail-Nina, and David Longhorn. "Mr. Wells's Goblins." *The Wellsian* 23 (2000): 56-58.
Arata, Stephen. *Fictions of Loss in the Victorian Fin de Siècle*. Cambridge: Cambridge UP, 1996.
Beer, Gillian. *Darwin's Plots: Evolutionary Narrative in Darwin, George Eliot and Nineteenth-Century Fiction*. London: Routledge, 1983.
Croley, Laura Sagolla. "The Rhetoric of Reform in Stoker's *Dracula*: Depravity, Decline, and the *Fin-de-Siècle* 'Residuum.'" *Criticism* 37.1 (Winter 1995): 85-108.
Darwin, Charles. *The Origin of Species by Means of Natural Selection or the Preservation of Favored Races in the Struggle for Life and The Descent of Man and Selection in Relation to Sex*. New York: The Modern Library, 1936.
Eckersley, Adrian. "A Theme in the Early Work of Arthur Machen: 'Degeneration'." *English Literature in Transition* 35.3 (1992): 277-87.
Fontana, Ernest. "Lombroso's Criminal Man and Stoker's Dracula." *The Victorian*

Newsletter 66 (Fall 1984): 25-27.

Galton, Francis. *Hereditary Genius: An Inquiry into Its Laws and Consequences.* 1892. Rev. ed. New York: Horizon Press, 1952.

Glover, David. *Vampires, Mummies, and Liberals: Bram Stoker and the Politics of Popular Fiction.* Durham, NC: Duke UP, 1996.

Greenslade, William. *Degeneration, Culture and the Novel 1880-1940.* Cambridge: Cambridge UP, 1994.

Gregory, Frederick. "The Impact of Darwinian Evolution on Protestant Theology in the Nineteenth Century." *God and Nature: Historical Essays on the Encounter between Christianity and Science.* Ed. David C. Lindberg and Ronald L. Numbers. U of California P, 1986. 369-90.

Halberstam, Judith. "Technologies of Monstrosity: Bram Stoker's *Dracula.*" *Victorian Studies* 36.3 (Spring 1993): 333-52.

Hurley, Kelly. *The Gothic Body: Sexuality, Materialism, and Degeneration at the Fin de Siècle.* Cambridge: Cambridge UP, 1996.

MacDonald, George. *The Princess and Curdie.* Harmondsworth: Puffin, 1994.

---. *The Princess and the Goblin.* Harmondsworth: Puffin, 1996.

Machen, Arthur. *The Great God Pan.* London: Creation, 1996.

---. *The Three Impostors.* London: Everyman, 1995.

Manlove, Colin. *Christian Fantasy: From 1200 to the Present.* U of Notre Dame P, 1992.

---. *Scottish Fantasy Literature: A Critical Survey.* Edinburgh: Canongate Academic, 1994.

Nordau, Max. *Degeneration.* 1895. Trans. George L. Mosse. New York: Fertig, 1968.

Prickett, Stephen. *Victorian Fantasy.* 1979. Rev. ed. Waco: Baylor UP, 2005.

Reis, Richard H. *George MacDonald.* New York: Twayne, 1972.

Stevenson, Robert Louis. *The Strange Case of Dr Jekyll and Mr. Hyde.* Ed. Martin A. Danahay. Peterborough, Ont.: Broadview, 1999.

Stoker, Bram. *Dracula.* Ed. Nina Auerbach and David J. Skal. New York: Norton 1997.

Wells, H. G. *The Definitive Time Machine: A Critical Edition of H.G. Wells's Scientific Romance.* Ed. Harry M. Geduld. Bloomington: Indiana UP, 1987.

Wilde, Oscar. *The Portable Oscar Wilde.* 1946. Ed. Richard Aldington and Stanley Weintraub. Harmondsworth: Penguin, 1981.

Chapter 13

Parent or Associate? George MacDonald and the Inklings

Colin Manlove

It is by now customary and beyond remark to link George MacDonald with the so-called Inklings: C. S. Lewis, J. R. R. Tolkien, Charles Williams and others. The assumption often is that MacDonald provided an early form of the ideas and the literary fantasy the later writers developed. Groupings together of the writers are found in the journal *Seven*, by the Mythopoeic Society, and by the *Inklings Gesellschaft* of Germany, which has held a symposium on MacDonald and has frequent articles on him in *Inklings Jahrbuch*. On the homepage of the George MacDonald website, Ian Blakemore of Rosley Books in England is described as specializing in "books by or about George MacDonald and the Inklings" (Website 1). Robert Trexler, editor of *CSL: The Bulletin of the New York C. S. Lewis Society*, speaks of "the mythology of George MacDonald and the Inklings" (Website 1a). Elsewhere we hear that "the Inklings claimed George MacDonald as their spiritual mentor" (Website 2), and find MacDonald being described as an "honorary Inkling" (Website 3). Seattle University has a course, "Theology and the Imagination: George MacDonald and the Inklings," run by Kerry Dearborn. And so on: this is only a random sample.

So there must be something in this connection between MacDonald and the Inklings, must there not? And certainly, some obvious general similarities among them exist. First, all of the Inklings and MacDonald were Christians. Second, all of the main figures wrote fantasy – and what may now be called 'major' fantasy at that. Third, all of them were Christian Romantics. By this many people understand that they have a Wordsworthian view of the universe with God at its root. Sometimes they are understood to be practitioners of "Romantic Theology," though while that term might find some justification in the different, partly invented, theologies of MacDonald and Williams, there is not often much, apart from the "dialectic of desire" (Lewis, *Pilgrim's Regress* 10), that is Romantic in the theology of Lewis or Tolkien, which is most commonly orthodox and resistant to liberalism.

These general likenesses have usually proved quite enough to bring them all together in people's minds without further ado. But let us look at them more closely. First, though Christians, they all had very different beliefs. MacDonald, brought up in a Scottish Calvinist household, and trained as a Congregationalist, later diverged from certain approved doctrines, and was forced to resign from his living in Arundel, Sussex; thereafter, influenced by F. D. Maurice, he developed a basic Christian faith of his own founded on the Gospels. C. S. Lewis, reared in an Ulster Protestant environment, became for some time an atheist, before re-entering the church as an Anglican. Charles Williams was High Church in tendency, with a strong belief in ceremonial. J. R. R. Tolkien was a Roman Catholic of more or less fervor throughout his life.

MacDonald renounces doctrine and dogma from his Christian belief; the later Inklings all bow to one or other established church and creed. (Not that they did not sometimes come to their own very original versions of doctrine, such as Charles Williams's idea of "the Coinherence.") MacDonald's theology downplays original sin and the whole idea of lost innocence and present corruption; denies the notion of Christ as redeemer or debt-payer; replaces hell with a longer or shorter purgatory; and is founded entirely on a loving relation required between man and God. All the others insist that we would not be fit for God but through Christ; and maintain the orthodox Christian belief in original sin, redemption, last judgement and hell. Charles Williams, and Tolkien as a Roman Catholic, make the Incarnation, the joining of heaven and earth, the central fact of their faith; but Lewis does not so often focus on it, seeing the earth rather as a blighted place; and MacDonald feels that God has always been incarnate in the world, and sent Christ as an example to man of a perfect loving relationship between Son and Father, man and God.

So far as the second similarity is concerned – the fact that all write fantasy – it is clear that they all write fantasy of very different kinds. MacDonald writes fairy tales with Grimm-like settings of kings and princesses, forests and castles, or fairylands peopled by forces of the imagination; Williams produces novels set in early 1930s England, into which fantastic events intrude; Lewis gives us fantasies that take place in a God-centred solar system, or fairy tales in which modern children enter other worlds; Tolkien creates an imagined prehistory of our own world, from which fantasy itself is shown disappearing. As to their literary sources, MacDonald looks to the revolutionary Blake, where Lewis values the more conservative Milton and Spenser; Williams's literary kinship is with Dante, while Tolkien's is with the author of *Beowulf*.

The third broad similarity among them is that they are all Romantics, and their shared beliefs are known as "Romantic Theology." This means that they believed God was immanent in the universe, which meant that fiction about that universe could be mystical; that the effect of a fantastic work was largely emotional; that the imagination was man's highest mental faculty; and that the ultimate direction of spiritual history was benign. All of them value God's role as creator, whether of nature or of art, and see the things of this world as capable of shadowing or embodying the things of God. They write "mythopoeia," by which Christian truth may be embodied in stories that are not overtly Christian. Lewis calls this getting "past watchful dragons" (*Of Other Worlds* 37) writing narratives stripped of the kind of religious associations that nowadays put people off: but the real effect is one of surprise, as we realise that the tale has depths we never imagined, and of persuasion, as it appears that all roads, as it were, lead to Rome.

However, so far as divine immanence is concerned, they all vary on the degree to which it is present in this world. Charles Williams, who sees the Incarnation as the central fact of this world, is a sacramentalist who finds the most common everyday things full of glory, from a railway porter or a traffic policeman to a mass of rubbish floating down the Thames. MacDonald, however, rarely writes about the contemporary world in his fantasy, and when he does, as in *At the Back of the North Wind*, he portrays little Diamond's London life as a poor thing beside the wonderful and mystical adventures he has with the lady of the North Wind. This is not because MacDonald prefers fantasy to reality, but because he finds the inner world of the imagination the one in which God is most present and creative: "God sits in that chamber of our being where the candle of our consciousness goes out in darkness, and sends forth from thence wonderful gifts into the light of that understanding which is His candle" (*A Dish of Orts* 25). And the world itself, seen by the light of the imagination, stands in the same relation to God, who continually imagines it into being (2-3). Thus at the end of *The Princess and Curdie*, the city of Gwyntystorm, the creation of man, is destroyed, and wild nature, the creation of God, returns. For Lewis, however, this world is a fallen one, from which God is largely absent, except in certain images and experiences through which He sends to us longings that can find no earthly satisfaction. "We are summoned to pass in through Nature, beyond her, into that splendour which she fitfully reflects" ("The Weight of Glory" 209). Tolkien's view seems less Platonic, in that he sees fantasy as potentially part of God's work, and the fairy tale, if well made, as caught up and sanctified in the great fairy tale that came true, the story of Christ. "The Evangelium has not abrogated legends; it has hallowed them" (*Tree and Leaf* 63).

As for "mythopoeia," the writing of narratives resonant with divine truth, this involves a particular attendance to a story and a sequence of events; and while this is certainly to be found in Tolkien and Lewis (who writes an essay on the subject), and in Charles Williams who writes what have been called "supernatural thrillers," it is less the case with MacDonald, at least in his adult romances *Phantastes* and *Lilith*, where the hero often wanders without direction and there is no causal sequence of events or suspense. In his essays, MacDonald speaks of the fairy tale working like an Aeolian harp and dealing with mysteries, more like an intermittent rapture than a logical series: "Let fairy tale of mine go for a firefly that now flashes, now is dark, but may flash again" (*A Dish of Orts* 321); and as an epigraph to *Phantastes* he quotes his spiritual mentor Novalis on fairy tales as "narratives without coherence but with association, like dreams." So it is that in *At the Back of the North Wind* little Diamond is visited seemingly at random, and at night, by the lady of the wind, and in the varying intervals between he gets on with his 'ordinary' life in London. And in *The Princess and the Goblin*, Princess Irene finds her way to her strange great-great grandmother in the attics not by design but by seeming chance; and her interviews with the lady have only intermittent relation to the rest of the plot with Curdie and the goblins.

Nor is the writing of mythopoeia an activity exclusive to the Inklings and MacDonald, either in the modern age or in the past. Though Romanticism certainly involves a revival of interest in myth and its powers, its use as a symbolic narrative shadowing divine truth can be seen as far back as Apulieus' *The Golden Asse*, in the medieval French *Arthuriad* and in Spenser's *Faerie Queene*, not to mention in many Renaissance readings of Greek and Roman myths. Even *Piers Plowman* and *The Pilgrim's Progress* are founded on the notion of finding Christian direction out by indirections. As for the modern period, mythopoeia can be seen from Coleridge's *The Ancient Mariner* (1798) or Kingsley's *The Water-Babies* (1863) to Evelyn Underhill's *A Column of Dust* (1909) or T. F. Powys' *Mr Weston's Good Wine* (1927), and from Graham Greene's *Brighton Rock* (1938) to D. M. Thomas' *The White Hotel* (1981).

MacDonald and the Inklings can, however, all be called Romantics in the sense that they put a high value on the emotional effect of their stories. Many of them have a lyric element so intense as to draw the reader into the story, to the point where the fact that it is a story is forgotten, and one treats the fiction as reality. This is what Tolkien calls "the art of Enchantment" in which the Elves are proficient, and to which all human stories aspire (*Tree and Leaf* 47-8). MacDonald says: "A fairy tale ... seizes you and carries you away" (*A Dish of Orts* 319). Williams' protagonists become whirled into the rapturous sequences of images in his novels; Lewis embodies his spiritual yearning or *Sehnsucht* through *Perelandra* or Aslan, the Uttermost East or the margins of Heaven; Tolkien, whose criteria for the fairy tale, Fantasy, Recovery, Escape and Consolation, are all emotional, believes that the ending of a successful fairy story can produce "a catch of the breath, a beat and lifting of the heart, near to (or indeed accompanied) by tears, as keen as that given by any form of literary art, and having a peculiar quality" (*Tree and Leaf* 60). In all these writers, however different the actual source of the emotion in their fantasy, the reader, like the writer, is to be drawn into a sympathy that, in stories having divine truth at their core, is a kind of mysticism.

To come now to influences on, rather than similarities among: how much do the Inklings owe directly to MacDonald? The answer as far as Charles Williams is concerned is, broadly, nothing. Williams includes a pastiche ballad, 'The Yerl o' Waterydeck' by MacDonald in his *A Book of Victorian Narrative Verse* (1927), but apart from that makes no reference to him; and not one of his seven novels shows a trace of MacDonald, whether in plot, characters, scenes or idiom. Since one of Williams' objects is to celebrate the glory in everyday contemporary life, where MacDonald's fantasies tend to go inwards to the world of the imagination, this is perhaps not surprising; and MacDonald's interest in the chaotic, the formless and the mysterious, is certainly at odds with Williams' continual panegyrics to order, clarity and coherence. MacDonald is concerned with deconstructing the patterns we put into the world; Williams may be said to be giving pattern to a world that is to twentieth century eyes much more a chaos.

On Lewis, however, MacDonald's influence would seem by contrast total. Lewis called MacDonald his "master" (*George MacDonald: An Anthology* 20); attributed the "baptism" of his imagination to a reading of *Phantastes* in 1916 (*Surprised by Joy* 171); introduced a figure of MacDonald into one of his own fantasies, *The Great Divorce* (1945); edited an anthology of extracts from MacDonald's writings (1946); and wrote on and continually mentioned MacDonald throughout his life. Lewis' first prose fiction, *The Pilgrim's Regress: An Allegorical Approach to Christianity, Reason, and Romanticism* (1933) may be deeply influenced by MacDonald's *Phantastes*, for both books have a common theme, that of the continual misidentification of a longing. MacDonald writes of a man wandering through Fairyland in search of an ideal that he continually misidentifies with beings in that world, when it actually lies beyond them, in "a great good" that is coming to him "through my tomb" (*Phantastes* and *Lilith* 182). Lewis' John, like Anodos, leaves home in search of a mysterious desire, which he tries to find in every figure he meets on his way, but always with disastrous outcome; until in the end he returns to his starting point to find the divine source of his longing, now transfigured to his opened mind. However, we may remark that in this theme in *Pilgrim's Regress* Lewis could be as readily indebted to a contemporary work by A. E. Coppard, *Pink Furniture: A Tale for Lovely Children with Noble Natures* (1930), in which one Toby travels the world in search of pink furniture, through a series of misidentified objects for his desire, only to journey back to find that Bridget the girl next door was his longed-for pink furniture all the time.

But apart from *The Pilgrim's Regress*, there is very little in Lewis' fiction that may be indebted to MacDonald's. In *The Silver Chair*, an underground journey recalls the one in MacDonald's short fairy tale "Cross Purposes"; and the giants in that book may owe a little to MacDonald's giants in *Phantastes* (though much more to the carnivorous giant Golithos in E. A.Wyke-Smith's *The Marvellous Land of Snergs* (1927)). What Lewis takes from MacDonald are more general interests: like MacDonald he has a yearning for God, if tinged with a Wellsian lust for the absolute, and he shares the same impulse to get clear of this world. However, Lewis' theology is much more of an apologetics than MacDonald's, which has an unquestioning certainty that makes it more a praise than a defence. It can fairly be argued that Lewis wrote his many works of theology, his *The Screwtape Letters* and maybe all of his fiction as a way of continuing to argue with God, to make his assurances more sure by showing to himself that Christianity rang logically true at every point. Certainly the degree to which Lewis believes in reason as a determinant of faith is quite unlike MacDonald, who often regards it as an impertinence. Again, throughout his books Lewis looks at himself having a relationship with God, where MacDonald is as much interested in the relationship God has with him. MacDonald wanted to abolish the self – "The one principle of hell is – 'I am my own'" – he wrote (*Unspoken Sermons* 495), and all his theology and fiction is directed at the destruction of the ego, the little island of 'me-ness' that stood outside the divine current of the universe. He wanted all things to lose their treasured identities, and become one; but Lewis preferred a measure of separation and independence. In *The Great Divorce* he has his fictional MacDonald espouse a belief in a final Hell to which the real one did not subscribe. Altogether Lewis is a remarkable example of someone convinced of a debt to another he does not really owe. (He also had an enthusiast's habit of drawing into the Inklings people who only partly belonged there.)

With J. R. R. Tolkien, however, there is altogether more similarity with MacDonald. Tolkien was reared on MacDonald's fairy tales and those of the Brothers Grimm, and MacDonald is one of the few modern writers to whom he refers with any frequency in his *Letters* and his essay "On Fairy-Stories" (1939, 1947). Both he and MacDonald share an interest in German fairy tales, though Tolkien tends to go to the original myths and folktales, where MacDonald prefers their reworkings in the Romantics Goethe, Novalis, Hoffmann or de la Motte Fouqué. Both have a considerable facility in languages. And both were trained in science, MacDonald in his undergraduate years at Aberdeen University, and Tolkien as a philologist at Oxford. The two also share certain views on fantasy, particularly in seeing it as one of the highest forms of literature, and in placing high importance on the inner consistency of reality, by which a fantasy remains true to the peculiar laws it has set up. They also particularly excoriate the use of allegory in fantasy, though in fact on occasion Tolkien accuses MacDonald himself of using it.

Tolkien said his orcs were based on MacDonald's goblins in *The Princess and the Goblin* (*Letters* 178), and we can find many other areas of his work that are influenced by the Scottish writer. The voracious Old Man Willow in *The Lord of the Rings* almost certainly comes from the no-less devouring Ash Tree in MacDonald's *Phantastes*. Tolkien's Galadriel is in the direct line of the immortal grandmother-figures in MacDonald's stories, and like the grand lady in *The Princess and the Goblin*, who gives Princess Irene a strange gold thread to lead her through the mines beneath the house, she presents Frodo with a magic phial that will help him through danger. The description of the Mines of Moria could well come from that of the mines in MacDonald; the portrayal of Théoden of Rohan disempowered by his flatterer Wormtongue probably comes from the account of the sick king in *The Princess and Curdie*; and the moment when the warrior eagles come to turn the final battle of Cormallen is almost certainly taken from the picture of the pigeons who become living darts to overthrow the evil army outside Gwyntystorm.

More generally – and this does not seem to be so far known – *The Lord of the Rings* as a whole is greatly indebted to MacDonald's "The Golden Key," a story Tolkien had admired all his life, until, oddly enough, when he came in 1964 to do an edition of it (Carpenter 242-3). The idea behind MacDonald's story is that a child who finds a golden key has then to follow a long journey to discover the lock into which it fits. *The Lord of the Rings* describes the finding of a ring that has to be taken over a long journey and put back where it belongs. When the golden key turns its lock, it disappears; so too when Tolkien's golden ring is put in its "keyhole," the crater of Mount Doom. In MacDonald's story, the way to heaven is then opened: in Tolkien's, the powers of hell are thrown down. "The Golden Key" also has a lady helper like Galadriel, who lives in a wood; and there is a journey from a wood land to a bare and rocky landscape, and mountain ranges to cross via tunnels. Then MacDonald's story has a division of the plot when the two children are separated, and go different ways (one more roundabout, through underground shafts and tunnels); and it has three successively wiser and more magical old men (like the two Gandalfs). Finally, it has stone stairs ascending into mountain walls (like Moria or the stairs of Cirith Ungol), and it ends in the centre of a mountain where one of the children has arrived from a place of subterranean fire. In retelling this story in *The Lord of the Rings*, however, Tolkien omits all its strange mystical imagery, to produce a literal narrative of adventure rather than a symbolic pilgrimage. He transforms what he called a fairy tale with its face, "the Mystical towards the Supernatural," into his own preferred kind, one whose face is "the Magical towards Nature" (*Tree and Leaf* 28).

Tolkien declared in his essay "On Fairy-Stories" that "Death was the theme that most inspired George MacDonald" (*Tree and Leaf* 59); but it was also one of the themes that most inspired Tolkien. The whole of *The Lord of the Rings* is full of the sense of time and mortality. Ancestries, past histories and legends are continually being recounted: the dead become almost as real as the living. And every step that Frodo takes with the Ring towards Mount Doom is not only towards the destruction of Sauron's power but also that of the Elves, the Ents and indeed magic itself in Middle-earth, which stands at the ending of the Third Age, on the verge of the dominion of men. Tolkien is much more elegiac than MacDonald here, for MacDonald sees death as desirable, the gateway to God; but Tolkien has admitted more of the dark vision of Beowulf to his story, in keeping with the Third Age of Middle-earth in which he has set it. (Elsewhere, in his short story "Leaf by Niggle (1964)", he is much more Christian in his treatment of death.)

But there the similarities end. One of Tolkien's concerns in *The Lord of the Rings* is to celebrate and delight in the world he has made: in "On Fairy-Stories" he calls it "Recovery," the regaining of a clear view of the identities of things. Frodo's journey involves slowly lighting up Middle-earth, bringing all its strange peoples and places before us. But MacDonald's fantasies often involve loss of the self and identity – Anodos and Vane, the ambiguous fading of little Diamond, the crushing of the self in *The Lost Princess*, the self-surrender of Curdie to the purposes of the grandmother. (Curiously, though, this is not so much the case in MacDonald's shorter fairy tales, where we sometimes have half-selves made whole, as in "The Light Princess," "Little Daylight" and "The Day Boy and the Night Girl.") And where *The Lord of the Rings* involves the exposure, the bringing to light, of hitherto mysterious or dark and terrible things, in MacDonald's fantasies identity becomes uncertain and mystery increases as the story proceeds. In Tolkien's story the loss of self that the Ring gradually produces in its bearer (most notably Frodo) is an evil. Then again, Tolkien's hero travels not by himself but as part of a group, a Fellowship made up of different races, and their journey not only involves many meetings with other peoples of Middle-earth, but also serves to bring them together after many years of isolation from one another. This socializing impulse is not found in MacDonald, whose protagonists are almost always solitary, and who are often shown being removed from their societies.

The fact is that the movement in MacDonald's fantasy is inwards, while that in Tolkien's is outward. MacDonald's fantasies go into the mind, ultimately of God, whereas Tolkien's move towards an outer and a solid world. MacDonald sees the creative and unconscious imagination as the home of God and the source of His speech through fantasy. Tolkien did not care for the inner world, nor did he put this value on it. Indeed it can be argued that the Ring contains the subconscious, which has usurped its proper place below stairs by assuming solid form, and which must be returned to the dark and abyssal places of the mind where it belongs. Significantly, the effect of the Ring on others is to remove solidity and identity, whether in the short term by making one invisible, or in the long by making one lose one's being, as with Gollum or the Nazgûl.

Actually here we are dealing with a difference between MacDonald and the Inklings generally. All of the Inklings could be said to take a delight in the solid identities of things central to their fantasies. For instance, the object of the evil Weston in Lewis' space trilogy is to reduce the individual worlds of Malacandra and Perelandra to one dead level of slavery; and this is what the White Witch has done to Narnia in *The Lion, the Witch and the Wardrobe*. It is the detail of the outside world, the landscapes of Middle-earth, of Narnia, or of this world seen as a pattern of divine ideas, that is often primary – though later works such as Williams' *Descent into Hell* and *All Hallows' Eve*, Lewis' *Till We Have Faces* and Tolkien's "Leaf by Niggle" tell a different story. All the Inklings have a distrust of the unconscious, particularly in its Freudian aspects: Charles Williams calls it P'o-L'u, the Incoherence (*The Region of the Summer Stars*, *The House of the Octopus*).

We are not dealing simply with the differences between MacDonald and the Inklings here, but with a difference between the kinds of fantasy they choose to write. MacDonald is a writer, broadly, of subversive fantasy: he belongs to the tradition that gives us such diverse works as Swift's *Gulliver's Travels* (1726), Voltaire's *Candide* (1759), E. T .A. Hoffmann's *The Golden Pot* (1814), Coleridge's *The Ancient Mariner* (1798), David Garnett's *Lady into Fox* (1922), George Orwell's *Animal Farm* (1945), Peter Ackroyd's *Hawksmoor* (1985) or Robert Irwin's *The Limits of Vision* (1986). He aims to undermine his reader's assumptions and ways of seeing the world – not, as with other subversive writers, for the sake of broadening our perspective on life, but for the purpose of leading us towards God. His fantasies are full of paradoxes, riddles and other reverses, to point us to a new and transcendent level of discourse. This is a level where an attic may open on to the stars, an apparent gulf beneath a child's feet hold her up, a fire burns a boy's hand not physically but spiritually, or where "The more doors you go out of, the farther you get in" (*Phantastes and Lilith* 194). MacDonald's fantasies are founded on words, scenes and events that continually reverse one another, pushing a deeper knowledge beneath a shallower one; and characters frequently change shape, according to their inner natures, or the spiritual nature of the person looking at them.

The Inklings, however, are writers of much more conservative fantasy. Their fantasies seek to preserve something, to keep things as they are. In all Williams' novels there is a supernatural invasion of the world that is in the end reversed. In Lewis' space trilogy, Ransom manages to keep the strange world of Malacandra as it is, and succeeds in preserving the innocence of the Lady on Perelandra. In the Narnia books, the story usually concerns the restoration of something – Narnia itself in the first books, variously dethroned princes in others, and Narnia as it was meant to be in the last. Tolkien's *The Lord of the Rings* is deeply conservative in impulse, in that Frodo is seeking to preserve the various worlds of Middle-earth from destruction by Sauron, and in that we have a celebration of the wonder of that world throughout: though Tolkien knows the bitter truth that the world will lose part of its essence in the very moment of being saved.

Another factor at work in these differences between MacDonald and the others is that in the end he is a Scottish fantasy writer, and they English. But there is not space to dilate on that here. Suffice to say that certain characteristics of MacDonald's fantasy are not his alone, but are found throughout Scottish fantasy generally. These include the focus on the unconscious mind, the movement inwards rather than out into the world, the isolation and spiritual reduction of the hero, the movement towards darkness rather than light (see Manlove *The Fantasy Literature of England* and *Scottish Fantasy Literature*). The point to be made from this is that MacDonald's differences from Williams, Lewis and Tolkien do not always stem from himself alone, but come from a wider cultural background of which he is a part.

So while with one, unexpected, Inkling there is specific debt to MacDonald's fantasy, with the other two there is less or none, and between all three of them and MacDonald there are real differences of outlook. While it is fair to say that they all have a broadly common programme and procedure, their individual natures – and this would go as much for differences among the so-called Inklings themselves – are so marked as to make any unity among them serve little more than a public purpose. It helps the importance and the persuasiveness of these writers if they are seen as part of a re-Christianising movement than simply as several people with merely individual visions. It helps MacDonald's significance to the common mind if he can be associated with more familiar and 'important' writers such as Lewis and Tolkien. And of course it makes things tidier to group more or less obstreperous individuals under more or less convincing intellectual categories; and it helps us to believe we are making sense of our cultural history. The topic must here be left. So far as MacDonald in particular is concerned, the main object here has simply been to show that he differs from Williams, Lewis and Tolkien much more than he is like them; and that we should be careful with our generalizations.

Works Cited

Carpenter, Humphrey. *J. R. R. Tolkien: A Biography.* London: Allen & Unwin, 1977.
Coppard, A. E. *Pink Furniture: A Tale for Lovely Children with Noble Natures.* London: Cape, 1930.
Lewis, C. S. *The Chronicles of Narnia.* London: Bles, 1950-56.
---. (ed.) *George MacDonald: An Anthology.* London: Bles, 1946.
---. *The Great Divorce: A Dream.* London: Bles, 1946.
---. *Out of the Silent Planet.* London: John Lane the Bodley Head, 1938.
---. *Perelandra.* London: John Lane the Bodley Head, 1943.
---. *Of Other Worlds: Essays and Stories.* London: Bles, 1966.
---. *Surprised by Joy: the Shape of my Early Life.* London: Bles, 1955.
---. *Till We Have Faces: A Myth Retold* London: Bles, 1956.
---. "The Weight of Glory" (1941), repr. in *They Asked for a Paper: Papers and Addresses.* London: Bles, 1962.
MacDonald, George. *A Dish of Orts: Chiefly Papers on the Imagination, and on Shakspere.* London: Sampson, Low, Marston, 1893.
---. *At the Back of the North Wind.* London: Strahan, 1871.
---.*The Light Princess and Other Tales.* Introduction Roger Lancelyn Green. London: Gollancz, 1961.
---. *Phantastes and Lilith.* London: Gollancz, 1962.
---. *The Princess and Curdie.* London: Chatto & Windus, 1883.
---. *The Princess and the Goblin.* London: Strahan, 1872.
---. *Unspoken Sermons. Series I, II, III.* Whitethorn, CA: Johannesen, 1997.
---. "The Yerl o' Waterydeck." In *The Poetical Works of George MacDonald,* 2 vols. London: Chatto & Windus,1893. Vol.2, 381-84.

Manlove, Colin. *The Fantasy Literature of England*. London: Macmillan, 1999.
   ---. *Scottish Fantasy Literature: A Critical Survey*. Edinburgh: Canongate Academic, 1994.
Tolkien, J. R. R. 'Leaf by Niggle' (1964). *In Tree and Leaf.*
   ---. *Letters   The Letters of J.R.R. Tolkien*. Edited by Humphrey Carpenter. London: Allen & Unwin, 1971.
   ---. *The Lord of the Rings*. London: Allen & Unwin, 1954-55.
   ---. "On Fairy Stories" (1939, 1947). Repr. in *Tree and Leaf*.
   ---. *Tree and Leaf*. London: Allen & Unwin, 1964.
Website 1   The Golden Key. George MacDonald WWW Page/ Homepage.
Website 1a   The Golden Key. George MacDonald WWW Page/ Resources/ Light Princess/ 'George MacDonald and the Light Princess' by Robert Trexler.
Website 2   The United Methodist Church/ My Spiritual Journey/ *The Chronicles of Narnia/ The Lion, the Witch and the Wardrobe*/ 'C.S. Lewis and the Prophetic Imagination' by Dan R. Dick [2005].
Website 3   'The Dancing Lawn', Official Forums of Narnia Fans/ Homepage [Dec. 2003].
Williams, Charles. [ed.] *A Book of Victorian Narrative Verse*. London: Oxford UP, 1927.
   ---. *All Hallows' Eve*. London: Faber & Faber, 1945.
   ---. *Descent into Hell*. London: Faber & Faber, 1937.
   ---. *The House of the Octopus*. London: Edinburgh House, 1945.
   ---. *The Region of the Summer Stars*. London: Editions Poetry, 1944.
Wyke-Smith, E. A. *The Marvellous Land of Snergs*. London: Ernest Benn, 1927.

Part 4: MacDonald's Reputation

Chapter 14

'Wolff' in Sheep's Clothing:
The George MacDonald Industry
and the Difficult Rehabilitation of a Reputation

John Pennington

In the first chapter of *Lilith* Mr. Vane is restless, trying to read in his library, when he notices a portrait hanging on the wall. He writes: "I knew it as the likeness of one of my ancestors, but had never even wondered why it hung there alone, and not in the gallery, or one of the great rooms, among the other family portraits" (9). Another portrait, one included among the photographs in Greville MacDonald's biography of his parents, depicts a literary family of sorts. This picture, titled "Group of Contemporary Authors," shows nine men seated in a library: J. A. Froude, Wilkie Collins, Anthony Trollope, W. M. Thackeray, Lord Macaulay, Bulwer Lytton, Thos. Carlyle, and Charles Dickens are featured with the author eulogized in 1905 by *The Athenaeum* as a man "distinguished for many years above the crowd of authors who were his contemporaries by virtue of the rich dower of lofty ideals and meditative insight which was his. His form was instinct with the nobility of his mind, and he leaves behind him many devoted friends who will cherish his memory" (400). That man is George MacDonald. This picture posing as a photograph included in Greville MacDonald's *George MacDonald and His Wife* (1924) is clearly a composite – or fake – photograph; however, it does suggest, along with *The Athenaeum* tribute, that MacDonald's literary stature and popularity at two defining periods were great – celebrating the centenary of his birth (1824) and the year of his death (1905).

By 1906, however, critics were bemoaning MacDonald's waning popularity, in America at least. In "A Neglected Novelist" for *North American Review* (1906), Louise Collier Willcox writes: "When one has said so much of MacDonald, one turns again to question why he is neglected. Compared with the people who are writing novels today, – and counting Meredith and Hardy amongst those who have ceased to produce, – he is a very giant amongst pigmies" (403). Willcox's concern must be tempered, at least in England, for in 1906, Chatto and Windus published *The Pocket George MacDonald*, "made" by Alfred H. Hyatt, who went on to compile *The Pocket Charles Dickens* in 1907, suggesting that indeed MacDonald was a giant among his literary peers. In fact, when *The Pocket George MacDonald* was published, only two authors were advertised in the MacDonald editions as having pocket volumes – Robert Louis Stevenson and Richard Jefferies. By the time *The Pocket Charles Dickens* hit the bookshops, Chatto and Windus was advertising editions for Thackeray, Emerson, Thomas Hardy, George Eliot, Charles Kinglsey, Ruskin, and Beaconsfield. Such company suggests that MacDonald was part of the Victorian literary ancestry as depicted in the 1924 picture. Willcox concludes her essay by stating that MacDonald "was to his own age shockingly liberal, and to ours he is amazingly orthodox. When another generation or two shall have passed, certain religious peculiarities will have become historical quaintness, and a fuller appreciation than he has yet had is awaiting him" (403).

Multiple generations have passed since Willcox made her claim. In 2005, we are at another crossroads, as we celebrate the centenary of MacDonald's death and reassess his lasting contributions. U. C. Knoepflmacher in the Penguin Classics edition of MacDonald's *Complete Fairy Tales* writes: "Valued in his own time as an original thinker and spiritual guide, [MacDonald] continues to command the attention of today's readers. But whereas the allure of his poems, sermons, novels, and essays has considerably faded, his fairy tales and longer fantasies such as *At the Back of the North Wind* and *The Princess and the Goblin* still fascinate" (vii). Knoepflmacher, however, underestimates the allure of MacDonald's nonfantastic work, for his realistic novels and sermons are attracting renewed interest. The Spring 2005 issue of *Christian History and Biography*, for example, is devoted to MacDonald. The cover of the journal describes MacDonald as "the Victorian poet, pastor, and storyteller who inspired C. S. Lewis." Associate Editor Jennifer Trafton admits the following:

> Like many people, I owe my discovery of George MacDonald to C. S. Lewis. I met him first in *Surprised by Joy* as the author of the book that marked a crucial turning point in Lewis' pilgrimage to faith. I met him again in *The Great Divorce* as the narrator's gentle Scottish guide through heaven. From there I found my way to *The Princess and the Goblin*, *Phantastes*, and *Sir Gibbie*. . . . So many of the theological ideas and emphases I associated with Lewis were waiting for me in MacDonald – the same abundant imagination, the same longing for something beyond, the same pervasive joy at the center of existence. (6)

Consequently, we find MacDonald relatively healthy 100 years after his death; his readership includes those who desire his fairy tales and fantasy, and those who seek spiritual guidance. In fact, MacDonald has been identified, to use Colin Manlove's term, as a writer of Christian Fantasy, whose goal "is to express the inner world of the imagination, and in so doing to make available, to those spiritually open to it, something of a sense of the immanent God" (166). The Armstrong Browning Library at Baylor University hosted a centenary conference in September, 2005 entitled "George MacDonald and His Children: The Development of Fantasy Literature," and its website call for papers described MacDonald "as the founder of a literary genre: religious fantasy – which, as the twentieth century has unexpectedly shown, has become a major and popular form."

This rising interest in religious or Christian fantasy assures that MacDonald will continue to have a readership for the foreseeable future. MacDonald's popularity, however, is inextricably intertwined with Lewis, as Trafton suggests in her personal discovery of MacDonald after reading Lewis. And we can pinpoint precisely the date – 1916 – with Lewis' discovery of MacDonald's *Phantastes* in a bookstall. Lewis would, in part, reclaim MacDonald as a serious writer—and gain a large audience for him – by referring to him in his scholarly *The Allegory of Love* (1936) and by making him a central character in his fictional *The Great Divorce* (1945). In many ways, Lewis revived MacDonald. As Lewis' popularity continues its ascent, with the release of the *Chronicles of Narnia: The Lion, the Witch and the Wardrobe* film (2005), and with the continued best-selling status of his children's series, MacDonald's popularity will be directly influenced by Lewis.

But Lewis has contributed unwittingly to the waxing and waning – to use an image from MacDonald's fairy tale "Little Daylight" – of MacDonald's reputation. Even with the opening of the canon and a historical focus centered on cultural materialism, academic scholars, for the most part, have relegated MacDonald to the margins of literary history, acknowledging, if at all, his weakness as a writer of moralizing novels whose style is ornate and clumsy. Lewis C. Roberts in the chapter, "Children's Fiction," in *A Companion to the Victorian Novel*, for example, mentions MacDonald but with a qualifier: "Fantasy might have signaled a significant shift away from purely moralizing fiction, but the didactic impulse was still operative. When moralists objected to this preoccupation with the imagination, writers would respond, as did George MacDonald, that 'the imagination of man is made in the image of the imagination of God" (361; qtd from *A Dish of Orts* 3). MacDonald is not referenced in any other chapter of the anthology, which includes chapters on "The Victorian Novel and Religion" (Hilary Fraser), "Scientific Ascendancy" (John Kucich), "Imagined Audiences: The Novelist and the Stage" (Renata Kobertts Miller), and "The Gothic Romance in the Victorian Period" (Cannon Schmitt). Nor is MacDonald mentioned, though Lewis is, in Terry Eagleton's *English Novel: An Introduction* (2005). Because of Lewis, in part, MacDonald has been pigeonholed as a religious writer, which further marginalizes him from the general reading public and from many critics, particularly those examining the canonical writers of the nineteenth century. More unsettling, though, is that MacDonald has been co-opted by Christian fundamentalists, who redact his work to fit a narrow theological agenda – that we must be obedient servants to an often-angry God who works in strange but powerful ways. Ironically, Lewis is simultaneously MacDonald's savior and his albatross.

In a 1987 piece in *North Wind*, titled "The George MacDonald Industry: A 'Wolff' in Sheep's Clothing?" I questioned whether the abridged editions of MacDonald's realistic novels by Dan Hamilton and Michael Phillips did a disservice to MacDonald's reputation by suggesting that he would not be read and appreciated on his own merits, an attitude driven primarily by Lewis' contention that MacDonald was a mythopoeic writer whose style was secondary to his imagined creations. This condescension toward MacDonald, I argued, could also be traced in later critics, in particular Robert Lee Wolff in *The Golden Key* (1961), the first full-length study of MacDonald published by Yale University Press. Wolff concludes his study by arguing that, "despite their Victorian conventionality in form, their often shoddy style, their lack of invention, their clumsiness, and frequent absurdity in plotting, MacDonald's novels strike one as off-key and somehow memorable" (379). Faint praise at best. W. H. Auden, a staunch fan of MacDonald, directly quotes Lewis' contention that MacDonald had a "'great inferiority in the art of words'" (84) but a gifted imagination, yet he concludes, "that is why, though there are many writers far greater than he, his permanent importance in literature is assured" (85). More contemporary critics followed suit. Even the insightful Rolland Hein has accepted MacDonald's secondary status as a writer. He writes in *The Harmony Within* (1982): "George MacDonald was first of all a Christian; secondly, an artist" (113).

This tension between flawed artist and spiritual guide haunts MacDonald, tarnishing his reputation. We can attribute this hesitant accepting of MacDonald as a major Victorian writer of the first order to Lewis' misguided attempt to make MacDonald relevant to his readers in his 1947 edited work, *George MacDonald: 365 Readings*, a work modeled, it seems, after Hyatt's 1906 *The Pocket George MacDonald*.[1] In this essay I explore how editors and writers have used Lewis' comments about MacDonald's style to grant themselves permission to redact his work in order, supposedly, to improve the readability and, often simultaneously, to highlight his Christian themes. More troubling, though, is the way some are misreading MacDonald's Christian stance from a fundamentalist perspective, which further marginalizes him, making the rehabilitation of his literary reputation a difficult task.

It appears that my concern in 1987 is alive and well over 18 years later. When I sent my original article to *North Wind*, then editor Kathy Triggs wrote to me, saying that "what you have to say is, of course, quite controversial. . . . I myself am firmly on the fence in the question of abridgements . . . . I do agree with you, that even for these consumers . . . any editing or abridging must produce a good work of art." William Burnside, in a 1988 article in the journal *Seven*, analyzed Phillip's Bethany House abridgements and concluded that, "theological ideas play a much lesser role in the modern abridgements than they do in the original novels. Is this a profit or a loss? His growing popularity indicates that there is indeed profit in modernizing George MacDonald. Perhaps Bethany House will now re-publish some of his better novels intact and thus reduce our losses" (127). Burnside would probably revise his comments today, for Phillips, in particular, has begun a crusade to make MacDonald a spokesperson for a fundamentalist teaching that prides itself on righteousness and intolerance of other viewpoints. All this is such a great irony when we remember that MacDonald was forced from his pulpit for preaching radical Christian beliefs about tolerance and acceptance.

No matter how brilliant George MacDonald is as a writer, consequently, he will be hounded by the supposed generosity of C. S. Lewis, who has categorized MacDonald as a second-to-third tiered writer of mythopoesis that focuses on Christian themes. It is no coincidence that Eerdmans, a religious publishing house in Grand Rapids, MI, continues to reprint Lewis' statements about MacDonald, from *George MacDonald: 365 Readings*, in its editions of *Phantastes* (2000) and *Lilith* (2000), the only mass-market paperback editions of these two works readily available for the general reader and the college classroom. Thus when readers, new or returning, begin MacDonald's great adult fantasies in the Eerdmans edition, they will be predisposed after reading Lewis to view MacDonald as an important, yet second-rate literary artist.

In his infamous introduction, Lewis writes that reading *Phantastes* was a turning point in his life: "What it [reading *Phantastes*] actually did to me was to convert, even to baptise . . . my imagination" (xxxiii). "I should have been shocked in my teens if anyone had told me that what I learned to love in *Phantastes* was goodness" (xxxiv), which to Lewis translates into "a certain quality of Death, good Death" (xxxiii), a sentiment echoed by J. R. R. Tolkien in "On Fairy-Stories." The words convert, baptize, and death provide fuel for the fundamentalists' fire, as they have misread MacDonald in light of conversion experiences. MacDonald "saves" Lewis and MacDonald "saves" readers by converting and baptizing them to God, while preparing them to accept the ecstasy or the Rapture, or the Second Coming when the world will be no more and God's justice will once again prevail. That Lewis converted from atheism to Christianity further enables such readings, and much of Lewis' popularity today resides in the fact that he is a voice of religion in the secular wilderness of contemporary society. To align MacDonald with Lewis, then, is to find another religious voice, another writer whose works are safe for fundamental Christians. It is common to find shelves devoted to Lewis' works in Christian bookstores; it is equally common to find a shelf below Lewis containing the works of George MacDonald. And it is common to find MacDonald's books marketed as Christian documents, as seen in Barbour Publishing's handsome 2005 edition of *At the Back of the North Wind*, which Barbour places in its "Christian Fiction Classics" series; Barbour claims on its copyright page of *North Wind* that "our mission is to publish and distribute inspirational products offering exceptional value and biblical encouragement to the masses."

Lewis, in addition, feels the need to apologize for MacDonald's limits as a writer, and justifies his claims by labeling him a mythopoeic writer, a label which tempts Lewis to make some of the most unintentionally damning statements about MacDonald as a literary artist. Lewis struggles to define the kind of art he finds in MacDonald:

> If we define Literature as an art whose medium is words, then certainly MacDonald has no place in its first rank – perhaps not even in its second. There are indeed passages where the wisdom and . . . the holiness that are in him triumph over and even burn away the baser elements in his style: the expression becomes precise, weighty, economic, acquires a cutting edge. But he does not maintain this level for long. The texture of his writing as a whole is undistinguished, at times fumbling. Bad pulpit traditions cling to it; there is sometimes a nonconformist verbosity, sometimes an old Scotch weakness for florid ornament . . . , sometimes an oversweetness picked up from Novalis. But this does not quite dispose of him even for the literary critic. What he does best is fantasy that hovers between the allegorical and the mythopoeic. And this, in my opinion, he does better than any man. The critical problem with which we are confronted is whether this art – the art of myth-making – is a species of the literary art. (xxvi)

The contention that MacDonald is primarily a Christian writer, whose words are secondary to his message, has prompted – and empowered – some to edit his work to profess a fundamentalist belief, and simultaneously edit his work to improve upon the written quality. And, thus, we continue to be in the midst of a "Wolff" in sheep's clothing, where MacDonald's reputation needs some dramatic rehabilitation so his legacy can truly reflect the remarkable writer that he was in the nineteenth and twentieth centuries, is in the twenty-first, and will continue to be in the future.

Dan Hamilton, Kathryn Lindskoog, and Michael Phillips are the most active in their enterprise to categorize MacDonald as a fundamentalist Christian writer; they have edited his works that are sold in Christian bookstores throughout the United States. In fact, Bethany House stated in a press release in June of 1999 that Phillips' books – books he both writes and edits – have sold over four million copies. Writer-editors such as Phillips, Hamilton, and Lindskoog are on a crusade to make MacDonald's Christianity more accessible to the general reader, and they have created a MacDonald industry that is based on a narrow ideological reading of his work. In effect, they want MacDonald to baptize the religious imaginations of targeted fundamentalist readers. In his edited versions for Victor Books, a division of Scripture Press Publications, Hamilton reminds readers of the primary reason for his editions – to make the Christian themes more explicit. He writes in *The Boyhood of Ranald Bannerman* (original title: *Ranald Bannerman's Boyhood*): "George MacDonald wrote his many books for the childlike of all ages – for any man, woman, boy, or girl who would receive God, the things of God, and things of God's world with open hands, warm hearts, and simple faith" (7).

MacDonald's "simple faith," for Hamilton, is concomitant with a simple style. Hamilton feels the need to defend his edition by claiming that "like many other writers of his time, MacDonald did have his technical faults," faults that Hamilton promises to correct, so that the reader can better appreciate the overall quality of his story: "His narrative skill was matched by the wise quality of his spiritual insights, for MacDonald spun his tales in order to tell us all about our Heavenly Father, His Son Jesus Christ, and the unbounded love with which They seek to persuade us to turn from our sins" (7). The edited *Bannerman*, it is important to note, is targeted for young readers; Hamilton's edition, consequently, emphasizes religious indoctrination through story. In *Home Again*, Hamilton claims that, "it is only fitting that George MacDonald should write a book about a man who first longs for a worldly fame as a poet, and then afterward comes to long for fame with God instead" (159). Not content with describing the plot in these Christian terms, Hamilton connects MacDonald to the struggles of contemporary readers, who see:

> the war of values between the worldly and the otherworldly; how the world squanders and kills time as a cure for boredom, while the follower of Jesus knows that time is passing all too quickly and should be redeemed and spent wisely. For is not our use of our time one of the talents give to us to invest? Some of us will have multiplied talents to surrender to our Lord, while others will have only dirt-crusted coins, for we cling to the treasures we have been given by hiding them in the earth. (160)

Hamilton's logic is paradoxical: he edits MacDonald because of his "technical faults," yet his editing highlights the didactic nature of MacDonald.

Not to be limited by conventional publishing houses, other redactors of MacDonald have shunted off to cyberspace, where their websites attract new converts to MacDonald and create a cyber-industry selling MacDonald wares. Kathryn Lindskoog is a case in point: her website, Lindentree, houses her work on Lewis and MacDonald (among many others), and the site is still maintained since her death in 2003 so that the important legacy of these writers, including Lindskoog, can live on. Like Hamilton, Lindskoog focuses narrowly on MacDonald as a Christian writer, particularly in her *Surprised by C. S. Lewis, George MacDonald and Dante: A Batch of Original Discoveries*. She has also edited a version of *Sir Gibbie*, which is published by P and R Publishing, which defines itself as a

> company . . . dedicated to publishing excellent books that promote biblical understanding and godly living as summarized in The Westminster Confession of Faith and Catechisms. Titles on our list range from academic works advancing biblical and theological scholarship to popular books designed to help lay readers grow in Christian thought and service. Our mission is to serve Christ and his church by producing clear, engaging, fresh, and insightful applications of Reformed theology to life. (www.prpbooks.com)

Lindskoog reminisces on *Sir Gibbie* in an online essay, "Adapting the Classics: Purists, Pirates, and Literary Liposuction":

> *Sir Gibbie* had been out of print for about thirty years when it was abridged by Elizabeth Yates, and it was her version I gobbled down with delight. . . . To my dismay, I discovered that along with the

unreadable old Northern Scots dialect, Yates had cut out much of MacDonald's Christian teaching ("digression from the story") and a key part of the plot. So I immersed myself in the book and adapted it from scratch, faithfully condensing each of the 62 chapters, to make it as readable for today's American children and adults as it was for British children and adults a century ago.

Lindskoog's focus on MacDonald's Christian didacticism does not stop here, however. She also has written a piece on MacDonald's "The Wise Woman." In "Plan for Curing: George MacDonald and Modern Child-Training Methods," she has an extended analysis on how the fairy tale teaches readers the proper child-rearing and training techniques, concluding that

George MacDonald never intended this 79-page fantasy to be a tract on child-training, and a prophetic one at that. But he knew very well that it was a mysterious, powerful story with at least two meanings. . . . One can read the story with one's forehead to glean MacDonald's insights about child training, and that is good. But he has been known to use a great feminine figure as his symbol for God, and he has been known to state that every child on earth is both the child of a king and the child of a shepherd. MacDonald's double story is about everyone, because he believed that everyone is part of God's ultimate plan for the curing.

Lindskoog's reading always turns at the end to the religious readying – "The Wise Woman" is ultimately about God.

But by far the most intriguing – and most suspect – figure in this Christian co-opting of MacDonald is Michael Phillips. He began his editing of MacDonald, as we have seen, at Bethany House Publishers, a Christian publishing company, where he also published his Christian hagiography-biography of MacDonald, *George MacDonald: Scotland's Beloved Storyteller* (1987); he writes in the Introduction, paraphrasing Lewis, that MacDonald is "so continuously close to the Spirit of Christ" (14). Phillips has more recently launched Sunrise Books, which publishes redacted versions of MacDonald's work as well as unabridged editions. Both are marketed as "The New Classics" on his website. Phillips has a clear agenda about MacDonald, as he focuses – some might say monomanaically – on a narrow range of MacDonald's Christianity, by either editing MacDonald's fictional works to highlight those themes, or by following Lewis and editing selections of MacDonald's words, these focusing entirely on MacDonald's Christian teaching. *George MacDonald: Knowing the Heart of God*, is subtitled "Where Obedience is the One Path to Drawing Intimately Close to Our Father." The book is a collection of quotations gathered by Phillips, in much the same way as *The Pocket George*

MacDonald and *Lewis' Anthology, 365 Readings.* But Phillips has only a narrow range of topics; in fact, he has only one topic – God. He writes in the volume that "to George MacDonald, all of life's truth could be discovered as part of an extremely simple two-step process: realizing who God is, then obeying him" (9). This simplifying of MacDonald – or indoctrinal reading of MacDonald – demonstrates the extent that Phillips, and the other redactors of MacDonald's work, will go to force MacDonald into a narrow theological category.

But Phillips goes one step further – he becomes George MacDonald, symbiotic with him in theological spirit. At Phillips' website – *www.macdonaldphillips.com* – the header for each web-screen section has the heading, "The writing, spiritual vision, and legacy of George MacDonald and Michael Phillips." Even a web-picture places MacDonald's portrait next to Phillips's own picture, as if they were doppelgangers. There is also an on-line journal – *Leben: The MacDonald/Phillips Magazine* – whose statement of purpose is the following:

> The fundamental essence of the Christian faith reduces to how one thinks and behaves. How one lives. At root, to be a disciple of Jesus Christ involves a revolutionary way of ordering one's thoughts, attitudes, priorities, perspectives, actions, responses, and moment-by-moment affairs. Only in the daily practice of obedience and a dedicated and total commitment to selfless Christlikeness does it avoid the fatal tendency toward religiosity.

Phillips calls this Christianity a "Bold" one, centered in the scriptures. His redacting of MacDonald replicates the fundamentalist way of literally reading the Bible that serves a particular ideological end.

In addition, Phillips has created the MacDonald-Phillips center in Eureka, CA, a physical retreat where one can immerse him or herself in a fundamentalist Christian think-tank. What is most disturbing about Phillips' appropriation of MacDonald is that he misreads MacDonald through a very narrow fundamentalist lens, which distorts MacDonald's overall reputation as writer and thinker. Phillips's narrow view of MacDonald's strict obedience to an Old Testament God, while embracing the salvation of the second coming of Christ, reflects what Bruce Lawrence in *Defenders of God: The Fundamentalist Revolt Against the Modern Age* describes as the fundamentalist spiritual quest: "The affirmation of religious authority as holistic and absolute, admitting of neither criticism or reduction; it is expressed through the collective demand that specific creedal and ethical dictates derived from scripture be publicly recognized and legally enforced" (27). "Fundamentalism is an ideology rather than a theology" (x), Lawrence avers. This ideology, in turn, becomes militant, focusing on the dualism between good and evil, right and wrong, and, as Martin Marty writes, they rely on battle metaphors: "fighting back," "fighting for," "fighting with," "fighting against," "fighting under [God]," all in the name of right (ix-x). This fight, Marty concludes, leads to a "politics of resentment" (22) that further ignites the holy crusade against those not yet saved, in keeping with the notion of the Rapture, or end of days, an eschatological hope for the believers, who, as Nancy Ammerman posits, "will one day soon simply hear the heavenly trumpet and disappear into the sky, leaving those around them bewildered" (6). In this context, MacDonald can be read alongside the *Left Behind* books. Thus the ending of *The Princess and Curdie* –"One day at noon, when life was at its highest, the whole city fell with a roaring crash. The cries of men and the shrieks of women went up with its dust, and then there was a great silence. . . .All around spreads a wilderness of wide deer, and the very name of Gwyntystorm has ceased from the lips of men" (320) – can be read in context of the Rapture, the end. In "Baptizing the Imagination: The Fantastic as the Subversion of Fundamentalism," Mara E. Donaldson concludes that the "fundamentalist Christian reader of the high-fantasy tradition cannot any longer even imagine another worldview, another framework – other than that of fundamentalist epistemology, society, and ethics – from within which this fantasy tradition might, much less must, be understood" (195).

If MacDonald should be categorized as a Christian fantasist, as Manlove argues persuasively, he is certainly not the same writer that Hamilton, Lindskoog, and Phillips depict. In fact, MacDonald subscribed to no such fundamentalist system, as Greville MacDonald stresses when he prints a letter from George to his father (April 15, 1851):

> I firmly believe people have hitherto been a great deal too much taken up about doctrine and far too little about practice. The word doctrine, as used in the Bible, means teaching of duty, not theory. I preached a sermon about this. We are far too anxious to be definite and to have finished, well-polished, sharp-edged systems – forgetting that the more perfect a theory about the infinite, the surer it is to be wrong, the more impossible is it to be right. I am neither Arminian nor Calvinist. To no system would I subscribe. (155)

In a later letter (January 20, 1889), MacDonald admits that he is "content in God. Rather than believe in the popular God, I would believe in none, with the agnostics . . . ." (535). Thus to place MacDonald into a fundamentalist system is to force him into a category that does not reflect his complexity. In other words, such fundamentalists misread MacDonald on the most fundamental – not fundamentalist – level. A major effect of this narrow systematizing of MacDonald is that he is marketed as a religious writer who espouses a narrow theological agenda. For the general reader, consequently, he may be seen as a didactic writer focused on indoctrination.

This narrowing of MacDonald to a conservative religious writer is exacerbated further by abridgements of his work that are edited precisely to highlight the religious focus of his work. Thus we have a two-fold contradiction: 1) MacDonald is redacted so his work can be seen in a fundamentalist light; and 2) these redactions are justified because MacDonald was not a strong literary artist, so he is in need of a strong editor. Such an editorial enterprise compounds the difficulty of rehabilitating MacDonald's reputation. Many abridgements are warranted, the editors claim, because MacDonald's style gets in the way of the imaginative world. These abridged versions are often considered "modernized" for "today's reader." In the Editor's Foreword to *The Genius of Willie MacMichael* (original title – *Gutta Percha Willie: The Working Genius*), Hamilton resorts to the clichéd reasons for abridgements, which he repeats verbatim in many introductions to the numerous redacted novels:

> Like many other authors of his time, MacDonald did have some technical faults as a writer. Yet he was a true storyteller, and always left his audience turning pages to see what would happen next. . . . This special edition has been slightly trimmed from the original and clarified for fuller enjoyment. May it bring all its readers delight in a 'new' author, and spur a growing interest in MacDonald at his fullest and best. And may such interest warrant the eventual reprinting of his complete, original works. (7-8)

This is interesting logic: Hamilton suggests that Victorian writing by its nature was flawed – and that contemporary writers have no such flaws. In addition, Hamilton has "trimmed" and "clarified" MacDonald so that the reader can better understand him. Yet Hamilton argues for reprinting of MacDonald's original work – one that he even renamed. Hamilton's arguments create confusion: why reprint the originals if they are stylistically faulty in need of clarification? In *The Boyhood of Ranald Bannerman*, Hamilton adds further particulars: "He often composed awkward and intricate sentences, repeated himself, sermonized, lost track of minor details, and sometimes wandered away from his subject. Yet he was a true storyteller . . ." (7). Here are his comments from *The Last Castle* (original title – *Saint George and Saint Michael*) as he justifies his editorial process, directly imitating Lewis' comments about MacDonald in *George MacDonald: 365 Readings*:

> MacDonald has few equals as a storyteller, but his writing is overlong, often uneven, and does not always rise to the same level as his story. The book in its original versions is lengthy and sometimes tedious; I have trimmed away the occasional outbreaks of irrelevancy, eliminated repetitive material, made consistent the choices of spelling and dialect, reshuffled out-of-sequence scenes, and tightened dragging narrative. However, I certainly do not represent my version as better than the original; it is only easier to read.... (288)

Hamilton's description of MacDonald as a writer is quite negative, yet he justifies such comments by returning to the notion that MacDonald is a true storyteller; in fact, Hamilton is recasting Lewis' comments but in a new way. In *The Parish Papers* (three novels in one, *Annals of a Quiet Neighborhood*, *The Seaboard Parish*, and *The Vicar's Daughter*), Hamilton boldly states at the beginning of the Foreword: "Writing styles change. Good stories don't. The first statement explains why George MacDonald's novels are not widely read these days. The second statement explains why they should be" (7).

Michael Phillips follows suit. Phillips states on his website that MacDonald's vision is spiritual, and spiritual vision is not in vogue today: "Today's 'average' reader is vastly different in world outlook than his or her counterpart a century ago and is not so concerned with spiritual matters. This is a new era of literary taste; happy endings are no longer in vogue as they were then." Phillips then justifies his editing:

> To understand MacDonald at all, one needs to experience his novels. When the reader does, however, two problems are immediately encountered in MacDonald's writing style. First of all, MacDonald frequently used lowland Scots dialect . . . which few now understand at a glance. And, secondly, MacDonald's tendency toward preaching and rambling often erupts without warning, and he lapses into off-the-subject discourses which slow up the story line considerably. For the loyal MacDonald follower, such idiosyncrasies lend a certain charm and flavor. But the average person is reading a novel, he wants to move through the drama without having to stop and wade through a sermonette or to unravel and decode a passage in Scotch dialect.

Again, Lewis' contention that story is more important than style dominates Phillips' attitude toward MacDonald's novels. And Phillips sprinkles testimonies on his website from readers who were able to finally understand MacDonald. One writes: "Understanding MacDonald's message has been a challenge for me. Having it in a language I understand has been a help." "Without your editing, I would never read George MacDonald's wonderful books," writes another reader of the redacted MacDonald. "Fabulous, for want of any word which would describe the editing of *The Curate's Awakening* by George MacDonald," concludes yet another reader. Of course, there is no such book by MacDonald – *Thomas Wingfold, Curate* is the book the reader is actually referring to.

As you can see, such editing of MacDonald's novels is justified by placing him as a second-rate novelist whose story is more important than his style – the mythopoeic haunting from Lewis continues to hover over MacDonald's reputation. Hamilton and Phillips, however, are primarily referring to MacDonald's novels – they say very little about MacDonald's fantasies and fairy tales, though Phillips has edited a "children's version" of *At the Back of the North Wind* (even keeping the title intact). It is more disturbing, however, when we recognize that Lewis' mythopoeic comment also impacts his fairy tale and fantasy contributions, which are some of the most original and important works of the nineteenth century, placing him on equal footing with, for example, Lewis Carroll, Hans Christian Andersen, and Oscar Wilde, writers who transformed fairy tale discourse during Victorian and late-Victorian times.

This tampering with MacDonald's style extends beyond fundamentalist appropriations – award-winning authors tend to view his work as religiously didactic and his style ornately Victorian. An example can be seen in Robin McKinley, the accomplished fantasy writer and Newberry Award winner of *The Hero and the Crown*. Harcourt Brace has published an edited edition by McKinley of "The Light Princess," lavishly illustrated by Katie Thamer Treherne. Unfortunately, McKinley falls for Lewis' seduction about MacDonald. McKinley writes in a preface to her retelling, "A Note about the Author," that "the strong strain of Christian doctrine in much of his work, and his often, ornate, old-fashioned style, has made him less popular than he deserves" (np). "The Light Princess," ironically, has no apparent Christian doctrine driving the fairy tale; in fact, most fairy tales by MacDonald have little direct references to God at all, including the most mystical tale of all, "The Golden Key." McKinley, obviously, is influenced by the critical view that MacDonald is religiously didactic. MacDonald becomes doubly doomed: McKinley chastises him for a didactic strain of Christian teaching, while others, like Hamilton, Lindskoog, and Phillips, praise that very strain, yet both camps find common ground by agreeing that his style is often shoddy. McKinley further writes in her preface to "The Light Princess" that MacDonald "had a first-rate imagination, although his literary style couldn't always keep up with it; and some of his dreariest historical romances were written under the pressing need to keep his eleven children fed" (np), a sentiment promoted by Lewis in *The Allegory of Love*. McKinley, it appears, intends to match his imagination to a style that is more deserving. She begins her enterprise in the first sentence. It will be instructive to compare MacDonald's original to McKinley's revised version:

> MacDonald: Once upon a time, so long ago that I have quite forgotten the date, there lived a king and queen who had no children. (1)
>
> McKinley: Once upon a time, so long ago that I have forgotten the date, there lived a king and queen who had no children. (1)

McKinley drops one word – quite – which suggests that she intends to edit moderately to eliminate, to her taste, unnecessary qualifiers. But such a change does nothing to improve the original. But her agenda is much more aggressive as readers move to the following sentences:

> MacDonald: And the King said to himself, "All the queens of my acquaintance have children, some three, some seven, and some as many as twelve; and my queen has not one. I feel ill-used." So he made up his mind to be cross with his wife about it. But she bore it all like a good patient queen as she was. Then the king grew very cross indeed. But the queen pretended to take it all as a joke, and a very good one too. (1)
>
> McKinley: The king said to himself, "All the queens of my acquaintance have children; I feel ill-used. (1)

To think that McKinley's revising is an improvement on the original is to think that Humpty Dumpty could be eliminated to improve Carroll's *Through the Looking-Glass*.

The key to MacDonald's passage is the humor, the play, the pun on "bore," that make the Queen's "joke" that much more subversive. Even the use of "cross" (twice) seems a pun on the religious iconography that MacDonald often used; this pun further delineates the King as a greedy, spiritually devoid bore. In fact, there is no way to improve the passage, a sentiment that Maurice Sendak had when he illustrated "The Light Princess" in the 1960s with no editing of the text. McKinley's audacious editing of a classic fairy tale needs to be seen in light of Lewis' comments, which shine down on MacDonald in unflattering ways.

"This collection, as I have said, was designed not to revive MacDonald's literary reputation but to spread his religious teaching" (xxx). So admits Lewis in his preface to *George MacDonald: 365 Readings*. Quite an ironic comment, it appears. Clearly, Lewis has done immense damage to MacDonald's literary reputation, and he has provided an example for others to follow in order to spread MacDonald's religious doctrine, further marginalizing him.

Despite some who seem heaven-bent on apologizing for or improving his work, MacDonald is a survivor, a resilient writer who preservers in spite of a MacDonald industry that attempts to apologize for him as a writer and co-opt him as a fundamentalist Christian. And, as we have seen, we can trace this tension back to C. S. Lewis, whose notion of mythopoeic writing has tempted critics into accepting MacDonald as a fumbling stylist in need of salvation. A great irony is that MacDonald's popularity will no doubt increase in the coming years because of Lewis: the filming of *The Chronicles of Narnia* (intended as a series of films to compete with the *Harry Potter* and *The Lord of the Rings* phenomena) will bring new readers to MacDonald, readers who will gain entrance to MacDonald through Lewis. If the Lewis "films" are popular – and there is no reason they will not be – one could imagine that movie producers may opt to bring other classic fantasies to life on screen. Will the animated *The Princess and the Goblin*, for example, be remade into a live-action feature? Or imagine screen versions of *Phantastes* or *Lilith*. One wonders if a great good is coming to MacDonald's work.

Some other positive signs point to a slow but assured rehabilitation of MacDonald's reputation. Currently, there are scholarly texts available through Penguin and Oxford World Classics, and Johannesen Publishing has made all of MacDonald's works available in unabridged, hardbound editions. *North Wind*'s editorial policy to use Johannesen editions (along with Knoepflmacher's Penguin fairy-tale edition) reminds readers that MacDonald's untouched words are important. One could hope that Johannesen would publish paperback editions so that teachers could consider adopting these texts for classroom use. The potential for MacDonald scholarship is also unlimited, with *North Wind* publishing a variety of essays geared for the general and specialized reader. Now may be the time when *North Wind* should move to make the journal totally peer-reviewed so that there is a clear distinction between scholarly pursuit and personal recollection.

If MacDonald were alive today, he might feel a little like Mr. Vane who looks at "the likeness of one of . . . [his] ancestors" (9) in a portrait that seems strangely unfamiliar. MacDonald might not recognize his own portrait, for many readers have painted him with narrow brush strokes or digitized his image in the likeness of a fundamentalist preacher. But when we back away from these images, and refocus our critical eye on the true legacy of MacDonald, we will encounter in his work that "great longing" that drives Mr. Vane into that literary realm, where he becomes "lost in a space larger than imagination" (50).

Endnote

1. It would be misleading to chastise Lewis solely for MacDonald's reputation without qualification. In *The Allegory of Love*, Lewis admits that, "a dominant form tends to attract to itself writers whose talents would have fitted them much better for work of some other kind. Thus the retired Cowper writes satire in the eighteenth century; or in the nineteenth a mystic and natural symbolist like George MacDonald is seduced into writing novels" (232). Greville MacDonald depicts an exchange between George Murray Smith, of the publisher Smith, Elder, and Co, and his father: "'Mr. MacDonald,' he said, upon the occasion of refusing his drama, *If I had a Father*, 'if you would but write novels, you would find all the publishers saving up to buy them of you! Nothing but fiction pays'" (318). When MacDonald began publishing *The Princess and the Goblin* in *Good Words for the Young*, a magazine that MacDonald edited, the readership dropped dramatically, which prompted MacDonald to claim that his publisher, Strahan, "thinks it is because there is too much of what he calls the fairy element. I have told him my story . . . shall be finished in two months more. . . . I know it is as good work of the kind as I can do, and I think will be the most complete thing I have done. . . . Perhaps I could find a market for that kind of talent in America – I shouldn't wonder. . . ." (Greville MacDonald 412).

In effect, MacDonald's fantasies and fairy tales were marginalized by publishers and the reading public, which preferred novels, or what became known as realistic fiction. George Levine writes that "whatever its difficulties and contradictions, however, realism was a historical impulse that manifested itself as a literary method and imposed itself on almost every form of prose narrative" (11). See also Ian Watt, *The Rise of the Novel*.

Let us not forget, however, that as much as Lewis apologizes for MacDonald being forced to write realistic novels, he continues to suggest that a natural symbolist – a mythopoeic writer of fantasy and fairy tale, that is – does not write in a form that ranks as Literature of the highest order.

Works Cited

Ammerman, Nancy T. "North American Protestant Fundamentalism." *Fundamentalisms Observed. The Fundamentalism Project. Vol 1.* Eds. Martin E. Mary and R. Scott Appleby. Chicago: U of Chicago P, 1991. 1-65.

Auden, W. H. Afterword. *The Golden Key.* By George MacDonald. Illus. Maurice Sendak. New York: Farrar, Straus and Giroux, 1967. 81-86.

Burnside, William. "Abridgement: Profit and Loss in Modernizing George MacDonald." *Seven* 9 (1988): 117-28.

Donaldson, Mara E. "Baptizing the Imagination: The Fantastic as the Subversion of Fundamentalism." *The Journal of the Fantastic in the Arts* 8.2 (1997): 185-97.

Eagleton, Terry. *The English Novel: An Introduction.* Malden, MA: Blackwell, 2005.

"George MacDonald." *The Athenaeum.* Sept. 23, 1905: 400.

"George MacDonald and His Children." Online posting. 3 Dec. 2005. http://www.browninglibrary.org/index.php?id=30300.

Hamilton, Dan, ed. Foreward. *The Boyhood of Ranald Bannerman.* By George MacDonald. Wheaton, IL: Victor, 1987. 7-8.

---. Afterward. *Home Again.* By George MacDonald. Wheaton, IL: Victor, 1988. 159-61.

---. Afterword. *The Last Castle.* By George MacDonald. Wheaton, IL: Victor, 1986. 287-88.

---. *The Parish Papers: Three Complete Novels in One Volume.* By George MacDonald. Colorado Springs: Victor Books, 1997.

Hein, Rolland. *The Harmony Within: The Spiritual Vision of George MacDonald.* Grand Rapid, MI: Eerdmans, 1982.

Lawrence, Bruce. *Defenders of God: The Fundamentalist Revolt Against the Modern Age.* New York: Harper and Row, 1989.

Levine, George. *The Realistic Imagination: English Fiction from Frankenstein to Lady Chatterley.* Chicago: U of Chicago P, 1981.

Knoepflmacher, U. C. Introduction. *The Complete Fairy Tales.* By George MacDonald. New York: Penguin, 1999. vii-xx.

Lewis, C. S. Preface. *George MacDonald: 365 Readings.* New York: Collier, 1986. xxi-xxxiv.

Lindskoog, Kathryn. "Plan for Curing: George MacDonald and Modern Child-Training Methods." Online posting. 3 Dec. 2005. <http://www.lindentree.org/plan.html>.

---. "Adopting the Classics: Purists, Pirates, and Literary Liposuction." Online posting. 3 Dec. 2005. <http://www.lindentree.org/plan.html>.

---. ed. *Sir Gibbie*. By George MacDonald. Phillipsbery, NJ: P and R Publishers, 2001.

---. *Surprised by C. S. Lewis, George MacDonald and Dante: A Batch of Original Discoveries*. Macon, GA: Mercer UP, 2001.

MacDonald, George. *At the Back of the North Wind*. Uhrichsville, OH: Barbour, 2005.

---. "The Imagination: Its Functions and its Culture." *A Dish of Orts*. Whitethorn, CA: Johannesen, 1996. 1-42.

---. *The Light Princess and Other Fairy Tales*. Whitethorn, CA: Johannesen, 2001.

---. *Lilith*. Whitethorn, CA: Johannesen, 2001.

---. *The Princess and Curdie*. Whitethorn, CA: Johannesen, 2000.

MacDonald, Greville. *George MacDonald and His Wife*. Whitethorn, CA: Johannesen, 1998.

MacDonaldPhillips.com. "The Writings, Spiritual Vision, and Legacy of George MacDonald and Michael Phillips." Online posting. 3 Dec. 2005. http://www.macdonaldphillips.com/index.html.

Manlove, Colin. *Christian Fantasy: From 1200 to the Present*. Notre Dame: U of Notre Dame P, 1992.

Marty, Martin E. "Fundamentals of Fundamentalism." *Fundamentalism in Comparative Perspective*. Ed. Lawrence Kaplan. Amherst: U of Massachusetts P, 1992. 15-23.

McKinley, Robin. *The Light Princess*. By George MacDonald. Illus. Katie Thamer Treherne. Orlando: Harcourt, 1988. P and R Publishing. Online posting. 3 Dec. 2005. < http://www.prpbooks.com/>.

Pennington, John. "The George MacDonald Industry: A 'Wolff' in Sheep's Clothing?" *North Wind* 6 (1987): 40-44.

Phillips, Michael. *The Curate of Glaston: Three Dramatic Novels from Scotland's Beloved Storyteller*. Minneapolis: Bethany House, 1986.

---. *George MacDonald: Knowing the Heart of God*. Minneapolis, Bethany House, 2000.

---. *George MacDonald: Scotland's Beloved Storyteller*. Minneapolis: Bethany House, 1987.

Pocket George MacDonald, The. Made by Alfred H. Hyatt. London: Chatto and Windus, 1906.

Pocket Charles Dickens, The. By Alfred H. Hyatt. London: Chatto and Windus, 1907.

Roberts, Lewis. "Children's Fiction." *A Companion to the Victorian Novel.* Ed. Patrick Brantlinger and William B. Thesing. Malden, MA: Blackwell, 2005. 353-69.

Trafton, Jennifer. From the Editor. *Christian History and Biography.* Spring 2005: 6.

Triggs, Kathy. Letter to the author. 16 June 1987.

Watt, Ian. *The Rise of the Novel: Studies in Defoe, Richardson and Fielding.* Berkeley: U of California P, 1957.

Willcox, Louise Collier. "A Neglected Novelist." *North American Review* 183 (July-Oct. 1906): 394-95.

Wolff, Robert Lee. *The Golden Key.* New Haven: Yale UP, 1961.

List of Contributors

David Robb is a senior lecturer at University of Dundee, Scotland. He was Joint General Editor of the Scottish Writers series and General Editor of the Scottish Classics series. David is the author of *God's Fiction: Symbolism and Allegory in the Works of George MacDonald.* and a past president of the Association for Scottish Literary Studies.

Gisela Kreglinger is currently working on a project tentatively titled: *Shock Reinvested: The Revelatory Hermeneutic of George MacDonald as a Way to Continue the Shock Experience of Jesus' Parables.* She is a holds an MCS degree from Regent College, Vancouver, British Columbia, Canada, and a ThD, from Regent College in conjunction with the University of Munich, Germany.

Robert Trexler is a marketing journalist in Connecticut and the managing partner of Zossima Press. He is also the editor of *CSL: The Bulletin of the New York C.S. Lewis Society.*

Fernando Soto holds a masters degree in Philosophy and has researched and published widely on Lewis Carroll and George MacDonald. He is the co-editor of *North Wind: A Journal of George MacDonald Studies.* He lives in Toronto.

David Neuhouser is the director of The Center for the Study of C.S. Lewis and Friends at Taylor University in Indiana and author of *George MacDonald: Selections From His Greatest Works.*

Jan Susina is an associate professor of English at Illinois State University and the author of several articles on MacDonald published in *Marvels & Tales: Journal of Fairy Tale Studies.* He was an editor for *The Lion and the Unicorn* for many years.

John Docherty is the author of *The Literary Products of the Lewis Carroll – George MacDonald Friendship*, and was the editor of *North Wind: A Journal of George MacDonald Studies* for many years. A retired research librarian, he lives in England and is soon to publish another book on children's literature.

Ginger Stelle is a PhD student at Baylor University. She graduated from Southern Illinois University with a B.A. in English and holds an M.A. from Hardin-Simmons University. She is currently pursuing her PhD on George MacDonald.

Kirstin Jeffrey Johnson is part of the 'Institute of Theology, Imagination, and the Arts', St Andrew's University, Scotland. She holds a BA in English Literature and Comparative Literature from the University of Alberta, and a Masters in Spiritual Theology and Literature from Regent College, Vancouver. She currently lives in France, working on her PhD, tentatively titled "The Mythopoesis of George MacDonald."

Susan Ang is an assistant professor of English literature at the National University of Singapore. Her specialties include 19th Century Literature (English and America), Children's Literature, and Science Fiction and Fantasy. She is the author of *The Widening World of Children's Literature*.

Roderick McGillis is Professor of English at the University of Calgary, Canada. His previous books include *For the Childlike: George MacDonald's Fantasies for Children*, *The Nimble Reader: Literary Theory and Children's Literature*, and *Voices of the Other: Children's Literature and the Postcolonial Context*.

Geoffrey Reiter, a PhD student at Baylor University, has published short stories in *Mythic Circle* and *Dragons, Knights, and Angels*, as well as an essay on Bram Stoker. He has presented conference papers on H. P. Lovecraft, Clark Ashton Smith, G. K. Chesterton, and Thomas Hardy.

Colin Manlove is a literary critic with a particular interest in fantasy. He is the author of several books including *C.S. Lewis: His Literary Achievement*, *Modern Fantasy: Five Sudies*, and *Christian Fantasy*. He was a lecturer in English literature at the University of Edinburgh until his retirement.

John Pennington is a Professor of English at St. Norbert College in Wisconsin and the current editor of *North Wind: The Journal of George MacDonald Studies*. He has published various works on John Ruskin, Lewis Carroll, and George MacDonald.

Some Contributors at the 2005 Baylor University
George MacDonald Centennial Conference

(Left to right)
Front row: John Docherty, Ginger Stelle, Jamie Crouse, Amy Vail, Stephen Prickett.
Second row: Louisa Smith, George Bodmer, John Pennington, Amber Malkovich, Fernado Soto.
Third row: Jennifer Koopman, Carolyn Kelly , Susan Ang, Roderick McGillis, Larry Fink.
Last row: Jan Susina, Kirstin Jeffrey Johnson, David Neuhauser, David Robb, Colin Manlove, Robert Trexler.

Index

Ackroyd, Peter, 235
Adamson, J.H., 54
Aeschylus, 73
Aitken, Hannah, 20
Allingham, William, 104
Ambrose Bishop of Milan, 90, 156
Amell, Barbara, 90
Ammerman, Nancy T., 249
Anderson, Gail-Nina, 225n
Andersen, Hans Christian, 104, 252
Ang, Susan, 4
Apollodorus, 67, 71
Apulieus, 230
Arata, Stephen, 217
Aristophanes, 69
Armstrong Browning Library, 1, 6, 241
Arnold, Matthew 4, 153, 154, 156, 157, 162, 163, 165-171, 176n, 178n
Auden, W. H., 132n, 242
Augustine, 156, 174n
Bach, Johann Sebastian, 156
Barclay, William, 95
Barfield, Owen, 25, 130n
Baxter, Richard, 58
Baylor University, 1, 6, 241
Blakemore, Ian, 227
Beer, Gillian, 218, 223
Behler, Ernest, 130n
Bellamy, Edward, 59, 61
Beowulf, 228, 234
Bible, 4, 7, 26, 59, 94, 95 123, 154, 156, 157, 163, 164, 165, 166, 167, 168, 169, 170, 172n, 173n, 211, 248, 249
Biser, Eugen, 40n

Blackie, J. S., 2
Blair, Hugh, 174n
Blake, William, 1, 4, 116-125, 127, 128, 130n, 131n, 132n, 133n, 156, 174, 202, 211, 228
Bodmer, George, 103
Brahms, Johannes, 156
Broome, Hal, 25, 38n
Brown, Curtis, 129n
Brown, Dr. John, 18
Browning, Robert, 45, 62
Bruford, Alan, 21
Buckley, J. H., 62
Bunyan, John, 49, 56, 129, 156
Burke, Edmund, 184, 198
Burns, Robert, 7, 17, 19, 61
Burnside, William, 243
Butts, Thomas, 118
Byrd, William, 156
Byron, Lord, 156
Campbell, John MacCloud, 85
Cambridge Platonists, 6, 54, 203
Carlyle, Thomas, 52, 62, 239
Carpenter, Boyd, 183
Carroll, Lewis, 87, 99, 100, 101, 102, 103, 105, 106, 117, 120, 131n, 132n,
 (Charles Dodgson), 133n, 134n, 252, 253
Chalmers, Thomas, 19
Chaucer, Geoffrey, 47, 156
Cheney, T. K., 167, 178n
Chew, Alistair, 179n
Clement of Alexandria, 84
Coleridge, S. T., 45, 51, 52, 61, 156, 162, 163, 164, 165, 166, 167, 168,

170, 171, 174n, 175n, 177n, 178n, 208, 230, 235
Collingwood, Stuart, 87
Collins, Robert, 210
Collins, Wilkie, 185, 239
Coppard, A. E., 231
Croley, Laura Sagolla, 220, 225n
Cromwell, Oliver, 50, 51, 140
Cusick, Edward, 143
Dante, 6, 38n, 49, 116, 117, 122, 156, 162, 164, 211, 228, 246
Darwin, Charles, 5, 217, 218, 219, 222, 224
Dearborn, Kerry, 25, 227
Denck, Hans, 90
De Quincey, Thomas, 50
Dickens, Charles, 62, 239, 240
Dijkstra, Bram, 130n, 132n
Docherty, John, 4, 25, 54, 116, 117, 127, 128, 131n, 132n, 133n, 134n, 165, 172n
Donaldson, Mara E., 249
Dunbar, William, 156
Durie, Catherine, 113, 117
Durer, Alberte, 128
Eckersley, Adrian, 219, 225n
Eliade, Mircea, 119, 132n, 133n
Eliot, George, 240
Emerson, Ralph Waldo, 46, 51, 52, 60, 61, 62, 240
Engel, Manfred, 27, 28, 29, 30, 32, 38n, 39n
Enlightenment, 1, 13, 22, 23, 27-28, 29, 33, 38n, 40n, 51
Erskine, Thomas, 85
Eumenides, 73, 76
Euripides, 73
Eusebius of Caesarea, 90
Finch, Martin, 58
Fontana, Ernest, 225n
Foucault, Michel, 195
Fouque, de la Motte, 232
Freud, Sigmund, 183, 187, 190-192, 194, 196, 207, 235
Froude, J. A., 239
Gaiman, Neil, 184
Galton, Francis, 218-19, 220, 223, 224
Garnett, David, 235
Gibbons, Lewis Grassic, 22
Glover, David, 225n
Goethe, Johann Wolfgang von 116, 130n, 179n, 232
Gollancz, Victor, 129n
The Gothic, 4, 5, 13, 183-198, 241
Graves, Robert, 65, 69, 70, 72, 73, 74, 75
Greek myth, 3, 6, 42n, 65, 69, 77, 78n, 128
Gregory, Frederick, 219
Gregory of Nazianzus, 90
Gregory of Nyssa, 90
Greeves, Arthur, 113
Greene, Graham, 230
Greenslade, William, 217, 218, 219, 223, 225n
Grimm, Brothers, 228, 232
Grimm, Gunther, 40n
Gunn, Neil, 22
Gurney, Russell, 85
Haggerty, George, 183
Halberstam, Judith, 225n

Hale, Dr., 107
Hamilton, Dan, 242, 245-246, 249-252
Handel, George Frederic, 155, 173n, 174n, 176n
Hanks, Patrick, 70
Hardy, Thomas, 239, 240
Harrison, Jane, 70, 72, 74
Hawthorne, Nathaniel, 45, 46, 51, 60-61, 62, 131n, 132n, 134n
Hayward, Deirdre Christine, 25, 29, 33, 36, 38n, 39n, 40n
Hein, Rolland, 25, 85, 86, 95, 139, 140, 142, 143, 144, 145, 207, 242
Herbert, George, 156, 175n
Herder, Johann Gottfried, 28
Herodotus, 71, 72
Hesiod, 68, 70
Hill, Robert W., 88
Hilty, Palmer, 41n
Himmelfarb, Gertrude, 225n
Hodge, Charles, 219
Hodges, F., 70
Hoffmann, E. T. A., 232, 235
Hogg, James, 3, 8, 22-23
Homer, 47, 65, 66, 72
Hooker, Thomas, 55
Hosmer, James, 51
Howells, Coral Ann, 184
Hughes, Arthur, 99, 100, 102-105, 108, 110, 222
Hurley, Kelly, 218
Hutchinson, Anne, 49
Hyatt, Alfred H., 239
Inklings, 5, 227, 228, 230, 231, 232, 235, 236
Iranaeus of Lyons, 90
Irwin, Robert, 235
Isaiah, Book of, 4, 94, 153-158, 160-165, 167, 170, 171, 173n, 174n, 175n, 176n, 177n, 178n
Jamieson, James, 13
Jefferies, Richard, 240
Jerome, 90, 156
Johnson, Joseph, 16
Johnson, Kirstin, 4
Kailyard novel, 16
Kant, Emmanuel, 51
Kasperowska, Ira, 29
Keats, George & Georgina, 197
Keats, John, 197
Kegler, Adelheid, 25
Kerenyi, Karoly, 68, 69, 72, 73, 74
Kingsley, Charles, 223, 230
Kooistra, Lorraine Janzen, 104
Knoepflmacher, U. C., 106, 107, 240, 254
Kranz, 25
Kreglinger, Gisela, 3
Kruger, Steven F., 40n, 42n
Lacan, Jacques, 206-210, 213
Lady Macbeth, 197
Landseer, Sir Edwin, 9, 18
Latourette, Kenneth Scott, 89
Lauder, Sir Thomas Dick, 3, 8-12
Law, William, 6
Lawrence, Bruce, 248
Lempriere, 68, 69, 70, 73
Lenardon, 73
Levine, George, 255n
Lewis, C. S., 1, 5, 7, 15, 58, 83, 94, 113, 114, 116, 117, 129n, 130n, 133n,

179n, 198, 201, 227-232, 235-237, 240-244, 246, 247, 250-254, 255n
Lindskoog, Kathryn, 5, 245-247, 249, 252
Lombroso, Caesare, 221, 222, 224, 225n
Longhorn, David, 225n
Lowth, Robert, 156, 174n
Ludlow, Morvenna, 90
Luther, Martin, 88
Lytton, Bulwer, 239
Macaulay, Lord, 239
Machen, Arthur, 5, 219, 221, 224, 225n
MacDonald, George
  Works:
Adela Cathcart, 84, 99, 100, 101, 102, 104-110, 185
Alec Forbes of Howglen, 10, 13, 22
Annals of a Quiet Neighbourhood, 154, 251
At the Back of the North Wind, 22, 38n, 39n, 102, 192, 193, 197, 202, 212, 229, 230, 240, 244, 252
Castle Warlock, 14, 15, 16
Creation in Christ, 95, 189, 192
"Cross Purposes", 94, 220
"The Cruel Painter", 4, 108, 155, 185-186, 188-189
David Elginbrod, 13, 17, 92, 109, 154, 175n, 176n, 177n
"The Day Boy and Night Girl", 234
Dealings With the Fairies, 99, 100, 101, 102, 103, 105, 106, 108, 110
The Diary of an Old Soul, 2
A Dish of Orts, 37, 40n, 52, 53, 54, 121, 131n, 201, 202, 203, 229, 230, 241
Donal Grant, 13, 91
The Elect Lady, 91, 93, 173n, 177n
England's Antiphon, 6, 87, 88
"The Fantastic Imagination", 99, 101, 103, 105, 106, 110, 111, 124, 189, 201, 202
The Flight of the Shadow, 131n
George MacDonald in the Pulpit, 184
"The Giant's Heart", 102, 107
"The Golden Key", 102, 130n, 205, 211, 233, 242, 252
"The Gray Wolf", 133n, 190
Hope of the Gospel, 155, 183, 192
"Imagination: Its Function and Culture", 52, 114, 121, 202
Letters from Hell, 93
Life Essential, 183, 192
"The Light Princess", 4, 21, 99-111, 128, 185, 211, 234, 252, 253
Lilith, 2, 3, 4, 25, 26, 29-32, 36, 37, 39n, 45-47, 53-56, 59-62, 90, 93, 113-118, 120-129, 130n, 131n, 132n, 133n, 134n, 155, 185-187, 190, 196-198, 203, 205, 207-211, 213, 215, 229, 231, 235, 239, 243, 254
"Little Daylight", 234, 241
The Lost Princess, 114, 205, 234
Malcolm, 13, 14
The Marquis of Losie, 17
Miracles of Our Lord, 5, 178n, 201, 203-204, 206, 211, 213-214
Paul Faber, Surgeon, 55
Phantastes, 4, 14, 19, 21, 25, 26, 29, 30, 38n, 113, 114, 115, 123, 126,

131n, 132n, 139-151, 157, 204, 205, 206, 212, 214, 229, 230-233, 235, 240, 241, 243, 254
Poetical Works, 25, 85
The Portent, 131n, 133n, 184, 185
The Princess and Curdie, 4,, 65, 67, 70, 72, 75, 76, 77, 78n, 79n, 103, 153, 154, 157, 160, 165, 170-171, 175, 185, 190, 214, 217, 222-224, 229, 233, 249
The Princess and the Goblin, 65, 67, 70-71, 77, 79n, 103, 153, 192, 194, 212, 217, 220, 221, 223, 224, 230, 233, 240, 254, 255n
Rampolli, 32, 33, 34, 35, 36, 40n, 164, 177n, 178n
Ranald Bannerman's Boyhood, 19, 245, 250
Robert Falconer, 17, 54, 84, 85, 92, 93, 95, 109, 110, 175
Sir Gibbie, 8, 9, 10, 13, 155, 240, 246
St. George and St. Michael 4, 55, 139-151
"The Shadows", 102
"Sketch of Individual Development", 168, 207
"The Snow Fight", 110
There and Back, 91, 155
Thomas Wingfold, Curate, 55, 116, 132n, 155, 252
Unspoken Sermons, 83, 94-95, 113, 127, 155, 189, 191, 232
  (Series 1, 2 and 3)
Weighed and Wanting, 84
What's Mine's Mine 17, 155
"The Wow O' Rivven", 154

MacDonald, Greville, 12, 22, 55-56, 62, 77, 85, 87, 89, 93, 99, 100, 107, 113, 130n, 133n, 155, 173n, 175n, 239, 249, 255
MacDonald, Lilia Scott, 85
MacDonald, Louisa (Mrs), 78, 173n, 176n
Mahl, Hans-Joachim, 40n
Manlove, Colin, 5, 25, 165, 172n, 209, 223, 236, 241, 249
Martin, John, 12
Martineau, James, 183
Marty, Martin, 248-249
Matthiessen, F. O., 61
Maurice, F. D., 4, 6, 45, 46, 55, 56, 59, 61, 62, 86, 87, 120, 153, 154, 156, 158-163, 165-168, 170, 175n, 176n, 177n, 178n, 223, 227
McKinley, Robin, 252-253
McGillis, Roderick, 25, 117, 153
McGrath, Alister, 157
Melville, Herman, 61
Mendelssohn, Felix, 156
Meredith, George, 239
Mill, John Stuart, 52
Millais, John, 104
Miller, Hugh, 11, 20
Miller, Renata Kobertts, 241
Milton, John, 45, 50, 61, 104, 110, 121, 122, 156, 164, 211, 228
Monaghan, Patricia, 69, 79n
Morel, Benedict Augustin, 218
Morford, 73
Morris, William, 59
Morrison, Isabella, 10
Mount Temple, Lord and Lady, 85,

177n
  (Cowper-Temple)
Mulford, Elisha, 61-62
Munro, Alexander, 99
Murray, Alexander, 68, 70, 72
Napier, Elizabeth, 183
Newman, Cardinal John Henry, 62
Neuhouser, David, 4
Nolan, Richard, 179n
Nordau, Max, 5, 220, 221, 222, 224, 225n
Novalis, 3, 25-37, 38n, 39n, 40n, 41, 42n, 88, 89, 164, 179n, 205,
  (Friedrich von Hardenburg)
    230, 232, 244
Origen of Alexandria, 6, 89-90
Orwell, George, 235
Ovid, 75, 118
Palma, James, 129n
Parnham, David, 56, 57, 58, 59
Parry, Robin A., 85, 87, 90, 96
Partridge, Christopher H., 85, 87, 90, 96
Patterson, Nancy-lou, 65, 68, 69, 79n
Pennington, John, 5, 127
Pfefferkorn, Kirstin, 38n
Phillips, Michael, 5, 90, 134n, 242, 243, 245, 247-249, 251-252
Plato (Platonic), 123, 203, 206, 207, 223, 229
Plotinus, 203
Plutarch, 71
Pope, Alexander, 156
Powys, T. F., 230
Prickett, Stephen, 1, 6, 25, 55, 113, 114, 116-117, 123, 153, 162, 163,

164, 165, 166, 167, 172n, 176n, 177n, 178n, 222, 224
Proverbs, 54
Psalms, 94, 173n
Pullman, Philip, 204
Queen Victoria, 155
Quixote, Don, 122
Radcliffe, Ann, 184
Raeper, William, 10, 17, 21, 25, 102, 106, 110, 132n
Reis, Richard, 25, 116, 139, 184, 222
Reiter, Geoffrey, 5
Richerz, Georg Hermann, 28
Richter, Jean Paul, 28
Riga, Frank P., 38n
Robb, David, 3, 13, 25, 139, 172n
Roberts, Lewis C., 241
Roder, Florian, 41n, 42n
Roemer, Kenneth, 52, 61
Rogerson, J. W., 163, 165, 168, 177n, 178n
Romanticism, 1, 3, 6, 9, 11-12, 13, 27, 28, 29, 30, 33, 35, 36, 38n, 42n,
  (Romantic)
51, 61, 130n, 156, 176n, 185, 210, 227, 228, 230, 231, 232
Rose, 73
Rossetti, Christina, 103, 104
Rossetti, Dante Gabriel, 104
Rossetti, William Michael, 103, 104
Ruskin, John, 62, 102, 105, 106-107, 116, 128, 131n, 134n, 157, 179n, 240
Sadler, Glenn Edward, 2, 60, 65, 85, 115, 154, 164, 172n, 173n, 177n
  (MacDonald Letters)
Sammuel, Richard, 40n

Sawyer, John F. A., 155, 156, 173n, 174n
Schelling, Friedrich Wilhelm, 51
Schlegal, Frederick, 130n
Schmitt, Cannon, 241
Schulz, Gerhard, 40n
Scott, Alexander John, 85
Scott, Sir Walter, 3, 7, 8, 13-15, 17, 19, 22, 50, 61
Scudder, Vida, 61, 62
Sepasgosarin, Wilhelmine Maria, 38n, 41n
Shakespeare, William, 14, 52, 156, 162, 164, 172n
Shelley, P. B., 156, 162, 203
Shklovsky, Viktor, 196
Sendak, Maurice, 211, 253
Sigman, Joeseph, 143, 172n
Sikes, George, 50, 58
Skeat, Walter, 74
Smith, George Murray, 255n
Soto, Fernando, 3, 6, 65, 132n
Spenser, Edmund, 104, 107, 126, 211, 228, 230
Spina, Giorgio, 25, 35
Spurgeon, Charles, 155
Stirling, J. H., 183
Strahan, Alexander, 102, 255n
Stelle, Ginger, 4
Stern, Jeffrey, 100
Stephen, Leslie, 157
Stevenson, Robert Louis, 8, 14, 15-16, 221, 224, 240
Stoker, Bram, 5, 220, 221, 224, 225n
Susina, Jan, 4
Sutton, Henry, 115

Sutton, Julie, 177n
Swift, Jonathan, 235
Talbot, Thomas, 87
Tam o' Shanter, 11
Tennyson, Alfred Lord, 62, 87, 88, 175n
Thackery, W. M., 62
Theodoret of Antioch, 90
Theophilus of Antioch, 90
Treherne, Katia Thamer, 252
Thomas, D. M., 230
Thoreau, Henry David, 38n, 45, 46-48, 51, 56, 60, 61, 62
Thucidides, 71
Todorov, Tzvetan, 188
Tolkien, J. R. R., 5, 179n, 201, 206, 215, 227-230, 232-237, 243
Transcendentalists, 46, 51, 62
Trafton, Jennifer, 240
Trexler, Robert, 3, 60, 131n, 134n, 227
Triggs, Kathy, 243
Trollope, Anthony, 239
Turner, J. M. W., 11
Twain, Mark, 59
Underhill, Evelyn, 230
Universalism, 3, 4, 83-96
Upham, Charles, 50
Vane, Sir Henry, 3, 45, 46, 47, 49-59
Vermaseren, R. J., 133n
Vidler, Alec R., 86
Voltaire, 235
Washington, George, 51
Watt, Ian, 255
Weinrich, Elizabeth McDonald, 53
Wells, H. G., 220, 221, 224, 225n,

232
Whitman, Walt, 61
Whittier, John Greenleaf, 83, 89
Wilde, Oscar, 186, 222, 224, 225n, 252
Wildman, Stephen, 104
Wiley, Basil, 54
Wilkinson, Garth, 133n
Willard, Nancy, 65
Williams, Anne, 183
Williams, Charles, 5, 227-231, 235, 236, 237
Williams, Roger, 50
Willcox, Louise Collier, 239, 240

Wilson, John ("Christopher North"), 18
Wilson, Keith, 142, 145
Wolff, Christian, 27-28, 39n
Wolff, Robert Lee, 2, 14, 25, 35, 38n, 153, 205, 207, 242
Wordsworth, William, 19, 52, 156, 174n, 210, 227
Wyke-Smith, E. A., 232
Yamaguchi, Miho, 55
Yates, Elizabeth, 246
Žižek, Slavoj, 201-206

Also from Zossima Press

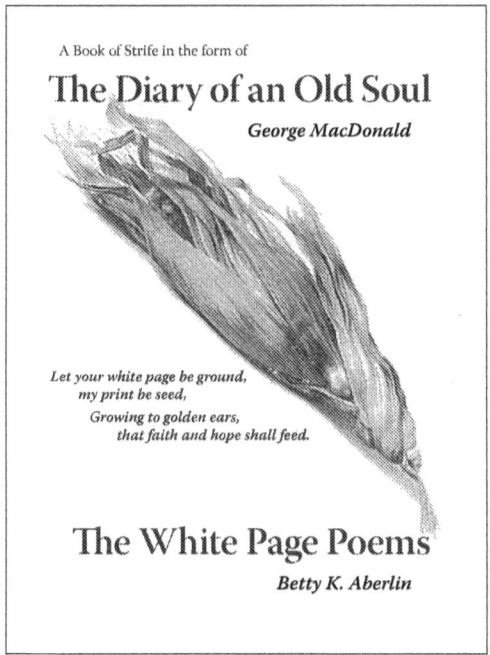

In this labor of love, Betty Aberlin's
close readings of George MacDonald's verses,
and her thoughtful responses to them speak clearly
of her poetic gifts and spiritual intelligence.

> Luci Shaw, poet and author of *Breath for the Bones*

A fascinating new book . . . fresh and incisive.
Aberlin's poems offer glimpses of her spiritual journey.

> Don King, author of *C.S. Lewis, Poet*

This is impressive indeed. George MacDonald treated as he would wish to be treated. Here is a truly dialogic book in which MacDonald's vision finds a receptive and sensitive reader who is prepared to respond in kind. A timely and generous publication.

> Roderick McGillis,
> Editor, *George MacDonald: Literary Heritage and Heirs*

www.ingramcontent.com/pod-product-compliance
Lightning Source LLC
Chambersburg PA
CBHW031238290426
44109CB00012B/340